Latin American Fighters, A History of Fighter Jets in Service with Latin A

By Iñigo Guevara y Moyano

LATIN AMERICAN FIGHTERS

A History of Fighter Jets in Service with Latin American Air Arms

By Iñigo Guevara y Moyano

HARPIA
PUBLISHING +

To Angela,
Who has inspired a unique passion for history,
Without who's strive I would never be what I am,
Thank you for all your knowledge and love,
I could never have asked for a better teacher or mother.

To Hector,
for inspiring me throughout your life so
that I may always take the right path,
you were a wonderfull father and guide,
may you rest in peace.

I would like to especially thank my wife Marcela, without whose support this book could not have been possible,
thank you for your love, critique and encouragement to continue, and to my son Patricio (Pato) for inspiring me
to write and fight for a better world.

Copyright © 2009 Harpia Publishing, L.L.C. & Moran Publishing, L.L.C. Joint Venture
2803 Sackett Street, Houston, TX 77098-1125, U.S.A.
laf@harpia-publishing.com

Layout by Norbert Novak, www.media-n.at, Vienna

Printed at Grasl Druck & Neue Medien, Austria

ISBN 978-0-9825539-0-9

Harpia Publishing, L.L.C. is a member of

Contents

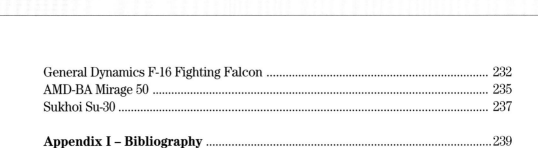

Introduction

In the immediate post WW-II years Latin American air forces received large amounts of surplus equipment from the US through military aid programmes. This comprised a broad number of types but can be generalized into P-51D Mustangs, P-47D Thunderbolts, B-25 Mitchells, B-26 Invaders and C-47 Skytrains. During these years there was little jet equipment available for export as the United States was keen in absorbing jet production into the newly created USAF, in an attempt to show a counterbalance to huge Soviet forces massing on Eastern Europe.

The UK was the only country capable and willing to sell advanced jet fighters to Latin American governments during this period. Peron's Argentina was the first country in the region to acquire jet combat aircraft. It was followed a few years later by Venezuela. The Gloster Meteor and DeHavilland Vampire first generation fighter jets became standard in several air forces during the following decade.

The period from 1950 to 1959 brought a further eight countries, Brazil, the Dominican Republic, Chile, Colombia, Ecuador, Cuba, Peru, and Uruguay into the jet club. These countries received an estimated 443 jet combat aircraft during this decade. Over a third of these were new built examples, with the bulk comprising first generation, second hand aircraft (mainly Lockheed's F-80 and T-33) from the United States. While the United Kingdom predominated in new aircraft sales, providing no less than 115 aircraft (Vampires, Meteors, Venoms and Hunters) to five air arms. Neutral Sweden supplied over 40 surplus jet fighters to the Trujillo regime in the Dominican Republic. Canada was also present through a small deal with Colombia. The most capable fighters delivered during this period were a small number of Hawker Hunters to Peru and F-86 Sabres to Colombia and Venezuela. The largest recipient of jets during this decade was Brazil by far, with over 100, followed by Peru who got 64, Colombia 57 and Venezuela 50. Meanwhile, Argentina geared towards local production of armed jet trainers.

During the 1960s, Latin American countries received some 639 jet fighters. That was a 44 per cent increase over the previous decade. The proportion of new aircraft compared to second-hand rose to almost one-half. Newcomers to the jet club included Mexico, Nicaragua and Guatemala. All of which obtained second hand armed jet trainers from the United States. The rather low level of sophistication was maintained throughout the region, with the exception of a huge amount of Soviet aid pouring into Cuba. This was in the form of supersonic MiG-21s, while modern western hardware was limited to a dozen Mirage fighter-bombers. Italy and Czechoslovakia became token suppliers, while British newly built exports dropped dramatically to just over a dozen armed trainers.

Acquisitions during the 1970s increased considerably, both in numbers and in quality. Latin American countries received over 850 fighter jets, over 70 per cent of which were newly-built models. Reasons for this was the widespread sales success of the French Mirage delta-fighter (undoubtedly triggered by its performance during the 1967 Six Day War), as well as the release of the American Cessna A-37B counter-insurgency and Northrop F-5E/F tactical fighters for export. The continued Soviet assistance to Cuba in the form of updated MiG-21s and MiG-23 variable geometry fighter-bombers was also a factor. Brazilian license production of the Italian MB-326 jet trainer was followed closely by several countries that wished to create their own production capabil-

ity, however, none of them prospered. The second hand market saw the debut of Israel as a main source of supply for a number of countries.

Bolivia, El Salvador, Honduras, and Paraguay became new to the jet community, all of them through second hand acquisitions from a variety of sources. Venezuela also became a source for transferring third hand equipment to Bolivia and Honduras.

The 1970s was clearly a period of re-equipment for several air forces, most of which managed to survive until the 21st century. Brazil received over two hundred jets, Argentina some 114 frontline fighters (in what can arguably be described as pre-Falklands preparations) followed by Cuba, who obtained at least 112 front-line fighters from the Soviet Union.

Arms races were evident during the 1970s, especially where border issues had escalated into mobilizations or even full scale warfare. For instance, Chile obtained some 80 fighters from the UK and the US, followed by Peru who bought from France, the U.S., and the Soviet Union. In an effort to counter this balance Ecuador obtained over 40 front-line fighters from the UK and US. Following up from the 1969 100-Hour War (also known as the Soccer War), El Salvador obtained 27 aircraft from Israel and France, while Honduras bought up to 44 from a variety of sources but focusing on Israel.

The 1980s saw a deceleration of this trend, although the decade began, undoubtedly fuelled by the 1970s as well as the height of the Cold War agenda with the acquisition of 3rd and 4th generation fighters such as the IAI Kfir, General Dynamics F-16, Dassault-Breguet Super Étendard, Mirage F.1 and Mirage 2000. Some 425 new fighter jets were delivered to the region during the 1980s, most of which continue to be in service.

Interestingly, regional powers such as Argentina, Brazil, or Chile did not procure fourth generation fighters during this decade but actually (in the case of Brazil and Chile) waited until the 21st Century to do so. The Soviet Union provided the bulk of new fighters with some 150 delivered to Cuba and Peru. France was the second most important source for new jet fighters and without any doubts the most profitable one, providing 60 fighter-bombers for about USD1 billion.

The United States sold new fighters only to oil-producing Mexico and Venezuela, yet it became the largest source for second hand fighters, with over some 170 delivered, mainly through military aid. Israel and France provided some 80 second hand fighters, while Spain and Czechoslovakia entered the Latin American market providing new examples of combat-capable jet trainers. Spain also became a granter of a license for the local production of armed jet trainers in Chile, and the later became the third Latin American country to license build European-designed jet aircraft.

The end of the Cold War and a wave of regional economic crisis had a devastating effect on the region's defence market during the 1990s, especially hitting the jet fighter market. The entire region acquired 45 brand new jet fighters and almost three quarters of these were remnants of licence production lines set up in the late 1980s, only France and Russia obtained some token orders for Mirage 50 and MiG-29 respectively. However the upgrades marketed showed an interesting increase with several countries subjecting their main fighter assets to different rejuvenation processes. Second hand purchases also suffered a decline, yet they included new comers such as Belgium and Belarus.

Into the 21st Century, Latin American militaries seem ever more conscious about the full range of implications (financial, industrial, political, social, etc.) of acquiring a new jet fighter type. From the year 2000 to early 2009 less than 90 fighter jets (new

and used) had made their way into Latin American squadrons. Most of the fleet is comprised by aircraft acquired in the 1970s and 1980s, and most of these will shortly need to be replaced. Technology transfers, industrial offsets and dual use technologies seemed to be the norm for the upcoming acquisition processes. In a region where conventional, territorial, symmetric warfare is said to be extinct, a squadron of AWACS-directed, tanker-supported, BVR and PGM-carrying fourth generation fighters is still a cherished instrument of deterrence.

Iñigo Guevara y Moyano, July 2009

Acknowledgements

The author would like to thank the following aviation professionals, enthusiasts and friends, who made this book possible:
Eduardo Ahumada (fach-extraoficial.com, Chile), **Milton Andrade** (El Salvador), **Virgilio Aray** (Ecuador), **Juan Arráez Cerda** (Brazil), **Johnson Barros** (FAB, Brazil), **Rodrigo Bendoraytes** (basemilitar.com.br, Brazil), **Michael Blank** (UK), **Eduardo Cardenas** (Peru), **Ian Caroll** (Mach III Publ., UK), **Juan Carlos Cicalesi** (Brazil), **Guido Chavez Acosta** (Ecuador), **Jorge Cobas "Pilotoviejo"** (Uruguay), **Andrés Contador Krüger** (Chile), **Rodrigo Conte** (Brazil), **Tom Cooper** (ACIG.org), **Tomas Cubero** (USA), **Cesar Cruz** (Peru), **Adrian DeVoe** (USA), **Rudnei Dias da Cunha** (Brazil), **Jonathan Derden** (USA), **Luis Dominguez** (Cuba), **André Austin Du-Pont Rocha** (Mexico Air Spotters), **Peter Elliot** (RAF Museum, UK), **Adrian English** (Ireland), **Carlos Alberto Espinosa**, **Oswaldo Flores** (Mexico), **Horacio Gareiso** (Argentinia), **Anno Gravemaker** (Netherlands), **Dan Hagedorn** (National Air and Space Museum, USA), **Jurgen Hesse Joya** (Air Museum Fund; Honduras), **Steve Homewood** (UK), **Martin Hornlimann** (Switzerland), **Erik Katerberg** (Netherlands), **Gustavo Kaufmann** (Brazil), **Gary Kuhn** (LAAHS USA), **Chris Lofting** (UK), **Beatriz López** (Peru), **Delso Lopez** (Venezuela), **Claudio Lucchesi** (Revista ASAS, Brazil), **Andres Luna** (Colombia), **Eduardo Luzardo** (ratones de hangar; AAMA; Uruguay), **Leandro Maldonado Barcelos** (Brazil), **Rafael Marti**, **Mario Martínez Hernández** (Mexico), **Fernando Mendoza**, **Ramiro Molina** (Nicaragua), **Enrique Munguia** (Nicaragua), **Carlos Augusto Narváez Díaz** (Colombia), **Carlos Filipi Operti** (Brazil), **Martin Otero** (Argentina), **Mario E. Overall** (LAAHS.com administrator; Guatemala), **Jonathan Parra Raya** (Mexico), **Ivan David Peña Nesbit** (Venezuela), **Luis Puesan** (Dominican Republic), **Andrés Ramírez** (Colombia), **José Ramón Rivas** (Nicaragua), **Santiago Rivas** (Argentina), **Hans Rolink** (Netherlands), **José Rosa** (Honduras), **Antonio Luis Sapienza** (LAAHS, Paraguay), **Casto Siñani** (FAB webmaster; Bolivia), **Wim Sonneveld** (Scramble, Netherlands), **Arturo Celestino Soto** (FAV-CLUB, Venezuela), **Tim Spearman** (UK), **Katsuhiko Tokunaga** (DACT, Japan), **George Trussell** (UK), **Cees-Jan van der Ende** (alfakilo.nl, Netherlands), **Roberto Vassali** (Nicaragua), **Christian Villada** (SAORBATS; Argentina), **Sergio Villalobos** (Mexico), **Hector Wong** (Mexico), **João Paulo Zeitoun Moralez** (Revista ASAS, Brazil)

Abbreviations

AAA	anti-aircraft artillery
AAM	air-to-air missile
AB	air base
AEW	aerial early warning
AFB	air force base
ALA	Armee de l'Aire/ French Air Force
AAMA	Asociación de Amigos del Museo de Aviación/ Society of the Friends of the Aviation Museum (Argentina)
AMARC	Aerospace Maintenance and Regeneration Center (US)
AMD	Aviation Marcel Dassault (1947-1971)
AMD-BA	Aviation Marcel Dassault-Breguet Aviation (1971-1990)
ARA	Armada de la República Argentina/ Navy of the Argentine Republic)
ASCC	Air Standardization Coordinating Committee (NATO)
BAC	British Aircraft Corporation
BAM	Base Aérea Militar/military air base (Argentina)
BPD	British Pound Sterling (£)
BVR	beyond visual range
CAF	Canadian Air Force
CAP	combat air patrol
CAS	close air support
CASA	Construcciones Aeronáuticas S.A. (Spain)
c/n	construction number
COAN	Comando de Aviación Naval/Naval Aviation Command (Argentina)
COIN	counter-insurgency
DoD	US Department of Defence
EMBRAER	Empresa Brasileira de Aeronáutica S.A.
ENAER	Empresa Nacional de Aeronáutica de Chile
FAA	Fuerza Aérea Argentina/Argentine Air Force
FLEC	Frente para a Libertação do Enclave de Cabinda/Front of Liberation of the State of Cabinda (Angola)
FMA	Fábrica Militar de Aviones/Military Aircraft Factory (Argentina)
FMS	Foreign Military Sales
FR	flight refuelling
HOTAS	hands on throttle and stick
HUD	head-up display
IAI	Israel Aircraft Industry
INS	inertial navigation system
IOC	initial operational capability
KAF	Kuwait Air Force
KLu	Koninklijke Luchtmacht/ Royal Netherlands Air Force
LIFT	lead-in fighter trainer
LMAASA	Lockheed Martin Argentina S.A.
MANPAD	man-portable air defence system

MAP	Military Assistance Programme (US)
MFD	Multi Functional Display
MLU	Mid-Life Update
NCO	non commissioned officer
OCU	operational conversion unit
PGM	precision guided munitions
R-3S	Soviet air-to-air missile (ASCC code AA-2D Atoll)
RAF	Royal Air Force
RCAF	Royal Canadian Air Force
RfP	request for proposals
RWR	radar warning receiver
SAAF	South African Air Force
SABCA	Société Anonyme Belge de Construction Aéronautique/
SAR	search and rescue
SEPECAT	Société Européenne de Production de l'Avion d'École de Combat et d'Appui Tactique/ European company for the production of a combat trainer and tactical support aircraft
SWAPO	South West African People's Organization
UM	Unidad Militar/Military Unit (Cuba)
UNITA	União Nacional para a Independência Total de Angola/ National Union for the Total Independence of Angola
USAF	United States Air Force
USD	US Dollar ($)
USN	United States Navy
VVS	Voenno-Vozdushnye Sily/ Soviet Air Force
WW-II	World War II

Chapter 1

ARGENTINA

Argentina had by far, the most technically advanced defence industry in Latin America by the end of World War 2. In 1947 Argentina was the first country in the region to develop and fly its own jet fighter, although it did not progress beyond the prototype stage. President Juan Peron's modern military machine was fuelled by expatriate designers such as the French collaborationist Emile Dewoitine, who built the Pulqui, a low-wing monoplane jet and the German Kurt Tank, one of WW-II's most famous Nazi designers, responsible for the Pulqui II, a swept wing jet prototype.

Argentina was also the first Latin American country to operate jet fighters. A first-generation British aircraft was to be the country's sole jet fighter from the late 1940s, until the Fuerza Aérea Argentina (FAA, Argentine Air Force) selected a French-designed liaison, training and light attack jet for a variety of roles in 1956. This aircraft was also the first jet to be license-assembled in Latin America. Argentina's Comando de Aviación Naval (COAN, Naval Aviation Command) was also the first – and for several more decades- the only Latin American naval air service to operate jet fighters.

In the 1960s the FAA transitioned from European to American-built aircraft, acquiring subsonic fighter and fighter-bombers. This was also the first time that the FAA acquired second hand aircraft, although major refurbishment and upgrades proved to be an economic solution.

The Pulqui was South America's first locally designed jet fighter. (via Eduardo Luzardo)

The Pulqui II was a swept-wing jet prototype, designed by famous German designer Kurt Tank. (via Eduardo Luzardo)

A return to European sources characterized the 1970s, with the first supersonic interceptors joining the air force and the first jet trainers joining the navy. French-built Mirages became the standard air-defence fighters, while U.S. built attack jets continued to replace earlier European fighter-bombers. By the late 1970s, economic problems prevented the local production of Mirages and the FAA settled for some 40 second-hand Israeli fighters.

As of the early 1980s, with a combined FAA and COAN strength over 120 operational fighter jets, Argentina managed to field the most powerful combat fleet in South America. In 1982 the fleet was committed against what turned out to be a formidable enemy. The might of the RAF and Royal Navy proved to be too much for this aspiring regional power and subsequently it lost about a third of its fleet. Actual military support to Argentina was almost non-existent during the conflict, although there are scarce reports that the Soviet Union offered to deliver up to some 100 jet fighters, with extremely attractive credit terms, however, the political strings proved too costly.

Rebuilding its fighter fleet was a top priority after the 1982 Falklands War, and Argentina approached several potential sources, including, Belgium, Denmark, France, The Netherlands and Spain. An U.S. imposed embargo as well as British pressure made it difficult to replenish its stocks. Israel was the main post-Falklands war supplier, delivering over 40 second hand Mirages. Israel also found a lucrative business in the upgrade market, and from then on became a major systems upgrade supplier. Brazil and Peru provided second hand combat aircraft to the air force and navy respectively.

During the late 1980s and early 1990s both services focused on upgrade programs that would keep the shrinking fleet in operational conditions. The economic debacle did not favour the acquisition of new front line fighters, and when the U.S. lifted its 12 year old embargo in 1994, the country was in dire need of a multi-role fighter. Second-hand updated fighters would have to do, as the country submerged into one of the worst economic meltdowns in modern history.

In the early 21st Century, the Argentine fighter fleet suffered severely from old age and lack of funds. The Mirage/Skyhawk combination was still in service, albeit with some upgrades that allowed mainly precision guided munitions, the fleet was a reminiscent of the early 1970s. A new generation fighter was indeed required, to replace at least the Mirage fleet of interceptors. Second handed USAF F-16Cs or former Armée de l'Air Mirage 2000Cs seem to be the preferred types, however this will only depend on the intention of the government and the capability of the economy. Such types as new-built F-16Cs, Rafales, or Gripens' seem to be out of the question in the foreseeable future. Likewise, the once mighty naval fighter fleet seems to be in demise, with no replacement or future carrier force envisaged.

Gloster Meteor (1947–1970)

Gloster Meteor I-089 in the early 1950s. (via Santiago Rivas)

Right after World War II, the UK offered to settle its trade deficit with Argentina with war surplus materials. This made the Fuerza Aérea Argentina the first in Latin America to field an operational jet fighter. Negotiations between the UK and Argentina over payment of food and raw materials provided to the UK during the war, led to an order for some 100 Gloster Meteor Mk.IV jet fighters in May 1947. The contract also included some 45 Lancaster and Lincoln bombers surplus to RAF requirements. The Peroni-

A group of FAA Meteors in formation sometime after 1958. (via Santiago Rivas)

sta Government's WW-II sympathy towards Nazi Germany had caused a US-promoted arms embargo, so the British decision to supply the country with 100 jets and 45 heavy bombers was highly criticized.

Training of 12 Argentine pilots in the UK started in June 1947 on a 60 hour course on 6 of its own Meteors (serial numbers I-007 to I-012). The first six Meteors (serial numbers I-001 to I-006) were delivered by ship to Buenos Aires in July 1947 and these formed the 4th Fighter-Interceptor Regiment at BAM Tandil. On April 1948 the FAA suffered the loss of its first jet, also, the first in Latin America, when serial number I-018 exploded in mid-air manoeuvres.

In 1949 the FAA received a replacement for serial number I-021, whose crate had fallen off the ship during its delivery efforts. It changed its organization designations, with BAM Tandil turning into the VI Brigade, which controlled the 4th Regiment. A new unit, the 6th Regiment was also created and it took charge of half the fleet of Meteors. These regiments were converted into the 2nd and 3rd Fighter Groups of the VI Brigade in 1951. Some 55 Meteors were then transferred to the newly-created VII Brigade at Moron Air Base.

On 16 June, during an insurrection against President Perón, the Meteor saw its first combat use: I-063 shot down a rebel AT-6 Texan armed trainer. On 16 September, a larger rebellion saw Meteors fighting on both sides, with loyal aircraft having the letter 'P' (for Peronista) painted on the fuselage and the rebel aircraft a large 'V'.

Rebel Meteors were used on bombing raids in June 1955 against the Casa Rosada (Pink House, the Presidential Residency) and downtown Buenos Aires, dropping 9½ tons of explosives and causing hundreds of civilian casualties. Loyal forces lost two Meteors, while the rebels, who took control of three aircraft in the city of Cordoba, lost one.

By 1957 an aerobatic demonstration team was organized with Gloster Meteors. They performed alongside the USAF Thunderbirds during Argentina's Aviation Week

festival. In 1958 the interceptors converted into the fighter-bomber role with the fitting of rocket rails and bomb racks, the designation was subsequently changed from the 'I' prefix to 'C' for 'Caza' (Fighter).

In January 1960 the remaining Meteors were concentrated at Moron, with the VII Brigade. On 21 September 1962, the Meteors were once again in service suppressing a new rebellion. They bombed the army's NCO school, where the rebels had taken refuge in Buenos Aires, and Punta Indio Air Base, from where navy's Grumman Panther fighters operated. The attack was performed using MS-760 Paris jets as FACs (Forward Air Controller) and F-86 Sabres as cover.

A slight upgrade to its weapon capabilities was performed during the mid-1960s, mainly to enhance them in the ground-attack role. The approximate remaining 20 Meteors were grouped into one mixed fighter-bomber/training squadron together with a few MS-760A Paris and Beech T-34 Mentors in the VII Air Brigade.

With new higher performance A-4 Skyhawk fighter-bombers entering service, and Mirage III interceptors on order, the Meteor's obsolescence was even more apparent. The last 12 fighters, C-005, C-027, C-029, C-037, C-038, C-051, C-057, C-071, C-088, C-093, C-094, and C-099, were retired from service by late 1970.

Manufacturer	Aircraft Type	Delivered	Number	Serial Numbers	Remarks
Gloster Ltd	G.41 Meteor Mk.4	1947	101	I-001 to I-0100	Prefix changed to C from 1958 onwards

The very first MS-760A Paris (A-01) in 1959.
(via Santiago Rivas)

Morane-Saulnier MS-760A Paris (1959–2007)

The FAA selected the French MS-760A Paris for its new advanced jet trainer requirement in 1956. An order for a dozen new-built MS-760s was signed in 1957 and was followed by an agreement for the license assembly of a further 36 aircraft.

Local workshops DINFIA, latter to be known as Fábrica Militar de Aviones (FMA) at Córdoba was in charge of assembling the aircraft using components provided by Tarbes-based Morane-Saulnier.

The French-built aircraft began to be delivered in September 1959 to the Escuela de Aviación Militar (EAM, Military Aviation School). They were assigned serial numbers A-01 to A-12 (A for Attack), although they were soon re-assigned as E-201 to E-212, E for Entrenador (Trainer). The first Paris, E-210, was lost in October 1959. The Paris, called 'Moraneta' by its pilots was used for advanced training after a T-34 Mentor and T-28 Trojan syllabus.

Locally-built aircraft started to be delivered in 1961 to the 2nd Fighter-Bomber Squadron at IV Brigade and a combat unit at VII Brigade for liaison duties. The jet trainers were armed with 7.5-mm GPMG pods and rocket launchers. FMA produced 13 aircraft during this year and they were numbered E-213 to E-225. E-203 was lost on 27 January 1961.

A further 15 aircraft were produced by FMA during 1962, being numbered E-226 to E-240, while attrition claimed yet another, E-216 on 26 April. Deliveries ended in 1963 with the final eight MS-760s (serial numbers E-241 to E-248). The first operational use of the MS-760s was in September 1962, when four aircraft escorted a flight of Gloster

This MS-760 Paris (E-202) serving with Grupo 4 at Mendoza Air Base was still used for advanced training in November 2005, some 46 years after delivery!
(Hans Rolink)

Meteors and F-86F Sabres to bomb Punta Indio Naval Air Base. They were used as observation and reconnaissance aircraft, and for bomb damage assessment done to the base.

E-231 was lost on 9 December 1964, and followed by E-228 on 16 August 1965. In 1966 VII Brigade transferred its aircraft to the IV Brigade, which became the main operating body. The MS-760s proved to be very popular in the FAA, being used as an advanced trainer, a weapons trainer, target-tug, forward air controller (FAC), liaison, and light attack. They were often 'loaned' from the IV Brigade to the V Brigade and to complement the EAM's fleet. In June 1968 an aircraft was written off, while E-238 was damaged and repaired. The Moranetas reached the peak of their career in 1968, logging over 15,000 flight hours in that year.

In 1973 a further two aircraft were lost, these being E-213 and E-217, both on 29 March. During the Beagle-Channel tensions, armed MS-760s were dispersed to Tandil and Rio Gallegos Air Bases and San Rafael Airfield. If they were to have been used in a conflict against Chile, their task would have been airfield attack, strafing enemy aircraft on the ground.

Studies to replace them with a locally-develop advanced trainer/ light fighter started in 1979 and the resulting aircraft, the FMA IA-63 Pampa. Thirty-three aircraft in strength, it seemed the MS-760's service years had been numbered. Pampa production was limited to 19 aircraft for financial reasons and the MS-760s continued in service for over 25 years. The fleet received new engines in 1979 and had two 7.62-mm machine guns installed in its nose, releasing additional hard-points.

During the Falkland's War, the Moranetas were kept for homeland air defence and performed costal patrol. They did not see any combat action. They received several novelties in the post-war period, including IFF and communication equipment. The remaining aircraft in service with the EAM were transferred to the IV Brigade in 1985.

The fleet had been reduced to 30 aircraft by 1990, although some more accurate sources indicated that only 17 aircraft were still in flying condition. A few aircraft were subjected to a partial upgrade that included GPS. By early 2007, some 48 years

after their introduction, the FAA still relied on 10 MS-760 Paris tactical trainers as part of the 1st squadron at its IV Brigade in Mendoza. The type was retired officially on 14 March 2007.

Manufacturer	Aircraft Type	Delivered	Number	Serial Numbers	Remarks
Morane-Saulnier	MS-760A Paris	1959	10	A-01 to A-10	Prefix changed to E-201 to E-210
Morane-Saulnier	MS-760A Paris	1960	2	A-11 & A-12	Prefix changed to E-211 to E-212
FMA	MS-760A Paris	1961	13	E-213 to E-225	
FMA	MS-760A Paris	1962	15	E-226 to E-240	
FMA	MS-760A Paris	1963	8	E-241 to E-248	

Grumman F9F-2B Panther (0453) flying over Bahia Blanca city. (via Santiago Rivas)

Grumman F9F Panther (1959–1970)

Sole international operator of this 1st generation naval jet fighter, the Argentine Navy received 20 single-seat Grumman F9F-2B Panthers in late 1956. The Panthers were acquired through a US Government USD 600,000 contract, plus refurbishment and delivery costs.

These former US aircraft formed the 1° Escuadrilla Aeronaval de Ataque (1st Naval Air Attack Flight) at Punta Indio Naval Air Base in January 1959. The single-seat fighters were assigned serial numbers 0416 to 0427, and then 0447 to 0458. The Escuadrilla was to form the main embarked element aboard a former USS *Essex* class aircraft carrier. However, the carrier purchase was dropped in favour of a former Royal Navy carrier, HMS *Warrior*. Renamed ARA *Independencia*, the old light carrier was not fast enough to allow jet operations.

An impressive line-up of COAN F9F-2B Panthers. (via Santiago Rivas)

By 1960 it was clear that the Navy Aviation needed a two-seat conversion trainer to ease the transition of naval fighter pilots from the T-6 Texan trainer to the F9F-2B Panther, and they bought two F9F-8T Cougars from the US Navy. The two-seaters were assigned the serial numbers 0516 and 0517 with the code numbers of 151 and 152 respectively, joining the 1° Escuadrilla Aeronaval de Ataque in 1962.

In April 1963 some units of the Argentine Navy started an insurrection against the government. Panthers flying from Punta Indio Naval Air Base attacked Argentinean Army armoured units on August 2. One of the Panthers is believed to have been shot down by AAA. Punta Indio was bombed the next day by FAA Gloster Meteors, F-86Fs and MS-760As.

Two F9F-8T Cougars sitting onboard of aircraft carrier ARA *Indepedencia* during the travel to Argentina.
(via Santiago Rivas)

The Panther's first and only embarked operation took place in July 1963, when 3-A-119 performed a landing on ARA *Independencia*. However, the Panthers were not usually embarked on Argentina's aircraft carrier, with piston-engine T-28F Fennecs used for the task. They were deployed to Rio Gallegos Naval Air Base during the 1965 conflict with Chile. The Panthers started to be withdrawn from use in 1967 and were completely replaced by MB-326 armed trainers in 1970.

Manufacturer	Aircraft Type	Delivered	Number	Serial Numbers	Remarks
Grumman	F9F-2B Panther	1959	20	0416 to 0427 0447 to 0458	
Grumman	F9F-8T Cougar	1962	2	0516 & 0517	

North American F-86 Sabre (1960–1976, 1982)

In November 1956 the FAA approached Canadian company Canadair Limited on the possible sale of up to 36 Sabre Mk.6 fighters. However, the U.S. protested the sale, as North American Aviation was also in negotiations with the Argentine government to supply brand new F-100 Super Sabres. Eventually, these negotiations were also cancelled, and the US State Department offered to provide reconditioned second hand F-86F Sabres as part of the US Military Assistance Program.

A three F-86F-30 Sabre line-up.
(Mario Martínez Collection)

In order to replace its old Calquin fighter-bombers, 28 F-86F-30 Sabre jet fighters were delivered in 1960. The first aircraft arrived in Argentina during September and were pressed into service with the IV Air Brigade. They received serial numbers C-101 to C-128.

By 1962 the unit had achieved IOC and had formed a six-aircraft aerobatic demonstration flight known as 'Escuadrilla Aerobatica Cruz del Sur' (Southern Cross Aerobatic Flight). Some of the aircraft employed by the flight were baptized with names from the Southern Cross constellation, so C-101 became 'Beta', C-108 became 'Alfa Centauro', C-113 'Gamma', and C-124 'Delta'.

Argentinean Sabres were used to suppress a military uprising in 1962. They attacked Punta Indio Naval Air Base, together with Meteors, destroying a rebel Douglas C-54.

By the early 1970s Argentinean Sabres were soldiering on in the interceptor role, but by 1976 they were replaced by Sidewinder-armed A-4C Skyhawk fighters. Sabres were stored and offered for sale in the international market, with Uruguay and Venezuela interested, but the sales never went through.

F-86F-30 Sabre (C-120) displayed in 1972 with a full range of weapons. The air-to-air component was limited to gun and unguided rockets. (via Santiago Rivas)

By the start of the Falklands campaign, the remaining Sabres were re-activated and dispersed to several coastal bases to act as point defence fighters. There was even a motion to deploy a flight of Sabres to the Falklands. It would have been an interesting account of 1950s vintage fighters versus Harrier jump jets.

Manufacturer	Aircraft Type	Delivered	Number	Serial Numbers	Remarks
North American	F-86F-30 Sabre	1960	28	C-101 to C-128	ex-USAF

Douglas A-4 Skyhawk (1966–1999)

The FAA selected the A-4B Skyhawk as a replacement for its aging fleet of Meteor fighter-bombers. The 1965 order comprised 50 surplus US Navy fighter-bombers worth USD 7.1 million. The Skyhawks were to be delivered in two batches after refurbishment at the Douglas facility in Tulsa in Oklahoma. The resulting aircraft was designated A-4P and had few modifications, including a revised ejection seat and new lift spoilers, however, it did not have Sidewinder missile capability.

A-4P (C-202) shortly after arrival in Argentina in 1966. (ARA)

A-4C (317) armed with Shafrir missiles and fuel tanks. (via Santiago Rivas)

The first batch of 25 aircraft were delivered in 1966 serial numbers C-201 to C-225 (C for Caza/Fighter), the second batch of 24 aircraft reached Argentina, but number C-203 crashed in the US. They formed the 3rd Fighter-Bomber Squadron at V Brigade in Villa Reynolds and the 1st Fighter-Bomber Squadron at IV Brigade based in El Plumerillo Air Base in Mendoza. On 10 November 1967 the first Skyhawk crashed in Argentina, this was C-205 to be followed less than seven months later by C-216.

The second batch was delayed by the US Government, as US naval air services were losing quite more fighter-bombers than they had thought in Vietnam. The 25 paid for Argentinean Skyhawks were kept back in reserve. The Argentinean owned fleet had been reduced to 20 aircraft after C-202 and C-211 had been written-off.

The second batch was finally delivered to Argentina in 1971, arming the IV Brigade's 2nd Fighter-Bomber Squadron and V Brigade's 4th Fighter-Bomber Squadron, displaying serial numbers C-226 to C-250. The first accident from this second batch occurred on 5 September 1972 (C-245) and was followed by C-249 in 1973. 1974 was a bad year for Skyhawks in Argentina, as the FAA lost three aircraft (C-210, C-223, and C-238) between August and December.

In order to replace the F-86F Sabre squadron, the Argentinean government ordered a third batch of Skyhawks. This time, they were radar-equipped and Sidewinder-capable A-4C. Twenty-five Skyhawks were obtained from US Navy surplus stocks and completely refurbished by Lockheed Aircraft Services at its Ontario, California facility. The refurbished 'Charlies' were modified with the external wing pylons, only seen on A-4E series onwards.

Delivery of this third batch started in 1976, with serial numbers C-301 to C-325. The 'Charlies' were put in flying condition at the Río Cuarto Air Material Area in Cordoba and were delivered to the IV Air Brigade at Mendoza, complementing A-4Ps. The first 'Charlie' to be lost was C-308 at the end of September 1976.

A-4C (C-314) preserved
in excellent conditions at
Mendoza.
(Chris Lofting)

Attrition was heavy during the next four years with the loss of 16 A-4s: in 1977 it lost three A-4Ps (C-201, C-217, and C-219), and two A-4Cs (C-316 and, C-317); in 1978 three A-4Ps (C-229, C-241, and C-243) plus one 'Charlie' (C-306); in 1980 one A-4P (C-213), two A-4Cs (C-315 and C-320); in 1981 two each for the A-4P (C-218, C-247), and the A-4C (C-311, C-323).

By the 1982 Falklands War, the FAA had some 49 Skyhawks operational out of 75 delivered. These were 19 A-4Ps, 17 A-4Cs with the IV Air Brigade at El Plumerillo and, 13 A-4Ps with the V Air Brigade at Villa Reynolds. The IV Air Brigade deployed its A-4C fleet to San Julian AB and the V Brigada's A-4Ps were deployed to BAM Rio Gallegos in order to engage enemy forces.

The first operational Skyhawk loss during the conflict occurred on 9 May, when two A-4Cs (C-303 and C-313) from IV Brigade were shot down, apparently by Sea Dart ship-borne SAMs.

The first successful action against the Royal Navy occurred on 12 May, when V Air Brigade's Skyhawks operating out of Rio Gallegos, damaged the destroyer HMS *Glasgow*. This proved to be a very bloody date, as the unit lost four fighters (serial numbers C-206, C-208, C-246, and C-248), two to Sea Wolf SAMs, one to friendly AAA fire over Goose Green and one on evasive manoeuvring. On 21 May the same unit damaged the frigate HMS *Argonaut*, but it was not until 23 May that it managed to sink the frigate HMS *Antelope* loosing another A-4P (C-242) to an unidentified SAM. On 25 May, Skyhawks sank the Destroyer HMS *Coventry* using free-fall bombs but lost an A-4P (C-244) in the attack to a Sea Dart SAM. That same day the unit also damaged the frigate HMS *Broadsword*. On 27 May, an A-4P (C-215) was shot down by anti-aircraft defences from HMS *Intrepid* or HMS *Fearless* over San Carlos.

The IV Air Brigade lost another pair of Charlies (C-309 and C-325) on 21 May to Sidewinders missiles from 800° Squadron Sea Harriers. The IV Air Brigade's 'Charlies', operating from Rio Grande and San Julian were committed against the British landing fleet in the San Carlos area on 24 May. They managed to damage or disable at least three landing ships (LSL) but suffered the loss of an aircraft (C-305) to anti-aircraft defences. The next day a pair of 'Charlies' was again shot down (numbers C-304 and C-319), one by a Sea Dart SAM from HMS *Coventry* and the other by an unspecified SAM.

On 30 May the Argentine Air Force mounted what was to be its most significant operation. An attack package of four 'Charlies' armed with three 250-kg bombs each, and two Naval Aviation Super Étendards (one armed with the last available Exocet) were to attack the British Carrier HMS *Illustrious*. Two of the 'Charlies' were lost (C-301 and C-310) during what turned out to be a mistaken attack against HMS *Avenger* by Sea Dart SAMs coming from HMS *Exeter*.

On 8 June, the V Air Brigade was again in action against British landing forces, sinking HMS *Fearless* (LCU) and damaging another two ships (HMS *Sir Galahad* and HMS *Sir Tristram*). Three A-4Ps (C-204, C-226, and C-228) were shot down by Sidewinder missiles coming from 800° Squadron Sea Harriers.

By the end of the conflict, the FAA had lost 10 A-4Ps and 9 A-4Cs, but worse of all, 17 Skyhawk pilots. British post-war pressure brought a US embargo on spares and the Skyhawk fleet quickly shrunk. The IV Air Brigade's seven surviving A-4Cs fleet was transferred to the V Air Brigade by 1983 in order to keep minimum strength levels.

Trying to rebuild its fleet, the Argentine government made efforts to obtain 24 A-4 Skyhawks from Israel. The deal was frozen by US pressure and collapsed. As compensation, Israel provided an estimated three IAI Gabriel III air-to-surface missiles per operational Skyhawk (including Navy variants).

A 1986 plan to rebuild several airframes at FMA's plant in Córdoba with assistance from McDonnell Douglas also collapsed. The once powerful fleet had been reduced to 16 A-4Ps and 7 A-4Cs fighters by the end of 1987. In 1988 C-318 was lost in an accident, the pilot ejecting successfully after a mechanical failure on 3 October, followed by C-236 the next day. With the advent of new A-4AR Fightinghawk fighter-bombers to No. 1 & No. 2 Squadrons of the V Group, the service's last five A-4Ps (C-207, C-214, C-221, C-222, and C-225) and two A-4Cs (C-314 and C-322) were retired at the end of March 1999.

Naval Skyhawks

The Argentine Navy selected the Douglas A-4B Skyhawk for its new embarked air group aboard the ARA *Veinticinco de Mayo* (former HMS *Venerable*, former HMNLS *Karel Doorman*) Colossus-class aircraft carrier in 1970. The Navy consequently ordered 24 second hand A-4Bs and refurbished 16 of them to the A-4Q standard, the rest were used as spare parts source. The refurbishment included new flaps, slats, Sidewinder missile capability, extra pylons, and a complete engine overhaul. They were delivered in December 1971 and started embarked operations in August the following year. They were operated by Escuadrón Aeronaval (Naval Air Squadron) 33rd (EA-33) at Base Aérea Naval 'Comandante Espora'. They used serial numbers 0654 to 0669 and radio call signs in the 3-A-301 to 3-A-316 range.

In 1973 the squadron lost two of its fighters, 0669/3-A-316 on 16 January and 0668/3-A-315 on 25 June. Further losses included 0666/3-A-313 on 13 May 1975, 0663/3-A-310 on 22 September, and 0664/ 3-A-311 on 18 July 1977.

In 1978 the A-4Q Skyhawks were deployed aboard the ARA *Veinticinco de Mayo* to the southernmost point of the country, performing CAPs over the Lenox, Picton and Nueva islands during a border dispute with Chile.

Latin American Fighters

A line-up of five COAN A-4Qs
on board of ARA *Veinticinco de
Mayo* in 1978.
(via Santiago Rivas)

By the time that Argentina invaded the Falklands, the Navy had ten operational
Skyhawks, with three aircraft deployed to Puerto Belgrano and seven aboard the ARA
Veinticinco de Mayo. The unit had been re-named the 3rd Attack Squadron.

During the Falklands War, Argentine Navy Skyhawks sank two British Frigates
HMS *Ardent* and HMS *Antelope*, damaged a County-class Destroyer and, a Type-21
Frigate. They first operated from the ARA *Veinticinco de Mayo* and latter from BAN
Rio Grande. Once restricted to land-based operations, the naval Skyhawks would have
to fly at they are limit range to reach their targets.

On 21 May 1982, a four ship formation of A-4Q Skyhawks led by Captain Philippi
sank the British Navy Frigate HMS *Ardent* after bombing it with Mk-82 bombs. Philippi, together with another A-4Q were shot down immediately afterwards by a Sea Harriers from °800 Squadron. A third A-4Q was lost as it was damaged by the sinking HMS

A-4Q (3-A-305/0658) seen
during launch preparations
onboard of ARA *Veinticinco de
Mayo*.
(via Santiago Rivas)

Ardent and a Sea Harrier with the pilot was forced to eject. On that same day a Type-21 frigate was also sunk and one of the attacking Skyhawks (0665/3-A-312) was shot down by a Harrier.

The COAN tried to replace it's loses after the end of hostilities. A pair of A-4B instructional airframes was overhauled to the A-4Q standard. They were serialled 3-A-317 and 3-A-318. Soon after, negotiations were started with Israel for up to eight A-4E fighter-bombers. British pressure on the US Government quickly froze the transfer of this US-made fighter to Argentina.

By December 1986 a lack of spare parts, attrition, and airframe fatigue had reduced the fleet to only five flying aircraft. The 3rd Attack Squadron was disbanded and the remaining aircraft were taken up by the 2nd Squadron. The last two operational Skyhawks were retired in 1988.

Manufacturer	Aircraft Type	Delivered	Number	Serial Numbers	Remarks
Douglas	A-4P Skyhawk	1966	25	C-201 to C-225	ex-US Navy; C-203 crashed before delivery
Douglas	A-4P Skyhawk	1971	25	C-226 to C-250	ex-US Navy
Douglas	A-4Q Skyhawk	1971	16	0654 to 0669	ex-US Navy
Douglas	A-4B Skyhawk	1971	2		Instructional airframes
Douglas	A-4C Skyhawk	1975	25	C-301 to C-325	ex-US Navy

Aermacchi MB-326 & EMBRAER EMB-326 Xavante (1969–2008)

In 1968 COAN selected the small Italian jet trainer and light attack aircraft MB-326GB to replace its fleet of F9F Panther fighters and AT-6 Texan trainers. Deliveries of the first batch of six aircraft began in 1969 and were applied serial numbers 0613 to 0618 and codes 4-A-101 to 4-A-106. They formed the I Escuadrilla Aeronaval de Ataque (1st Navy Attack Squadron) at Punta Indio Naval Air Base (BAN).

EMB-326 Xavante (4-A-137/0782) with gun pod on a training mission. (ARA)

One MB-326 (4-A-104/ 0616) and one EMB-326 Xavante (4-A-137/ 0782) from COAN are patrolling off the Argentinean coast.
(ARA)

The MB-326 received the local designation MC-32 and it started working up mainly on close air-support and armed reconnaissance training. The MC-32s were equipped with Vinten 360 photographic reconnaissance pods for this last mission. They were joined by another two aircraft, numbers 0646 and 0647 (codes 4-A-107 and 4-A-108).

During the 1982 Falklands War, the MB-326s were dispersed to Comandante Espora and Almirante Zar naval bases to serve as emergency point defence fighters. They were then deployed to Rio Gallegos and Ushuaia naval air stations for border patrol missions, in case a foreign (Chilean or British) enemy would invade continental Argentina. This was the extent of their participation in the Falklands campaign.

MB-326 serial number 0614 (4-A-102) was lost on 29 May 1982, on 28 October, another MB-326, serial number 0613 (4-A-101) was also written off. The six remaining aircraft soldiered on, although they soon encountered serviceability problems, as the Rolls Royce Viper engine became the subject of a British embargo.

Urgent attrition replacements were sought from Brazil, who's local aerospace company EMBRAER had built the MB-326GB under license as the EMB-326 Xavanate. The Forca Aerea Brasileira (FAB) offered 11 second-hand aircraft: serial numbers 0775 to 0779 (former FAB numbers 4576, 4573, 4588, 4602, and 4545) received the codes 4-A-131 to 4-A-135, number 0780 (former FAB 4609) replaced 4-A-101, numbers 0781 and 0782 (former FAB 4574 and 4612) received the codes 4-A-136 and 4-A-137, numbers 0783 and 0784 (former FAB 4606 and 4610) received the codes 4-A-102 and 4-A-104. Serial number 0785 was coded as 4-A-138. All the aircraft were delivered on 21 September 1982.

The original MB-326 4-A-104 was apparently stored or cannibalized, although it was reported as operational during 2000.

By 1985 Argentina's CITEFA (The Armed Force's Centre for Scientific and Technical Research) begun a weapon integration programme using an MB-326 and the locally developed, radio-guided Martin Pescador (Kingfisher) air-to-surface missile. The missile had an active range of 8 km. Eventually, the entire MB-326/Xavante fleet was modified to fire the Martin Pescador missile. They were also equipped with the Macchi 850-21 reconnaissance pod.

The first Xavante loss occurred to 0780/4-A-101 (again 101) on 21 December 1988. It was followed by 4-A-134 during 1991 and by 4-A-135 in 1994. In that year, the original surviving MB-326GB fleet was relegated to reserve status and stored. The 4-A-133 was cannibalized for spare parts to keep the 4-A-138 operational.

As the annual training output was down to five new naval aviators by 1997 the Xavante unit, by now known as Escuadrón Aeronaval 41, offered to train Brazilian naval aviators. The two year course includes ground, basic, advanced and weapons training with the aid of two simulators. A pair of Xavantes was still in service by late 2007. However they were officially retired on 26 April 2008, marking 39 years of MB/EMB-326 operations in Argentina. There is no replacement in sight.

Manufacturer	Aircraft Type	Delivered	Number	Serial Numbers	Remarks
Aermacchi	MB-326GB	1969	8	0613 to 0618 0647 to 0648	
EMBRAER	EMB-326GB	1982	11	0775 to 0784	ex-FAB

Aviation Marcel Dassault Mirage III (1973-)

The French-designed delta fighter was first offered to Argentina as early as 1965 in order to replace its ageing Meteor fighters. After a prolonged study that involved the North American F-100 Super Sabre and the Swedish Saab Draken, the Fuerza Aérea Argentina (FAA) ordered 12 Aviation Marcel Dassault (AMD) Mirage IIIEA supersonic interceptors and 2 Mirage IIIDA conversion trainers in October 1970. Original plans called for these 14 fighters to form a squadron within the III Air Brigade at Jose C. Paz Air Base, while up to 70 more Mirages would be locally produced under license. The license production program was cancelled for financial reasons and the single-seat order was cut to ten.

The Mirage IIIEAs (serial numbers I-003 to I-012) and Mirage IIIDAs (numbers I-001 and I-002) were delivered aboard Argentinean C-130Es during 1973, and assembled by

Two Mirage IIIEAs in different paint schemes. I-007 is armed with a pair of R.550 Magic missiles.
(via Santiago Rivas)

Mirage IIICJ (C-717) drops a SAMP 400 parachute retarded bomb during weapon trial tests. (via Santiago Rivas)

a team of French technicians at a civilian airport, latter to become Mariano Moreno AFB. The Mirages were assigned to the 1st Fighter-Interceptor Squadron.

Mirage pilots were trained by French instructors in Argentina and at El Libertador Air Base in Venezuela, were they had access to the sole Mirage simulator in the Americas at the time. The Mirage IIIEA was a pure interceptor variant, armed with Matra R.530 air-to-air missiles, 51 of which were purchased. In January 1976, after a re-organization program, the unit became the VIII Air Brigade, and Grupo 8 was its operational title.

Mirage I-009 was lost on 23 March 1976, but was followed that year with an order for a follow on batch of seven Mirage IIIEAs in 1977. The first operational deployment of the type occurred in 1978 when tensions with neighbouring Chile saw six Mirage IIIEAs sent to Comodoro Rivadavia Air Base.

Second batch of Mirages had the capability to fire the R.550 Magic short-range air-to-air missile and seven Mirages were delivered during 1979 (serial numbers I-013 to I-019). That same year Mirage number I-001 was lost on 30 March.

During the Falklands War, the Mirage IIIs were deployed to the naval air bases of Rio Gallegos and Comodoro Rivadavia, from where they could perform CAP missions over the islands. The Mirage fleet had 21 fighter pilots (12 at Gallegos and 9 at Comodoro) in strength to be distributed among 13 available aircraft. Another three Mirages were held back to defend Buenos Aires from a possible attack by British Vulcan bombers. The original idea of positioning them at BAM Malvinas (Falklands Air Base) was abandoned, as the air base lacked the required infrastructure.

First contact with the enemy was a disappointment, with two 'second-batch' Mirages (I-015 and I-019) shot down by a pair of Royal Navy Sea Harriers. Allegedly a Mirage shot down a Sea Harrier from 801° Squadron using a Matra R.530. After a third Mirage was shot down by friendly fire, the surviving fleet was held back to defend the mainland. They performed a total of 170 combat sorties.

The FAA started to re-build its Mirage force in the immediate post-war period. Two former Armée de l' Air (ALA, French Air Force) Mirage IIIBE two-seat fighters (former ALA 271 and 272) were converted into IIIDA standard and delivered (wearing serial numbers I-020 and I-021) by Dassault in December 1982. However British pressure

Mirage IIIEA in grey overall paint scheme with toned-down markings prepares for take-off. (Santiago Rivas)

prevented anymore former ALA Mirages to be delivered to Argentina. In October 1983 the fleet lost I-016 during an operational deployment to Rio Gallegos.

Israel was not subject to British pressure and it supplied 19 former Israeli Defence Force Mirage IIICJ fighter-bombers and 3 two-seat Mirage IIIBJs between March 1984 and November 1985. These Six-Day War veterans were delivered to the 1st Fighter-Bomber Squadron of the IV Air Brigade at El Plumerillo Air Base assigned the serial numbers C-701 to C-719 (IIICJs) and C-720 to C-722 (IIIBJs).

On 29 April 1985 the first IIICJ (C-707) was lost, followed on 26 August 1987 by I-014 during a training flight. This had reduced the second batch aircraft to three flying aircraft. Plans to buy 12 Mirage IIIEE fighters from Spain failed, mainly because of British pressure. However, at least eight Argentinean pilots received training on the Spanish Mirage IIIEEs, and some sources suggest that the training focused on DACT with Spanish Navy Harriers (Matadores). The Spanish Mirages were eventually sold to Pakistan.

The VIII Air Brigade was dissolved in March 1988 and the aircraft were re-assigned to the VI Brigade at Tandil. In 29 July 1988 Mirage IIIBJ serial number C-720 was lost, to be followed by Mirage IIICJ C-705 on 25 June 1989. By the early 1990s the FAA's Mirage fleet almost had been halved, with some 11 Mirage IIIEAs, 1 IIIDA, 12 IIICJs, and 2 IIIBJs in inventory. At this time, service levels effectively reduced the fleet to about 15 operational aircraft. The remaining former Israeli Mirages were retired in 1995 from operational service, although one IIICJ was kept for weapon testing. One of the retired Mirage IIICJ (713), a veteran of the Yom Kippur War, was donated to the Israeli Defence Force Museum at a ceremony on 20 May 2003.

By 2002 only 12 Mirage IIIEA/DA fighters were operational. These were concentrated with the remaining M-5 Maras and Fingers at Grupo de Caza 6, VI Air Brigade at Tandil Air Base and tasked with air superiority armed with Matra Magic and Super R.530F missiles. A secondary ground-attack capability can be performed using BK-BR PG 50-kg, 125-kg, or 250-kg precision guided bombs. They are also used for target towing of CECAPEM 90 targets for ground air defence gunnery.

Original plans called for their replacement by 2005 with a new interceptor that would protect Argentinean skies. Spanish (former Qatari) Mirage F.1 interceptors were

evaluated, but negotiations did not proceed. On 3 July 2009, a Mirage IIIEA crashed near Tandil, its pilot ejected safely but this brings the number of Mirage III interceptors in service to eight. Without a replacement program in place, former ALA Mirage 2000s seem to be the favoured choice, however France has announced it will be able to provide a dozen fighters until 2014. Replacement of the fleet now appears to be for former ALA Mirage 2000s, however France has announced it will be able to provide a dozen fighters until 2012.

Manufacturer	Aircraft Type	Delivered	Number	Serial Numbers	Remarks
Dassault	Mirage IIIEA	1970	10	I-003 to I-012	
Dassault	Mirage IIIDA	1970	2	I-001 & I-002	
Dassault-Breguet	Mirage IIIEA	1976	7	I-013 to I-019	
Dassault	Mirage IIIBE	1982	2	I-020 & I-021	ex-ALA
Dassault	Mirage IIICJ	1982	19	C-701 to C-719	ex-IDF/AF
Dassault	Mirage IIIBJ	1982	3	C-720 to C-722	ex-IDF/AF

Israel Aircraft Industries Dagger (1978–)

The relationship between the Argentinean and Israeli air forces began in 1971, when a group of Argentinean pilots were sent to Israel to learn the tactics employed during the Six Day War.

Israel assembled 51 single-seat Nesher S (Eagle) and 10 two-seat (trainer) Nesher T fighter-bombers, using Mirage 5 with Israeli avionics and Shafrir AAMs. The aircraft were delivered by USAF transports wearing Aerospatiale plates, but there is no indication that it ever built the fighter jets. Neshers brought down some 100 enemy aircraft during the 1973 Yom Kippur War.

As the US-imposed Humprey-Kennedy amendment was still in place, which prevented the sale of aircraft with US-made parts to Argentina, the desired Kfir C-2 fighters could not be delivered. The remaining 35 'Nesher S' and 4 'Nesher T' fighter-bombers

Dagger A (432) loaded with fuel tanks and Mk.82 bombs, pairs with an unidentified Mirage IIIEA armed with R.550 Magic. (via Santiago Rivas)

A FAA Finger in grey overall paint scheme with two long range fuel tanks over southern Patagonia.
(Cees-Jan van der Ende/alfakilo.nl)

were negotiated under a swift and secret deal, code named 'Dagger'. Aircrew training was speeded, with dozens of pilots being sent for advanced training in Peru (on its Mirage 5Ps) and Israel (to Eitam AB).

The first batch, comprising 25 Dagger As (serial numbers C-401 to C-424, and C-427) and 2 two-seat versions (numbers C-425 and C-426) was delivered from November 1978 to July 1979 and entered service with the VI Air Brigade at Tandil. The first accident claimed Dagger A C-406 on 26 November 1979 and was followed by a two-seat write-off on 07 October 1980 (C-425). The second batch comprised ten Dagger As (serial numbers C-428 to C-437) and two Dagger Bs (serial numbers C-438 and C-439). It was delivered during 1981.

During the Falklands War the Dagger fleet and its 33 fighter pilots, operating out of San Julian and Río Grande were completely committed to the operations. Daggers attacked the Royal Navy fleet starting on 1 May, damaging the destroyer HMS *Glamorgan*, the frigates HMS *Alacrity*, and HMS *Arrow*. The first Dagger (C-433) was shot down by a Sidewinder missile from a Sea Harrier belonging to 800° Squadron over East Falkland.

On 21 May, Dagger fighters attacked the British fleet at San Carlos, bombing the destroyer HMS *Antrim*, the frigate HMS *Ardent*. Also minor damage was caused to the frigates HMS *Brilliant* and HMS *Broadsword*. However the price toll was high, HMS *Broadsword* managed to shoot down one Dagger with a Sea Wolf SAM near Fanning Head, a second Dagger A fell to an AIM-9L Sidewinder from 800° Squadron Sea Harriers near Teal River Inlet. At West Falkland three more Daggers were shot down by 801° Squadron Sea Harriers, all victims of the deadly Sidewinder AIM-9L. In total, the FAA lost five Daggers (C-403, C-404, C-407, C-409, and C-428).

On 23 May Dagger A (C-437) was shot down over Pebble Island again by a Sidewinder missile from a Sea Harrier. On 24 May, three more Daggers (C-410, C-419, and C-430) were shot down by the Sidewinder missiles north of Pebble Island. On 29 May the last Dagger (C-437) was lost to a Rapier SAM over San Carlos Bay. By the end of the war, the FAA had lost 11 Daggers.

After the war, the FAA still had 23 Dagger As and 3 Dagger Bs. In 1980 a program named FINGER, which included new Elta EL/M-2001B radar, Marconi HUD, mission computer and electronic unit, a Doppler system from Canadian Marconi and a Sfim INS, started to upgrade the FAA's Dagger fleet. One aircraft (C-427) was upgraded before the Falklands War. However, the program had to be modified, as Marconi, a British company, was not able to provide the required systems.

The program was launched again in 1983, with C-408 receiving a development FINGER II upgrade, and C-427 being brought up to the same standard. The interim FINGER III upgrade included a new HUD in 1985. The first Finger upgraded model that was lost was C-431 on 16 May 1985, to be followed by C-418 on 12 June 1987.

By the early 1990s the remaining 21 Finger IIIs were earmarked to be upgraded to 'Finger IIIA' version, with a Kfir C2 type nose, canards and a new INS. Only 20 fighters were upgraded as C-427 was lost on 25 October 1993. Finger III, C-413 was lost on 14 July 1995 followed by C-429 on 18 October 1995.

By 1999 the fleet had been reduced to 14 operational aircraft, comprised of 11 As and 3 Bs. The As were subjected to the USD 39 million FINGER IIIB follow-up upgrade, which included an Elta EL/M-2001B multi-mode radar, Elbit/IAI WDNS-41 navigation and attack system, an Elbit S-8600 navigation system, GPS, an El-Op HUD (similar to the Kfir C-10 upgrade) and Python Mk. IV air-to-air missiles.

Finger C-434 was reported lost on 21 June 2004 over Rio Cuarto due to engine failure during a training flight from Tandil. The pilot, 1st Lt. Sebastian González Iturbe managed to eject and escape without harm.

Optimized for strike missions, the Fingers are armed with LAU-68A 70-mm rocket launchers, BK-BR 125-kg, 250-kg, and 500-kg general purpose bombs, EXPAL BR-S 250-kg retarded bombs, Mk.117 820-kg demolition, TL-1/-2 cluster bombs, and FAS-260 plus the FAS-300 anti-runway bombs. The upgraded Finger IIIB fleet will stay in service until 2010.

Manufacturer	Aircraft Type	Delivered	Number	Serial Numbers	Remarks
IAI	Dagger A	1979	25	C-401 to C-424 & C-427	ex-IDF/AF Nesher
IAI	Dagger B	1979	2	C-425 & C-426	ex-IDF/AF Nesher
IAI	Dagger A	1981	10	C-428 to C-437	ex-IDF/AF Nesher
IAI	Dagger B	1981	2	C-438 & C-439	ex-IDF/AF Nesher

Aermacchi MB-339A (1980–1990)

The Argentinean Naval Aviation Command (COAN) selected the Italian MB-339A to operate as a lead-in fighter trainer for the service's Super Étendard fighters. A fairly good service record with the MB-326GB was a decisive factor.

An order for 14 aircraft was placed and deliveries started in 1980 with 5 aircraft receiving the serial numbers 0761 to 0765 and the codes 4-A-110 to 4-A-114. Another five aircraft were received in 1981, wearing the serial numbers 0766 to 0770 (codes 4-A-115 to 4-A-119). They joined the eight MB-326GBs in service with the 1st Attack Squadron at

The only survivor of the COAN MB-339 fleet during the Falklands War, 0766/4-A-115, seen during the conflict in full armament. On 25 May 1982 it successfully attacked HMS *Argonaut* in that weapon configuration.
(via Santiago Rivas)

Punta Indio Naval Base. The 1982 Falklands war prevented the order to be completed, as the MB-339AA was powered by a British Rolls Royce Viper engine.

Due to its good short runway capability, six MB-339AAs (0761, 0763 to 0766 and 0768) were deployed to the Falklands, together with four armed T-34C-1 Turbo Mentors, two Shorts Skyvan transports, and one Puma helicopter. The MB-339AA was to be the only Argentine combat jet to operate from the Falklands, performing armed reconnaissance and CAS missions.

On 3 May 1982, 0764/4-A-113, part of a two-aircraft patrol flying out of Port Stanley crashed over Camp Pembroke due to bad weather killing its pilot. On 21 May, 0766/4-A-115 flying from Goose Green detected the British invasion forces near San Carlos and attacked (and damaged) a Leander-class frigate (HMS *Argonaut)* with cannon fire and rockets. Curiously, this was the only deployed MB-339 to survive the war.

On 28 May, 0765/4-A-114 was shot down by a Royal Marine Blowpipe SAM and its pilot killed after attacking British positions at Darwin during the battle for Goose Green. Three MB-339AAs were captured by British forces in Stanley.

The five remaining MB-339AAs suffered immediate effects from a British arms embargo that prevented delivery of the remaining four aircraft on order and any spares

COAN MB-339 4-A-117 exhibited as museum piece.
(via Iñigo Guevara y Moyano)

support for its RR engines. The aircraft were soon stored pending a replacement. A naval version of the IA-63 Pampa capable of embarked operations was planned and the COAN developed a requirement for between nine and twelve aircraft to supersede the MB-339 fleet, but the order never materialized.

Manufacturer	Aircraft Type	Delivered	Number	Serial Numbers	Remarks
Aermacchi	MB-339AA	1980	5	0761 to 0765	
Aermacchi	MB-339AA	1981	5	0766 to 0770	

Aviation Marcel Dassault-Breguet Aviation Super Étendard (1981–)

In order to replace its A-4Q Skyhawks in the embarked strike role, the Argentine Navy selected the longer range AMD-BA Super Étendard in 1979. A contract worth some USD 150 million was signed in 1980. Its missions were to be anti-ship strike, fleet air defence and CAS. A group of 50 pilots and mechanics was sent to France for conversion training on the type in September 1980. But the Super Étendard's capabilities were not the only reason why COAN selected it, the combination with the AM-39 Exocet was set to modernize the service.

The trained group of pilots returned to Argentina in late 1981 where it formed the 2nd Attack Squadron at Base Aeronaval Comandante Espora (BACE) at Bahia Blanca. In November 1981 it received five Super Étendards, wearing the codes 3-A-201 to 3-A-205 and five AM-39 Exocet missiles.

By the time the campaign to retake the Falklands started, the 2nd Squadron had received five aircraft and was still working up on the type with French technicians preparing the aircraft to operate the Exocet missile. The second batch comprising another

A Super Étendard during the Falklands War being armed with an AS-39 Exocet anti-ship missile.
(ARA)

COAN Super Étendard (0761/ 3-A-211) from 2° Escuadrilla Aeronaval de Caza y Ataque was refuelled by a Lockheed KC-130H TC-69 (FAA, 1° Brigada Aérea) during the Exercise "Mosquito" in October 2007. (Martin Otero)

five Super Étendards was to be delivered during late April, but delivery was suspended due to the European arms embargo, halting also any Exocet deliveries. In fact, France delayed delivery of Exocet missiles to Peru, in fear that they would be sent to Argentina during the conflict. Still, some Dassault technicians remained in the country and were able to put four Super Étendards in operational condition.

With only two weeks in operation, the 2° Attack Squadron equipped with the available Super Étendards and Exocet Missiles were pressed into service. Operating from Rio Grande Air Base, they managed to perform 12 combat sorties, sinking the British destroyer HMS *Sheffield* and the transport HMS *Atlantic Conveyor*. Both ships were sunk by Exocet missiles fired from Super Étendard 0753/3-A-203.

The Super Étendard-Exocet combination proved to be such a psychological weapon, that the British forces even considered a suicide SAS operation to destroy them at their base. No Super Étendard was lost during the war. Post war deliveries saw the order completed (including a further 28 Exocet missiles) by December 1982, with the aircraft receiving the codes 3-A-201 to 3-A-214.

By early 1983 the ARA *Veinticinco de Mayo's* flight deck had been modified to operate the Super Étendards and the squadron was completely operational. Although their main armament continued to be the Exocet, they were also armed with R.550 Magic air-to-air missiles, LAU-32 70-mm rocket pods, and Mk.82 bombs. They could also perform reconnaissance missions with the Vinten 360 pods.

In August 1989 the first Super Étendard (3-A-210) was lost, followed by 3-A-212 in December. The remaining 12 aircraft continued in service during the 1990s. On 29 May 1996, Super Étendard 0753/3-A-203 crashed into the tarmac at BAN Punta Indio, killing its pilot. Once the ARA *Veinticinco de Mayo* was sold, the Super Étendard pilots would train ship landings on the Brazilian aircraft carrier NAeL *Minas Gerais*,

Super Étendard (0757/ 3-A-207) being prepared for take-off with four SAMP 250 bombs. (ARA)

although these 'landings' were actually touch-and-go as the Brazilian ship lacked to required equipment to land the aircraft.

By the early 21st Century, the number operational aircraft had been reduced to just seven, these being 3-A-204, 3-A-206, 3-A-207, 3-A-209, 3-A-211, 3-A-213, and 3-A-214, with the remaining aircraft stored for economic reasons.

Manufacturer	Aircraft Type	Delivered	Number	Serial Numbers	Remarks
Dassault-Breguet	Super Étendard	1981	5	0751 to 0755	naval call signs 3-A-201 to 3-A-205
Dassault-Breguet	Super Étendard	1982	9	0756 to 0764	naval call signs 3-A-206 to 3-A-214

Aviation Marcel Dassault Mirage 5 (1982–)

Ten Peruvian Mirage 5P fighter-bombers arrived in Argentina during June 1982, marking this act the single, most significant symbol of Latin American military cooperation in the post Falklands era. Peruvian Mirages were quick to fill a void left by wartime losses. They formed the X Air Brigade based at Rio Gallegos Air Base, the FAA's main operating base during the conflict.

The Mirages were originally on loan, but the FAA decided it would buy them at a very reasonable USD 5 million price tag each. Officially the 'transfer' had been signed in December 1981, but the real negotiations took place during the Falklands War. Some sources state that the Mirages were delivered armed with AS-30 guided missiles.

The Mirage 5s were upgraded by Israel Aircraft Industries (IAI) to a standard similar to the Dagger's FINGER II configuration. They received the Dagger's old nose, new HUD, and the Shafrir missile capability. Addition of the Matra Belouga BGL-66 cluster bomb to the air fleet was also included in the programme, the resulting upgrade known as the 'M-5A Mara'. They were later enhanced by a local company – AeroCuar SA with a new Canadian Marconi computer, OMEGA navigation system, RWR and other improvements. Studies to modify the aircraft with FR probes similar to those of the SAAF Cheetahs were made, but abandoned.

This is one of ten ex-Peruvian Mirage 5P delivered to FAA in 1982. Those received a modest upgrade and were then called M-5A MA Mara. (Hans Rolink)

A FAA Mirage 5P armed with
R.550 missiles after Mara
upgrade over Argentina.
(via Santiago Rivas)

When armed for ground-attack missions, the Maras can carry a wide-variety of weapons that include TL-1/-2 250-kg cluster bombs, LAU-68A 70-mm rocket launchers, BK-BR 125-kg, 250-kg or 500-kg GP bombs and EXPAL BRP-S retarded bombs. In 1996 the M-5A Maras were transferred to the VI Air Brigade at Tandil, where they formed the 10th Fighter-bomber squadron, operating alongside two-seat Mirage IIIDA and Finger IIs.

Manufacturer	Aircraft Type	Delivered	Number	Serial Numbers	Remarks
Dassault	Mirage 5P	1982	10	C-603, C-604, C-607, C-609, C-610, C-619, C-628, C-630, C-633, C-636	ex-Peruvian AF

Fábrica Militar de Aviones IA-63 Pampa (1984–)

The State-owned Fábrica Militar de Aviones (FMA, Military Aircraft Factory) was assigned to supervise the design of a new basic/advanced jet trainer in 1979. The aircraft was to supersede and replace the aging MS-760A Paris fleet. FMA contracted Dornier for the initial design phase, which is why the aircraft bares a slight resemblance to the Dassault-Breguet/Dornier Alpha Jet.

The first prototype flew on 6 October 1984 (former 01) and was assigned to the Centro de Evaluación de Vuelo-CEV (Flight Test Center). Another two prototypes were delivered in 1985 (former 02 and former 03). A light attack capability was included, with a provision for a centreline DEFA (Aero Cuar) 30-mm gun pod, and four hard points for up to 1,160-kg weapons load. Main armament includes two 7.62-mm gun pods, LAU-61A 70-mm, ARM-657A 57-mm rocket launchers, BK-BR 50-kg, 125-kg, 250-kg GP bombs, INC 50-kg, or 100-kg napalm bombs.

At a fly-away USD 3 million price tag, a first order for 64 aircraft to replace the Paris jet trainers was to be followed by another 40 aircraft to be used as light attack fighters. The first Pampa (serial number E-801) was delivered in late 1987 and followed by another two in April 1988, declaring the first Pampa flight operational that year. The unit received a further ten aircraft (serial numbers E-804 to E-813) during 1989, and

IA-63 Pampa (818) built by LMAASA displaying during FIDAE 2008.
(Santiago Rivas)

IA-63 Pampa (815) built
by LMAASA with Andean
mountains in the background.
(Cees-Jan van der Ende/alfakilo.nl)

another (E-814) in 1990. Argentina's new liberal economy could not bear the 100 plus
Pampa production cost, and FMA began various export offers. The type was offered
to Bolivia, who had a requirement for up to 12 Pampas. Brazil was also approached
with an offer for 10 Pampas, as an offset for the 30 Tucano turboprop trainers that the
FAA bought from EMBRAER. Israel was to select the Pampa for 60 to 100 jet trainer
requirements. None of these ventures came to fruition. The first accident was over
Mendoza province in 1991 and the E-802 was written-off.

In 1990 FMA teamed with LTV Aerospace to offer the Pampa 2000 for the US JPTAS
(Joint Primary Trainer Aircraft System) to replace the USAF Cessna T-37 and the USN
T-34 Mentor trainers. former 01 and E-812 were shipped to the US, where LTV performed several modifications, including fuel system layout, revised avionics, strengthened landing gear, and a new cockpit layout. The Pampa 2000 was evaluated in August
1994 but the Argentine jet was deemed as 'too advanced for young pilots' and unit price
was too high. The contract was eventually won by the Pilatus/Raytheon team.

The FAA lost another aircraft in 1992 (E-813) during a demonstration at Farnbor-
ough air show in the UK. This was followed by E-810 in December 1994, reducing the
fleet to 11 operational Pampas, and the 3 prototypes. In December 1994 Lockheed-
Martin took control of FMA, creating Lockheed-Martin Aircraft Argentina Sociedad
Anónima (LMAASA). The LMAASA line delivered an IA-63 Pampa jet (E-815) in September 1999, anticipating a 'Pampa return-to-work' period in the 2000-2005 timeframe.
Each Pampa was returned to LMAASA after 800 hours, with 9 aircraft being kept operational at any one time. E-815 served to replace E-808, which was lost in that same
month over San Juan. Final assembly of E-816 was suspended, with some 55 per cent
of the work finished.

In June 2000, LMAASA re-started production of an upgraded IA-63 Pampa (using the
E-816 airframe) known as the AT-63. The new light fighter/trainer features a new Hon-
eywell TFE-731-2C turbofan, HOTAS, an Elbit-designed avionics suite incorporating
two Multifunction Colour Display Units (MCDU), GPS navigation, a mission computer

and an integrated weapons system that includes a 30-mm Aero Cuar FAS 460 cannon pod, Mk-81 and Mk-82, BK-BR 125-kg, 250-kg, and 500-kg general purpose bombs, 70-mm LAU-61, and 57-mm ARM-657A Mamboreta rocket launchers. The FAA signed an USD 230 million contract with LMAASA for the construction of 12 new AT-63 light fighters, with an option for a further 12. It would also upgrade 12 out of the existing 12 Pampas to the AT-63 configuration. They were to join the 1st and 2nd squadrons of the 4th Fighter Group/IV Brigade at El Plumerillo Air Base in Mendoza.

Financial problems forced the contract to be re-negotiated, and the FAA was to receive only six new AT-63s. Ten production Pampas (excluding E-807) and two of the prototypes (former 02 and former 03) would be upgraded to the same standard. The remaining six new aircraft would be privately financed by Lockheed-Martin and a buyer would be sought. Bolivia was the targeted customer, and the upgraded AT-63 was presented to Bolivian officials in May 2003, however without success.

The small Pampa fleet logged over 22,500 flying hours by 2003, but its future was still quite uncertain. With an operational fleet of less than 20 aircraft, the Pampa's spares supply is not assured in the long term and unit cost is quite high. On 10 December 2004 another Pampa (former 01) was lost while on a performance demonstration flight over Punta Indio Naval Air Base to a group of Chinese representatives. 1st Lt. Juan Pablo Martinez, an experienced Pampa pilot with over 560 hours on the type was killed.

First flight of the upgraded AT-63 was performed on 22 June 2005, with the conversion of one of the original prototypes (former 03) to the new configuration. Deliveries of upgraded aircraft began in 2006 and new aircraft followed from November 2007 until December 2008. The MoD announced a new contract with LMAASA in December 2007 for 10 new airframes and has initated studies into fitting a new turbofan engine. The LMAASA was bought back by the Argentine Government in early 2009 and is now known as the Area Material de Córdoba (AMC).

Manufacturer	Aircraft Type	Delivered	Number	Serial Numbers	Remarks
FMA	IA-63 Pampa	1984	1	EX01	
FMA	IA-63 Pampa	1985	2	EX02 & EX03	
FMA	IA-63 Pampa	1987	1	E-801	
FMA	IA-63 Pampa	1988	2	E-802 & E-803	
FMA	IA-63 Pampa	1989	10	E-804 to E-813	
FMA	IA-63 Pampa	1990	1	E-814	
LMAASA	IA-63 Pampa	1999	1	E-815	
LMAASA	AT-63 Pampa II	2005	6	E-816 to E-821	
LMAASA	AT-63 Pampa II	2007	10	E-822 to E-831	

Lockheed-Martin A-4AR Fightinghawk (1997–)

The US-imposed arms embargo on Argentina ended in 1994 and the FAA quickly started negotiations to obtain modern fighter aircraft. They required some 50 front-line fighters with the F-16 Fighting Falcon as the preferred choice. The McDonnell Douglas F/A-18 Hornet was runner up. US Congress immediately denied the sale, arguing that it would break the fragile balance of power in the region.

FAA's latest fighter – the A-4AR Fightinghawk. The second aircraft is armed with AIM-9M Sidewinder missiles.
(Cees-Jan van der Ende/alfakilo.nl)

With a large A-4 Skyhawk infrastructure in place, the FAA started looking for a modernized Skyhawk variant. Offers came from McDonnell Douglas and the Kuwaiti Air Force, Smith Industries and the US Navy, McDonnell Douglas and CASA, and Lockheed Aircraft Services and the USMC. The last offer, which included 48 A-4Ms single-seat, and 6 OA-4Ms two-seat fighter-bombers were selected. It was latter reduced to 32 A-4Ms and 4 OA-4Ms. The deal included 13 inoperable airframes (4 A-4Ms, 1 OA-4M, 6 A-4Fs and, 2 TA-4Js) to be used as a spare parts source.

The A-4M/OA-4M fleet was completely re-worked, with the installation of new ARG-1 (a down-rated version of the F-16's AN/APG-66V2) radar which led to the capability of firing AGM-65 Maverick missiles, LGBs, and AIM-9M Sidewinder AAMs. Avionics included Sextant Smart HUDs, a new INS, HOTAS, and an ALR-92 RWR. The new aircraft was renamed the A-4AR (for ARgentine) Fightinghawk (for sharing some capabilities of the F-16 Fighting Falcon).

Deliveries started in December 1997 to the V Group at Coronel Pringles AB in Villa Reynolds wearing the serial numbers C-901 to C-904 (OA-4ARs) and C-905 to C-936 (A-4AR). Half the fleet was upgraded at the Lockheed-Martin Aircraft Argentina SA (LMAASA) facility in Cordoba (what used to be FMA). Further weapon trails brought the A-4AR fleet to a new upgraded block, known as Block C3B with enhanced avionics. Training on the Fightinghawks starts with some 400 hours or simulator time followed by to 18 hours on the OA-4AR.

With the new fighter-bombers in service with 1st & 2nd squadrons of the V Group, the last five operational A-4Ps (C-207, C-214, C-221, C-222, and C-225) and two A-4Cs (C-314 and C-322) were retired during March 1999. By August 2000, the FAA had 24 pilots qualified to fly the new fighters. However it decided to place half the fleet in storage on reserve status at the V Brigade's base in Villa Reynolds.

A proposed plan for the replacement of the FAA's MS-760A Paris II LIFTs with 18 former US Navy TA-4J Skyhawk trainers was latter scrapped, as the airframes were considered too old. On 6 July 2005 the FAA suffered its first Fightinghawk loss, when one aircraft from V Brigade crashed some 30 km south of its base in Villa Reynolds.

Manufacturer	Aircraft Type	Delivered	Number	Serial Numbers	Remarks
Lockheed-Martin	A-4AR Fightinghawk	1997	32	C-905 to C-936	ex-USMC; upgraded before delivery
Lockheed-Martin	OA-4AR Fightinghawk	1997	4	C-901 to C-904	ex-USMC; upgraded before delivery
McDonnell Douglas	A-4M Skyhawk	1997	4		for spares; ex-USMC
McDonnell Douglas	OA-4M Skyhawk	1997	1		for spares; ex-USMC
McDonnell Douglas	A-4F Skyhawk	1997	6		for spares; ex-USMC
McDonnell Douglas	TA-4J Skyhawk	1997	2		for spares; ex-USMC

A-4AR (905) is the first of 32 former USMC A-4Ms being converted to Fightinghawk standard.
(Cees-Jan van der Ende/alfakilo.nl)

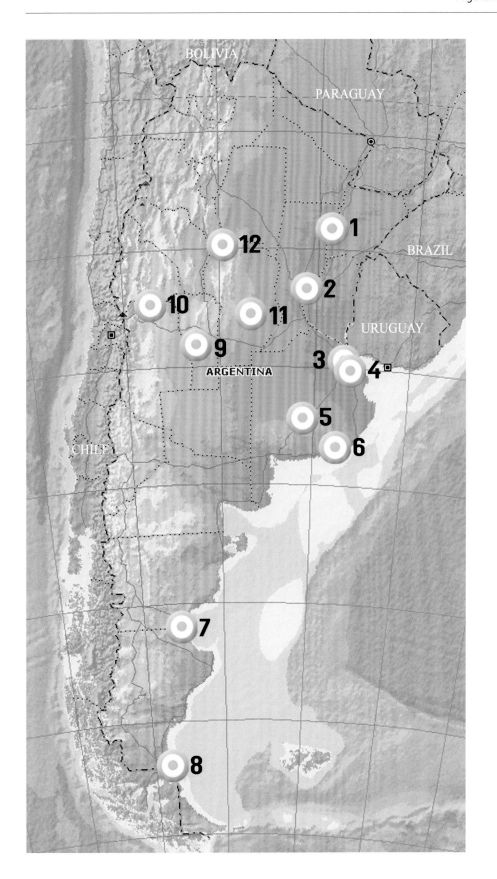

FAA Bases
1. Reconquista, Santa Fé
2. Paraná, Entre Ríos
3. Morón, Buenos Aires
4. El Palomar, Buenos Aires
5. Tandil, Buenos Aires
6. Mar del Plata, Buenos Aires
7. Comodoro Rivadavia, Chubut
8. Río Gallegos, Santa Cruz
9. Villa Reynolds, San Luis
10. El Plumerillo Air Base,
    Mendoza, Mendoza
    (now an IAP)
11. Río Cuarto, Córdoba
12. Córdoba, Córdoba

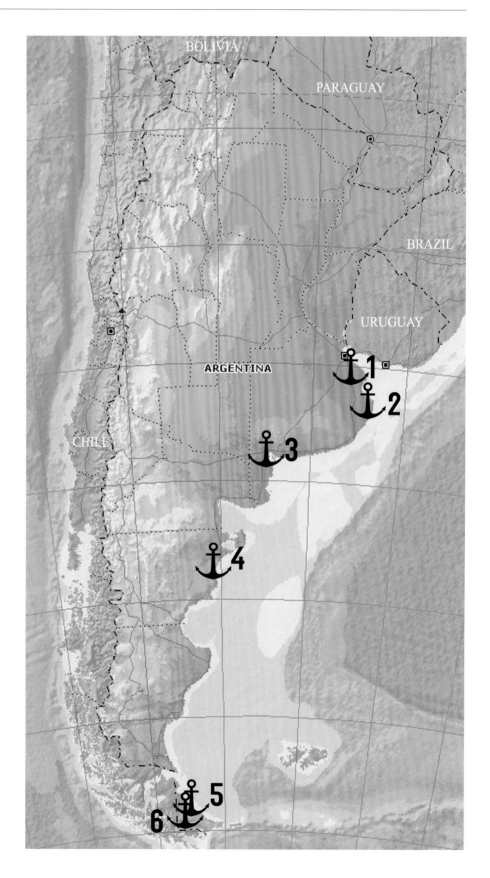

COAN Bases
1. Base Aeronaval Ezeiza (BAEZ), Buenos Aires
2. Base Aeronaval Punta Indio (BAPI), Buenos Aires
3. Base Aeronaval Comandante Espora (BACE), Buenos Aires
4. Base Aeronaval Almirante Zar (BAAZ), Chubut
5. Base Aeronaval Almirante Hermes Quijada, Rio Grande
6. Base Aeronaval Ushuaia, Tierra del Fuego

Chapter 2

BOLIVIA

The absence of external threats and a poor performing economy, has kept the Fuerza Aérea Boliviana (FAB, Bolivian Air Force) at a very low-technology state. Surplus, second-hand and obsolete, Canadian, French and Venezuelan aircraft have formed its jet fighter fleet since the early 1970s.

Bolivia has the privilege of being the last military operator of the ancient North American F-86 Sabre. An operational unit was kept in service as the country's first line of defence until the early 1990s. The similar-generation Lockheed T-33 has been the core of the fleet, and attempts to augment the force with 10 former Spanish Air Force HA-200 light attack jets or 18 Brazilian-built EMB-326 Xavante ground-attack fighters during the late 1970s were unfruitful. Similar attempts to acquire new multi-role fighters during the early 1980s, in the form of the SEPECAT Jaguar, IAI Kfir C-2 and AMD Mirage F.1 proved also disappointing due to lack of funds. By the late 1980s negotiations switched again seeking either former Belgian F-104G Starfighters, new Chinese F-7M Airguards or, Argentine IA-63 Pampa jets, but again, these too failed to materialize.

To date (early 21st Century), the venerable T-33 continues to be the backbone of Bolivia's air-combat capabilities. A thorough upgrade of the type performed by a Canadian company in 2000 will keep the T-bird in Bolivian skies well into the 2010s. Bolivia's President Evo Morales has bowed to modernize the country's air arm, but again, this will depend on the country's financial capabilities. In 2008, Morales announced a USD 57 million contract with the Czech Republic for six L-159 ALCA light jet fighters.

North American F-86F Sabre (1973–1993)

A group of six experienced Bolivian pilots received conversion training on the F-86F Sabre jet fighter with the Venezuelan Air Force at Maracay during 1972. They formed the Bolivian nucleolus that received a Venezuelan donation of nine F-86F Sabre jet fighters in 1973. These fighters received FAB serial numbers 650 to 658 once delivered. A further five pilots graduated from Venezuelan F-86 training in 1974 and joined the original contingent that formed the Grupo de Caza 31 (31st Fighter Group) at El Alto Air Base.

By 1975 the type's poor performance at such high altitude (El Alto is situated some 13,300 feet/ 4,054 meters above sea level) forced the FAB to re-organize its operational units and transferred the Sabres to the Grupo de Caza 32 (32nd Fighter Group) at Santa Cruz de Sierra Air Base.

Two F-86Fs patrolling Bolivian skies with the Andean mountains in the background. (via Santiago Rivas)

Local F-86 pilot training, as well as ground crew training began in 1975 with the help from an Argentinean military mission. The Argentine mission remained in Bolivia until 1977.

By 1982 the unit was down to six operational aircraft. Plans to replace them with six Dassault Mirage 50 fighters had to be scrapped due to financial constraints, and the Sabres remained at the forefront of the country's defence during the 1980s. In 1984 a civilian Cessna crashed into a FAB hangar destroying two Sabres and reducing the fleet by a third. The type remained in service until February 1993, when it was officially retired. The last aircraft in Bolivian colours, FAB-651 was sold to a private collector in 1994.

The People's Republic of China (PRC) offered to supply a squadron of Chengdu F-7M Airguard air-defence fighters to replace the void left by the Sabres, and to provide a true air defence capability to the land-locked country. However, this offered was refused by the Bolivian government. Air defence responsibilities were transferred to the T-33 units.

Manufacturer	Aircraft Type	Delivered	Number	Serial Numbers	Remarks
North American	F-86F-30 Sabre	1973	9	FAB-650 to 658	ex-Venezuela

F-86F (656) still in silver colour scheme and colourful national markings. (Ramiro Molina)

The same F-86 (656) this time in three-tone camouflage. (Ramiro Molina)

Canadair CT-133 Silver Star (1973–)

In February 1973 Bolivia bought 15 former Royal Canadian Air Force CL-30 Mk.3 Silver Star armed trainers via an arms broker, Northwest Industries Ltd. Canadian Silver Stars also known as T-33AN, differed from US-built T-33s in that they had a 5,100-lbs Rolls-Royce Nene 10 turbojet instead of the General Electric J-33. Bolivian pilots were sent to Edmonton CAFB, Alberta in Canada, where they received conversion training on the type by CAF personnel. Once delivered, the Silver Stars received FAB serial numbers 600 to 614, and formed the Grupo de Caza 32 at El Alto Air Base from August 1973. Attrition begun almost immediately, as FAB-603 was lost on its delivery flight during October 1973 and was followed soon by FAB-611, the first record of a Bolivian ejection.

By late 1977 the fleet had suffered heavy losses, with FAB-600 crashing in April, followed by FAB-601 and FAB-605 in August, so the FAB ordered five attrition replacements through Northwest Industries. Six FAB P-51D Mustangs were taken by Northwest as part of payment for the Silver Stars that became FAB-615 to 619. FAB-615 was lost during February 1980.

A group of experienced pilots formed an aerobatic demonstration team known as the Escuadra Escorpio (Scorpion Flight) in 1983.

Attempts to acquire similar, albeit modern light attack jets, in the form of the EMBRAER Xavante were hampered by a lack of resources. However, the FAB managed to negotiate the transfer of 18 former Armée de l'Air (ALA, French Air Force) T-33SF armed trainers in 1985.

French T-33SF (Standard Françoise) also differed from the US version as they had used their old Nene turbojets transplanted from their retired Dassault Ouragan fighter bomber. They received the serials FAB-620 to FAB-637 and formed a new fighter unit at El Trompillo Air Base in Santa Cruz.

Two more fatalities struck the fleet, one aircraft was lost in May 1988, followed by yet another in the same month during 1989. Both incidents occurred in the vicinity of

CL-33 (FAB-612) at their home base at El Trompillo Air Base. (Fernando Mendoza)

FAB's CL-33s, here FAB-612, have to soldier on well into 21th century due to lack of funds. (Fernando Mendoza)

El Alto AB, and the second crash was fatal to its crew of two. A further two T-33SF were delivered by 1989, these being FAB-638 and FAB-639. On 19 October 1991, another trainer was lost, this time over Cochabamba, killing both its crew members. FAB-632 was lost in September 1992.

In 1997 the entire fleet was grounded for security reasons. However, a Grupo de Caza 33 aircraft exploded over Tarija, and this led to the decision to ground the entire fleet and consider its future. The FAB selected a British Columbia-based company Kelowna Flightcraft Ltd to perform a comprehensive upgrade. FAB-606, FAB-607, FAB-610, FAB-612, FAB-614, FAB-620, FAB-621, FAB-623, FAB-625 to FAB-628, FAB-631, FAB-634 to FAB-637, and FAB-639 were selected to undergo the rejuvenation process.

The November 1998 programme included new glass cockpits, BARCO MFD-6.8/1 multi-function cockpit displays, LCDs, a flight computer, HUDs, airframe modification and enhanced communication capabilities. The entire programme was to end by December 1999, but several problems plagued its development. A US offer for up to 18 second hand TA-4J Skyhawks complicated and extended negotiations with Kelowna, floating the final price tag up from USD 12 million to about USD 20 million.

In 1999 Ecuador announced plans to donate eight of its retired AT-33A armed trainers to the FAB. Negotiations continued in May 2001, when the FAB announced it would receive them shortly. Some reports indicated that they would be used as spare parts source, while attrition replacements also seemed to be likely, however the transfer has had not come into effect by late 2007.

The first three upgraded aircraft (FAB 608, 612, and 614) arrived in August 2000. The first upgrade loss was recorded during May 2003, when FAB-623 crashed into the sea while flying from Peru, killing both its pilots. The Bolivian government suspended payments to Kelowna and decided to terminate the program, with 16 out of the 18 aircraft completed. The remaining Kelowna T-33s are operated by the Escuadrón de Caza 311 (311th Fighter Squadron) from the Grupo Aéreo de Caza 31 out of El Alto Air Base. A handful are deployed to the Escuadrón de Caza 320 (320th Fighter Squadron) operating from Santa Cruz and the Escuadrón de Caza 330 (330th Fighter Squadron) at Tarija Air Base. The FAB intends to continue operating its upgraded T-33s up until 2015, however if funding is available for a replacement it will cease T-33 operations by 2010.

Manufacturer	Aircraft Type	Delivered	Number	Serial Numbers	Remarks
Canadair Ltd	CL-33 Silver Star Mk.III	1973	15	FAB-600 to 614	ex-RCAF
Canadair Ltd	CL-33 Silver Star Mk.III	1977	5	FAB-615 to 619	ex-RCAF
Canadair Ltd	T-33SF	1985	18	FAB-620 to 637	ex-ALA
Canadair Ltd	T-33SF	1989	2	FAB-638 & 639	ex-ALA

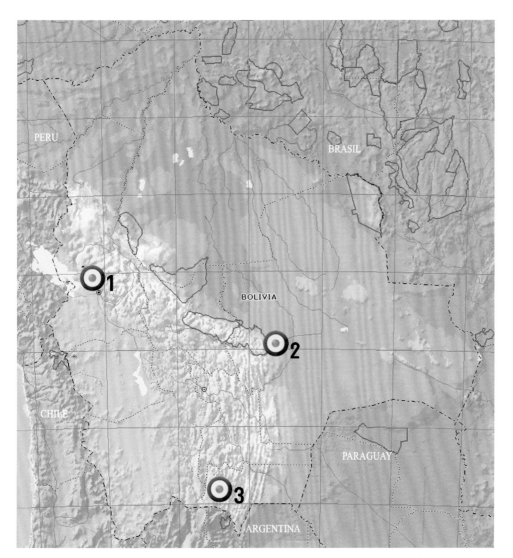

1. El Alto Air Base, La Paz
2. El Trompillo Air Base, Santa Cruz de Sierra
3. Tarija Air Base

Chapter 3

BRAZIL

By the post-World War II years, the Força Aérea Brasileira (FAB, Brazilian Air Force) was the most combat proven and largest air arm in South America. Its pilots had served with the 1st Brazilian Fighter Group as part of USAAF's 350th Fighter Wing in northern Italy, performing thousands of ground-attack sorties and nearly 500 missions against Axis forces. Brazilian maritime patrol aircraft had also played an important role in defending south Atlantic waters from foreign aggression. Brazil had proven to be a reliable U.S. ally. However, by the early 1950s, the United States refused to sell modern jet fighters to the FAB, arguing that this would severely alter the balance of power in the region. Truth is to say, that jet-fighter production lines were quite busy supplying USAF units in Korea, as well as building up their USAF and NATO allies in Europe.

Neighbouring Argentina had embarked upon a major modernization of its fighter assets, and by 1950 its air force boosted some 90 fighter jets. The United Kingdom was keen in obtaining new markets for its defence products and they became the source for Brazil's modernization plan.

A latter rethink by the US Government brought the famous T-bird to Brazilian colours by the late 1950s, which helped the FAB to diversify its jet assets, and obtain new experiences in US-built jets. The T-bird proved to be a much better alternative than the British jets, mainly because of its roughed and multi-role (COIN, ground-attack, reconnaissance, training) characteristics. It was soon followed by its single-seat fighter version, the F-80 Shooting Star.

Brazil is one of the few Latin American countries to operate jet trainers in an actual 'training-only' role. In 1960 it bought 30 Morane-Saulnier MS-760 jets, most of them were traded just a couple of years later to Potez in exchange for seven or so CM-170-2 Magister trainers. The Magisters were used by the Esquadrilha de Fumaça (Smoke Squadron) aerobatic team. The MS-760's place in the air force academy was taken by up to 61 Cessna T-37 basic jet trainers from 1968. Since these were never used in an armed role, they are not featured in this book.

The need for a large fleet of multi-role subsonic jets that could cover the entire country led the Brazilian Government to encourage the local production, in order to gain some experience. The Italian MB-326GB was chosen to fulfil this requirement and over 160 were produced locally. This programme contributed significantly to the development of a very successful indigenous aerospace industry. French supersonic air defence fighters arrived in the early 1970s followed by U.S. supplied tactical fighters. These formed the basis of Brazil's air defence force for the next three decades. Top up batches of both types were received during the 1980s, 1990s through to the early 2000s. Continued collaboration with Italian aerospace industries led to joint development of a light fighter-bomber – the AMX.

During the 1990s major upgrades for most of the fighter fleet were planned and this started to take place by the end of the century. Plans for the introduction of a new generation of fighter began in the mid-1990s through a programme dubbed the F-X-BR. The first phase of F-X was to include the off-the-shelf acquisition of a dozen fighters for about USD 700 million. The second phase was to include heavy participation of local industry with the selected airframe to be assembled and eventually licensed built. F-X saw major international aerospace companies such as Dassault and Sukhoi developing relationships with players such as EMBRAER and AVIBRAS to offer their products. Production projections ranged from 60 to 150 depending on the selected platform as well as the prospect of regional export success. The project was eventually cancelled and the requirement satisfied by a dozen former French fighters acquired for about USD 100 million. In late 2007 the Brazilian government, in a defence policy shift, launched a USD 2.2 billion programme for the acquisition of up to 36 new multi-role fighters.

On 2 July 2008, the Brazilian MoD re-launched its long standing requirement for a new generation multi-role fighter in a program known as FX2. It is to be implemented in two phases. Phase 1 will cover acquisition of up to 36 new fighters through a USD 2.2 billion budget. The MoD issued an RfP from Dassault for its Rafale, Sukhoi's Su-35 Super Flanker, Boeing's F/A-18E/F Super Hornet, the SAAB JAS-39 Gripen NG and the Eurofighter Typhoon. The competition culminated in the September 2009 with the apparent selection of the Rafale. The first phase should be implemented by 2015, at which time the second phase should be in progress. The second phase comprises local production for an anticipated total requirement for around 120 fighters which are to replace the FAB's entire F-5EM/ FM/ A-1M/ Mirage 2000 fleet by around 2025.

In 1998 the Brazilian Navy became the second naval force in Latin America to operate jet fighters. After a lengthy evaluation that included several options, Boeing managed to off-load a fleet of former Kuwaiti Air Force Skyhawks. Although it was an old design, the aircraft were in good shape as proudly gave the Marinha do Brasil (Brazilian Navy) an embarked combat asset.

In a historical sense, Brazil is the largest operator of fighters in Latin America, and about 70 per cent of these have been new-built aircraft (mainly due to local production), a percentage that separates it from its neighbours.

Gloster Meteor (1953–1973)

The FAB got its hands on a large batch of first-generation jet fighters in 1952, when it reached a barter agreement with the UK which involved a fleet of 71 Gloster Meteors to be paid for with 15,000 tons of raw cotton.

The order included 60 Gloster Meteor F.8 single seat fighters (serial numbers 4400 to 4459), the last of which were aircraft originally destined for the Egyptian Air Force (serial numbers 4455 to 4459) and 10 Meteor T.9 conversion trainers (serial numbers 4300 to 4309). A 61st single seat Meteor was kept in its crate to serve as an attrition replacement. The Meteors were concentrated at Santa Cruz with the 1st Fighter Group (1° GAVCA) in its 1st and 2nd Fighter Squadrons.

Meteors suffered the burden of being Brazil's first jet. Most of the pilots assigned to fly them were former WW-II veterans, which flew 145 ground attack missions with the USAAF's 350th Fighter Group in northern Italy. They pushed the aircraft in the same

Gloster Meteor F.Mk.8 (4449) armed with 50 lbs. bombs and unguided
rockets during landing at a Brazilian airfield.
(via Santiago Rivas)

This Gloster Meteor F.Mk.8 (4413) is preserved at Pirassununga. Armed
with unguided rockets it is painted in livery of 2°/1° GAVCA.
(Rodrigo Conte)

way that did their rough P-47D Thunderbolts, causing severe structural damage and
airframe fatigue on the Meteor fleet.

An initiative to restore the cracked wings did not attract any industrial support, and
a general alarm quickly grounded half the fleet. By 1960 only some 27 aircraft were
operational. Most of the fleet was grounded in 1966 and only three aircraft survived
by 1967, by which time the FAB started negotiations to replace them with Canadian-
built CF-5 Freedom Fighters. The deal was denied by US export controls and the FAB
started replacing its front-line fighter fleet with armed T-33A jet trainers.

The last Meteor (the 61st single-seat aircraft) was assembled in 1969 and assigned
to duties of towing aerial targets. This was officially withdrawn from service in 1973,
although it was kept in flying condition until April 1974. Some sources state that a 62nd,
built by the FAB using spare parts, was assembled and flew in 1973.

Manufacturer	Aircraft Type	Delivered	Number	Serial Numbers	Remarks
Gloster Ltd	G.41K Meteor F.Mk.8	1953	61	4400 to 4459	One unmarked
Gloster Ltd	G.43 Meteor FT.Mk.7	1953	10	4300 to 4309	

Lockheed T-33 (1956–1976)

The United States allowed the sale of the Lockheed T-33A jet trainer for use as a close
air support fighter, armed reconnaissance and light attack missions to Latin American
countries. Brazil was keen to augment its jet units and acquired a first batch of four
factory fresh T-33As in 1955. These four T-33As (serial numbers FAB-4310 to FAB-4313)
were delivered during 1956 and entered service with the 1st Squadron of the 4th Aviation
Group at Fortaleza Air Base.

A second batch comprising four aircraft (serial numbers FAB-4314 to FAB-4317)
were delivered in 1960. These last T-birds had served briefly with the Dominican Republic in 1957-58 but were withdrawn by the US Military Mission there.

Lockheed TF-33 (4346) parked at the ramp at Santos Dumont Air Base during the mid 1970s. (via Eduardo Luzardo)

In 1962 the FAB obtained two former USAF examples (built in 1952–53), giving them the serial numbers FAB-4318 and FAB-4319. In order to boost its combat squadrons, the FAB started negotiations for the transfer of up to 48 T-33A-LO-5s from USAF stocks. The former USAF T-birds, originally built in 1952-53 were refurbished and converted into the AT-33A (Brazilian designation TF-33A) close-support/light attack configuration, with nose fixed 12.7-mm machine guns and the capability to carry two 454-kg bombs and up to ten HVAR unguided rockets.

The first five TF-33As entered service in 1965, followed by another eight in 1966 and, the final thirty-five in 1967, assigned the serial numbers FAB-4320 to FAB-4367. On 22 June 1965 the first T-bird (4313) was lost in an accident. The TF-33As arrived at Fortaleza Air Base in 1966, complementing the F-80C Shooting Stars and T-33As of the 4th Aviation Group. Canoas was the next air base to receive the type, replacing old Gloster

The majority of FAB's T-33s have been the machine gun armed version - AT-33A. (Juan Arráez Cerda)

Meteors in the 14th Aviation Group during February 1967. With the final examples delivered, the FAB also equipped the 1st GAVCA (Fighter Aviation Group) at Santa Cruz Air Base, replacing the remaining Meteors. The first TF-33A, (4359), was lost on 3 June 1969. In 1970 the fleet suffered two more accidents, losing FAB-4366 and FAB-4330 on 30 September and 4 November, respectively.

The remaining T-birds were concentrated in the 14th Fighter Group during 1974, where they remained in service until 1976, after being replaced by Northrop F-5E tactical fighters. In October 1975 the first of the former Dominican T-birds (FAB-4314, ex FAD3301) was lost in an accident.

Manufacturer	Aircraft Type	Delivered	Number	Serial Numbers	Remarks
Lockheed	T-33A	1956	4	4310 to 4313	
Lockheed	T-33A	1960	4	4314 to 4317	ex-Dominican; via MAP
Lockheed	T-33A	1962	2	4318 & 4319	ex-USAF
Lockheed	AT-33A	1965	48	4320 to 4367	ex-USAF; refurbished

Lockheed F-80 Shooting Star (1958–1973)

The Lockheed F-80C Shooting Star was selected by the US as the fighter that would replace Latin America's P-47D Thunderbolt fleet. Both new and refurbished aircraft previously offered to every P-47 operator in the region.

The FAB acquired 29 F-80C-10-LO Shooting Star single-seat fighters and deliveries started from May 1958 to the 1st Squadron of the 4th Aviation Group (1°/4° Gav), replacing its elderly P-47D Thunderbolts at Fortaleza AFB. They were painted in the standard silver finish of most USAF Shooting Stars and received serial numbers FAB-4200 to FAB-4228. FAB-4228 was lost soon after it was delivered as final aircraft.

A further four aircraft, with applied serial numbers FAB-4229 to FAB-4232, were delivered from 1960. Aircraft number 4206 was lost on 18 May 1965. The 1°/4° Gav operated the type as its sole fighter until 1966, when it began to receive some TF-33 fighter-trainers. The F-80s were kept on strength until 1973, when they were completely retired, and replaced by the new AT-26 Xavante light attack fighters. Only two losses

Lockheed F-80A (4232) is the last one out of 33 ex-USAF aircraft delivered to FAB until 1960. It can be seen inside a hangar at Santos Dumont AB. (via Santiago Rivas)

F-80A (4201) armed with unguided rockets is now on display at FAB's Museo Aeroespacial. It has been the first F-80A being delivered to FAB in 1958.
(Claudio Lucchesi)

are recorded during their 15 year career in the FAB, and the two surviving F-80s have been preserved as monuments.

Manufacturer	Aircraft Type	Delivered	Number	Serial Numbers	Remarks
Lockheed	F-80A-10-LO Shooting Star	1958	29	4200 to 4228	ex-USAF
Lockheed	F-80A-10-LO Shooting Star	1960	4	4229 to 4232	ex-USAF

Embraer EMB-326 Xavante (1970–)

The FAB operated a large number of North American T-6 Texan armed trainers in several mixed COIN squadrons dubbed Escuadrao Misto Reconhecimento e Ataque (EMRA, Mixed Reconnaissance & Attack Squadron) in a wide variety of roles that included close air support (CAS), counter insurgency (COIN), border patrol, armed liaison, reconnaissance, basic, advanced, and tactical training. By the late 1960s it was clear that a replacement was needed and the selected type would need to be definitely a subsonic multi-role aircraft that could be produced locally for financial as well as national development reasons. The Italian Aermacchi MB-326G was selected after trials were completed in 1969. Aermacchi offered full technology transfer participation and EMBRAER obtained a license in May 1970 to produce the EMB-326GC (Brazilian version of the MB-326GB) for the Brazilian order as well as for export to South America or Africa.

Production began in 1971 and the aircraft was designated AT-26 (Attack-Trainer) Xavante (a local Indian tribe). A reconnaissance version was designated RT-26, although only a handful were ordered. The initial order was for 120 aircraft, to be followed by a second order for 54 aircraft. The first 38 aircraft were assembled from Aermacchi-provided kits before full license production would be achieved. Deliveries started in 1971 with seven aircraft received that year and lasted until 1981 with Xavantes receiving serial numbers ranging from FAB-4462 to FAB-4627. They equipped the 1st Squadron of the 4th Fighter Group at Fortaleza AB, the 2nd Squadron of the 5th Group and the 1st and 3rd Squadrons of the 10th Fighter Group. The 3rd EMRA at Santa Cruz Air Base and the

One of the last built EMBRAER EMB-326GB Xavante (4621). (Rodrigo Bendoraytes)

FAB obtained as attrition replacement from SAAF 10 Atlas Impala Mk.2 single seater. Seen here as AT-26A (4632, top) together with EMB-326GB (4625, bottom).
(Cees-Jan van der Ende/alfakilo.nl)

4th EMRA at Santa María Air Base also received Xavantes, replacing not only the lightly armed Texans, but also B-25 Mitchell and B-26 Invader attack-bombers.

A few aircraft entered service with the 1st Squadron/1st Fighter Group alongside TF-33A armed trainers, but the type was soon phased out of service with that front line combat unit making way for the F-5E tactical fighter in 1975. Three Xavantes were taken up by the 5th EMRA at Santa María Air Base in 1975, although their life with this unit was also brief, as two of the aircraft were lost on 20 July 1976 in a mid-air collision and the remaining Xavante was transferred to its sister unit, the 4th EMRA based also at Santa María.

In early 1979 the remaining Xavantes of the 4th EMRA were transferred to the 3rd Squadron/10th Group, while the Xavantes of 3rd EMRA were transferred to the 1st Squadron/4th Group and to the 3rd Squadron/10th Group before the unit was disbanded in 1980.

Xavantes had a limited export success in the international market, with three sold to Togo in 1976 and nine to Paraguay in 1979. These were brand new aircraft, and follow-up orders included an additional three for Togo in 1977 and an attrition replacement for Paraguay in 1981.

After the Falklands campaign Argentina approached the Brazilian government and acquired a squadron of Xavantes for its Naval Aviation Command. The Argentine Navy's MB-326GB and MB-339 fleets had been severely affected by combat losses and a UK-embargo on Viper engine spare parts. Brazil provided 11 former FAB Xavantes comprising serial numbers 4545, 4561, 4573, 4574, 4576, 4588, 4602, 4606, 4609, 4610, and 4612. They were completely re-assembled by EMBRAER before delivery.

FAB Xavante number 4470 from the 2nd Squadron/5th Fighter Group was lost during May 1989 during a reconnaissance flight. During May 1990 two other Xavantes, number 4486 from the 1st/5th Group and number 4496 from the 1st/4th were both lost.

On 26 December 2002 an AT-26 had a mid-air collision with an EMB-110 Bandeirante transport, killing three people over Sao José dos Pinhais, Paraná. One day later,

Another ex-SAAF Atlas Impala
as AT-26A (4630).
(via Santiago Rivas)

another AT-26 crashed into the sea while it was performing a test flight after receiving some maintenance work at the Parque de Material Aeronáutico de Recife.

By 2003 only some 48 Xavantes remained in operational service, with an additional 40 aircraft being used by the Comando de Entrenamiento (CATRE, Training Command) on purely training tasks. Xavantes were completely replaced by 2008.

In order to keep the Xavante fleet in operational conditions, the FAB acquired a package from the South Africa Air Force in 2005, comprising two Atlas Impala Mk.1 two-seat trainers and ten Impala Mk.2 single-seat attack fighters. The aircraft were intended to serve as a spare parts source but after a comprehensive examination, FAB determined that the aircraft were in better operational conditions that the Xavantes, so they were brought into service during 2006. The Impalas are slightly different from the Xavantes, as they are more 'combat capable' armed with 30-mm canons, equipped with RWR and chaff/flare dispensers. They were applied the FAB designation AT-26A and serial numbers 4630 to 4641. Impalas formed the 1st Squadron/4th Air Group 'Pacau' at Santa Cruz from 2006.

Manufacturer	Aircraft Type	Delivered	Number	Serial Numbers	Remarks
EMBRAER	EMB-326GB Xavante	1971–1981	166	4462 to 4627	
Atlas	MB-326 Impala Mk.1	2005	2	4630 & 4631	ex-SAAF; FAB designation AT-26A
Atlas	MB-326 Impala Mk.2	2005	10	4632 to 4641	ex-SAAF; FAB designation AT-26A

Aviation Marcel Dassault Mirage III (1973–2005)

The Mirage III's history in the Brazilian Air Force can be traced back to the late 1960s, when the Ministry of Aeronautics outlined the requirement for a supersonic combat aircraft that could provide national air defence coverage. A study commission known as the CEPAI (Comissao de Estudos do Projeto da Aeronave da Interceptacao, Comission for the Study of the Interceptor Aircraft Project) selected the McDonnell Douglas F-4E Phantom II as its preferred choice. However, the strict US arms-export policy towards Latin America forced the CEPAI to re-evaluate the candidates.

FAB received 12 Mirage IIIEBR, known in Brazil as F-103, until 1973. They served with 1° ALADA at Annapolis Air Base. Note the Matra R.530F missile below fuselage. (Gustavo Kaufmann)

A close-up look of one of the
two Mirage IIIE delivered to
FAB. Serial number 4929 is seen
here with three long range fuel
tanks.
(Cees-Jan van der Ende/alfakilo.nl)

The French Aviation Marcel Dassault (AMD) Mirage IIIE was selected as winner
and a contract for 12 single-seat IIIEBR and 4 two-seat IIIDBR fighters was signed in
May 1970. They equipped the 1° Ala de Defesa Aerea (ALADA, Air Defence Wing).

A group of Brazilian pilots were sent to Dijon in France for conversion training
on the Mirage and returned to Brazil where they would begin operations starting in
April 1973. By this time six Mirages were in operational condition. AMD completed
deliveries in October 1973 to Annapolis, a new fighter base located some 144km from
Brasilia.

The single-seat IIIEBR was officially known as F-103E in the Brazilian Air Force
while the IIIDBR two-seat version was known as the F-103D. They displayed a natural
metal finish with red markings next to the air intakes and were assigned the serial
numbers 4910 to 4921 (F-103Es) and 4900 to 4903 (F-103Ds).

Aircraft number 4921 was lost on 5 September 1974, and a seventeenth aircraft,
serial number 4922 was ordered to replace it. Almost a year later, serial number 4920
was lost on 2 September 1975. Further attrition replacements would soon be needed
and the FAB signed a contract with the French Government for three former ADLA
Mirage IIIE fighters in 1977. These were delivered by 1980, wearing serial numbers
4923 to 4925.

In April 1979, as part of a major re-organization program, the 1°ALAD was disbanded and replaced by the 1er Grupo de Defesa Aerea (1st Air Defence Group) as the main
component of Base Aérea Annapolis (BAAN, Annapolis Air Base).

By late 1980 another two Mirages had been lost, these being serial numbers 4912
(on 28 June 1979) and 4900 (on 20 November 1980). The loss of the first two-seater
was followed by another two (number 4902) in August 1981 and (number 4903) in May
1982. Two additional Mirage IIIDs were ordered from the French Air Force, these were
to become numbers 4904 and 4905. They were delivered in June 1984. Aircraft number
4905 was lost less than two months after, followed by number 4901 just one day later,
on 26 July. This series of accidents left number 4904 as the only available two-seater
until numbers 4906 and 4907 entered service in 1989.

Several Mirage IIIs were obtained from French Air Force. Mirage IIID (4904) and Mirage IIIEX (4927) seen here in current grey overall colour scheme. (Cees-Jan van der Ende/alfakilo.nl)

An offer from the French Air Force for up to 20 Mirage IIIE fighters at an estimated USD 70 million was not accepted by the Brazilian Government. However, in 1988 Dassault was selected to modify four former French Air Force models to an upgraded IIIEX configuration, incorporating several enhancements presented in the Mirage IIING (Nouvelle Generation) program. The eight-year program included addition of an in-flight refuelling probe, canards, and new air-to-air weaponry such as Python III and MAA-1 Piranha missiles.

In 1999 the FAB received another two Mirages IIIDs from France, being serial numbers 4908 and 4909. Original plans called for the F-103 Mirage fleet to be withdrawn from service by 2005 and replaced by up to 12 new multi-role fighters acquired through the failed F-X-BR program. This programme was cancelled by late 2004 leaving the FAB to soldier on with the Mirage as its main air defence fighter until 15 December 2005, when the last F-103 was officially retired.

Manufacturer	Aircraft Type	Delivered	Number	Serial Numbers	Remarks
AMD	Mirage IIIEBR	1972	12	4910 to 4921	
AMD	Mirage IIIDBR	1972	4	4900 to 4903	
AMD	Mirage IIIE	1980	3	4923 to 4925	ex-ALA
AMD	Mirage IIID	1984	2	4904 & 4905	ex-ALA
AMD	Mirage IIIEX	1988	2	4926 & 4927	ex-ALA
AMD	Mirage IIIE	1989	2	4928 & 4929	ex-ALA
AMD	Mirage IIID	1989	2	4906 & 4907	ex-ALA
AMD	Mirage IIID	1999	2	4908 & 4909	ex-ALA

Northrop F-5 Tiger II (1975–)

The Força Aérea Brasileira was the first Latin American country to receive the F-5E Tiger II tactical fighter. It first negotiated an order for F-5A/B Freedom Fighters in 1967, together with a requirement for F-4B Phantoms, but the US quickly declined to provide them. Inquiries into buying Canadian-built examples soon shared the same fate.

Negotiations started again in October 1974, this time for the updated F-5E Tiger II. The FAB ordered a fleet of 43 fighters under a program known as FMS *Peace Amazon*, comprising 37 single-seats F-5Es and 6 two-seat F-5B Freedom Fighters to be used as conversion trainers. The 1974-built F-5Bs were the last 'B' models built by Northrop. These Block 50 models arrived in March 1975 and wearing the serial numbers 4800 to 4805. Aircraft numbered 4803 was written off in an accident just two months after delivery. The F-5Es had the serial numbers starting from 4820 and replaced Gloster Meteors F.8 and P-80 Shooting Stars in service with the 1st and 14th Fighter Groups.

By 1986 only 29 F-5B/Es where operational (six more had been written off) and the FAB decided to boost its fighter fleet. Several types where considered, including second hand F-104G Starfighters and new Chengdu F-7M Airguards, but the final decision was for expanding the fleet of F-5s. The Chilean Government offered its 17 remaining F-5E/Fs but, the US discouraged this transaction, offering the FAB a package of 26 former USAF machines in 1987. The program known as FMS *Peace Amazon II* comprised 22 single-seaters drawn from the 405th TFTS at Williams AFB and 57th TTW (the Aggressor Squadron) at Nellis AFB. Some of the F-5Es where actually former South Vietnamese aircraft, that managed to escape Vietnam and had been pressed into USAF service. The aircraft arrived in 1989, with the former USAF F-5Es (serial numbers 4857 to 4879) going to the 14° Group at Canoas AB. The F-5Fs were new models assembled from spare parts. They replaced the old F-5B Freedom Fighters. These aircraft displayed the

In 2005 FAB celebrated 30 years of F-5 operations with a special markings aircraft. It is paired with a regular painted F-5E (4845).
(DACT/Katsuhiko Tokunaga)

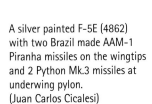

A silver painted F-5E (4862) with two Brazil made AAM-1 Piranha missiles on the wingtips and 2 Python Mk.3 missiles at underwing pylon.
(Juan Carlos Cicalesi)

One of the upgraded F-5 (4830), called F-5EM, prepares for another load of fuel during CRUCEX 2008.
(Chris Lofting)

Beside a large fleet of 59F-5Es FAB operates only four F-5Fs.
(João Paulo Zeitoun Moralez)

serial numbers 4806 to 4809. Attrition was high as number 4809 was written off in 1996, while aircraft numbered 4868 and 4878 crashed in 1995, in separate incidents.

In October 1998 the FAB announced that Elbit's proposed F-5UP upgrade programme, also known as F-5BR had won a contract to provide the air force with modernized F-5s. EMBRAER served as systems integrator, producing the upgraded F-5BR variant which included the installation of a new FIAR Grifo X radar, self defence suite, new avionics and navigation systems as well as Python III and (eventually) Derby BVR air-to-air missiles. Brazilian F-5Es already carried the local Mectron MAA-1 Piranha AAM. In March 2001 the Brazilian Congress approved USD 285 million for the modernization of 45 F-5Es single-seat and 3 F-5Fs two-seater fighters. The aircraft are locally designated F-5EM and F-5FM and deliveries were scheduled to end by 2007. The first F-5F to be converted was number 4808.

In 2001 the FAB announced that it was negotiating the purchase of second-handed F-5Fs from the Swiss Air Force. The Swiss F-5Fs where intended to replace the old Xavante tactical trainers of the 4th Aviation Group at Natal Air Base. As the Swiss did not want to part with all of their two-seaters, the deal was never finalized. A Swiss offer to transform up to 15 F-5Es into F-5Fs was not accepted. During early 2006, the FAB struck an USD 24 million deal with the Royal Saudi Air Force, via C&C International Inc. for the supply of six F-5Es and three F-5Fs. The deal however fell apart and again in September 2007 the FAB announced it was negotiating the acquisition of eight F-5Es and three F-5Fs fighters from the Royal Jordanian Air Force (RJAF). Deliveries took place during summer 2008, with the first batch of four arriving in an Antonov An-124 Ruslan.

The FAB has also announced that four F-5Es fighters will be upgraded to the new F-5EM standard but fate of the remaining aircraft is unknown.

Manufacturer	Aircraft Type	Delivered	Number	Serial Numbers	Remarks
Northrop	F-5B Freedom Fighter	1975	6	4800 to 4805	Last F-5Bs built
Northrop	F-5E Tiger II	1975	37	4820 to 4856	
Northrop	F-5E Tiger II	1989	22	4857 to 4879	ex-USAF
Northrop	F-5F Tiger II	1989	4	4806 to 4809	ex-USAF
Northrop	F-5E Tiger II	2008	8	???? to ????	ex-RJAF
Northrop	F-5F Tiger II	2008	3	???? to ????	ex-RJAF

Embraer AMX (1989–)

As the FAB received its final batch of license-produced MB-326GC light strike/armed trainers, it soon developed a requirement for a new interdiction strike fighter-bomber that would complement and eventually supersede the Xavante fleet. On 27 March 1981 the FAB instructed Brazilian aircraft maker EMBRAER to join its European partner Aermacchi, together with Aeritalia, in the development of the AMX (Aeritalia Macchi Xperimental). EMBRAER got roughly a 30 per cent work share.

The AMX programme was being developed by these two companies since 1977 to replace Italian Air Force Fiat G.91 and F-104G fighter-bombers. The AMX was supposed to operate as a CAS fighter, attacking Soviet/Warsaw Pact mechanized forces on approach to NATO's front-lines with a secondary role as counter air and anti-shipping roles. It is a true interdiction/strike fighter. The FAB had an original requirement for up to 144 AMX but this was soon changed to 79 due to financial constraints.

An Embraer AMX A-1 (5539) equipped with a Vicon 57 reconnaissance pod. It is a rare configuration as only three were delivered together with A-4KUs. (Carlos Filipi Operti)

Embraer AMX A-1 (5517) with a load of one Mk.82 bomb under each wing.
(Carlos Filipi Operti)

Delivery of AMXs to the FAB started in 1989 to the 1st Squadron of the 16th Group, shortly after the first flight of the Brazilian model on 12 August. The Brazilian version differed from the standard Italian version in some respects. The Brazilian AMX, designated A-1, has two DEFA 30-mm cannons instead of the single US-built M-61 Vulcan 20-mm cannon installed on Italian aircraft. The Vulcan cannon was not available for export to a non-NATO country such as Brazil.

Another difference is in its navigational system, the Brazilian examples having a much simpler version. With the export market in sight, EMBRAER was entrusted the development of a two-seat version known as AMX-T from 1986. Deliveries of the first two seat examples began in 1992 and the FAB had a requirement for 14 of them.

A revised (financial) requirement called for fewer aircraft to be acquired, comprising 45 AMX (A-1) and 11 AMX-Ts (A-1B) to equip 3 squadrons. Production ended in 1999 and serial numbers included FAB-5501 to FAB-5545 for the single-seat AMX. The serial numbers included FAB-5650 to FAB-5660 for the AMX-Ts. A reconnaissance version, equipped with a removable reconnaissance pod and known locally as RA-1 or RA-1B (depending on either single or two-seat version) entered service from 1999. Although only 6 aircraft have been identified (FAB-5539, -5540, -5541, -5543, -5659, and 5660), up to 15 may be designated as such.

The 'Adelfi' Squadron (1° Squadron / 16° Aviation Group) began to work on the type from 1989. It is based at Santa Cruz and its role is centred on long-range interdiction and penetration, using the standard A-1 and A-1B armed with Mk.81 and Mk.82 GP bombs, SBAT 70-mm rocket launchers, and Piranha air-to-air missiles. FR probes and KC-130 tankers extended the squadron's legs considerably. The first A-1 loss of an AMX occurred on 6 June 1997, when FAB-5532 crashed. It was followed by FAB-5516 that crashed some 45 km south of Rio de Janeiro on 24 July 1998.

A naval version of the AMX was offered to the Brazilian Air Force, who was responsible for embarked operations on the deck of the Brazilian carrier NAeL *Minas Gerais*. But this was discarded in favour of experienced, second-hand A-4 Skyhawks.

The 'Centauro' Squadron (3° Squadron / 10° Aviation Group) received its first A-1s starting in 1998, replacing its maritime-attack dedicated AT-26 Xavantes. The squadron, with its base in Santa Maria, focuses on providing CAS to the Brazilian Navy. Although the AMX has been fitted with AM-39 Exocet anti-ship missiles for trial purposes, this has not been adopted.

Located at Santa Maria Air Base, the 'Poker' Squadron (1° Squadron / 10° Aviation Group) is the main tactical reconnaissance unit in the FAB. It began receiving its first

An early built AMX A-1 (5504) in two-tone green/gray colour scheme flies over Santos Dumont Air Base. (Katsuhiko Tokunaga / DACT)

of 15 RA-1 attack- reconnaissance fighters starting in 1999 to replace the older RT-26 Xavantes.

The FAB announced in 2004 that it would submit its 53 strong fleet of AMX attack aircraft to an USD 400 million upgrade programme. The work includes a new radar, HOTAS, a new data link, night-vision goggles and, a laser designator among other refinements, will be the stepping stone for a more comprehensive USD 1.1 billion project. This will include a 300-km cruise missile to be developed by CTA and a new family of GPS-guided munitions developed by Avibras. First deliveries were scheduled to start in 2003 with the final aircraft to be handed over in 2010. Funding constraints caused the programme to stall and the first AMX was handed over for upgrade until mid-2007. The upgraded aircraft is known as the A-1M.

Manufacturer	Aircraft Type	Delivered	Number	Serial Numbers	Remarks
EMBRAER	A-1/AMX	1989	45	5501 to 5565	
EMBRAER	A-1B/AMX-T	1992	11	5650 to 5660	

McDonnell Douglas A-4 Skyhawk (1998–)

After more than 30 years of being restricted to rotary-wing operations, the Marinha do Brasil (MB, Brazilian Navy) obtained US Congressional approval to acquire a squadron of fixed-wing fighter jets for operation aboard its NAeL *Minas Gerais* (former HMS *Vengeance*) light aircraft carrier.

After considering several options, which included former UK Fleet Air Arm Sea Harriers, French Aeronavale Super Étendards or, developing a naval version of the

One A-4KU (N-1004) being prepared for a catapult launch during deck trials on board of aircraft carrier NAeL *Minas Gerais* in May 2001.
(Erik Katerberg & Anno Gravemaker)

AMX. The Brazilian Navy signed an USD 79 million contract with Boeing for the acquisition of 23 former Kuwait Air Force A-4KU Skyhawk fighter-bombers during 1997.

The A-4KUs were built and delivered between 1976 and 1977 to the Kuwaiti Air Force (KAF) and they participated in the defence of their homeland during the Iraqi invasion during August 1990, performing operations from highways in the south of the country before fleeing to Saudi Arabia. They then participated in the liberation of their country as part of Operation Desert Storm (ODS). McDonnell Douglas (now Boeing) had been trying to offload the Kuwaiti Skyhawks since the late 1980s, as the KAF had conditioned the re-sale of its aircraft as part of its F-18C/D Hornet deal.

The deal included low-hour airframes at a reasonable price tag, with most of them averaging 1,800 hours. The 20 single-seat A-4KUs and 3 two-seat TA-4KUs were deliv-

One A-4KU (N-1004) during deck trials on board of aircraft carrier NAeL *Minas Gerais* in May 2001.
(Erik Katerberg & Anno Gravemaker)

A-4KU N-1017 armed with 2 AIM-9H Sidewinder missiles is parked in front of its hangar at Sao Pedro de Aldeia. (Rodrigo Bendoraytes)

ered via ship during September 1998 to Arraial do Cabo. The unit in charge of operating the Skyhawks was the newly created 1st Fighter and Attack Squadron VF-1 'Falcoes', from naval air base Sao Pedro de Aldeia. The air base had to expand its runway from 1,800m to 2,400m to accommodate the fighters.

Brazilian Naval fighter pilots where trained by the FAB on Tucano basic trainers, and later received naval instruction on T-34C Turbo-Mentor and EMB-326GB Xavantes of the Argentine Naval Aviation Command, as well as T-45 Goshawk and TA-4J Skyhawks of the VT-7 US Navy at NAS Meridian in Mississippi.

Original plans call for 15 aircraft to be operational with VF-1, the other 8 kept back as attrition reserves. The operational aircraft are to receive a large upgrade, to include new HUD, HOTAS, INS, and multi-mode radar. New weapons, such as Piranha AAMs and maybe Derby BVR missiles will give them an enhanced capability.

Sea-trails, including the first ever ship landing by a Brazilian jet fighter where included in CATRAPO I exercises off the Atlantic coast. Only eight pilots had actually qualified to fly the Skyhawks when VF-1 embarked on Brazil's new aircraft carrier (former French Navy Foch) A-12 NAe Sao Paulo in May 2001.

Designated as AF-1 and AF-1A, the Skyhawks are armed with AIM-9H Sidewinder air-air missiles, Zuni rockets, and GP bombs. By 2007 the fleet had been depleted to some 15 A-4KUs and 3 TA-4KUs in the inventory with 5 A-4KUs being cannibalized for spare parts. On 14 April 2009, the Brazilian Navy awarded EMBRAER a contract to upgrade nine AF-1 and the three AF-1A to a new configuration, with a new avionics suite and radar among other improvements. The 5-year contract was valued at USD 140 million.

Manufacturer	Aircraft Type	Delivered	Number	Serial Numbers	Remarks
McDonnell Douglas	A-4KU Skyhawk	1998	20	N-1001 to N-1020	ex-KAF
McDonnell Douglas	TA-4KU Skyhawk	1998	3	N-1021 to N-1023	ex-KAF

Aviation Marcel Dassault-Breguet Aviation Mirage 2000 (2006–)

The Mirage 2000BR, and upgraded Mirage 2000-5 Mk.2 version was one of the front-runners for the FAB's much publicised F-X programme to find a replacement for the long service Mirage IIIs. As part of the technology transfer agreements, Dassault (AMB-DA) had offered to transfer production of the Mirage 2000 line to EMBRAER's new Gavião Peixoto plant. However, F-X was cancelled by President Lula da Silva and France offered a squadron's worth of Mirage 2000 fighters to fulfil the gap in air defence capabilities.

An USD 104 million contract between the governments of France and Brazil comprised ten single-seat Mirage 2000C interceptors and two twin-seat Mirage 2000B fighter-trainers. The contract also included missiles, training, and support infrastructure. Deliveries began during September 2006 to the 1er Grupo de Defesa Aerea (1st Air Defense Group) at Base Aérea Annapolis (BAAN) and the type has been designated as the F-2000C and F-2000B by the FAB. All aircraft were delivered by end of August 2008.

Manufacturer	Aircraft Type	Delivered	Number	Serial Numbers	Remarks
AMD-BA	Mirage 2000C	2006	10	4940 to 4949	ex-ALA
AMD-BA	Mirage 2000B	2006	2	4932 & 4933	ex-ALA

The latest fighter in FAB's inventory are ex-ALA Mirage 2000. As shown here, s/n 4940 takes off for another training mission, equipped with just one central fuel drop tank. (Leandro Maldonado)

A total of ten Mirage 2000C and two Mirage 2000B, as they are dubbed in Brazilian service, serve with 1st Air Defence Group.
(Leandro Maldonado)

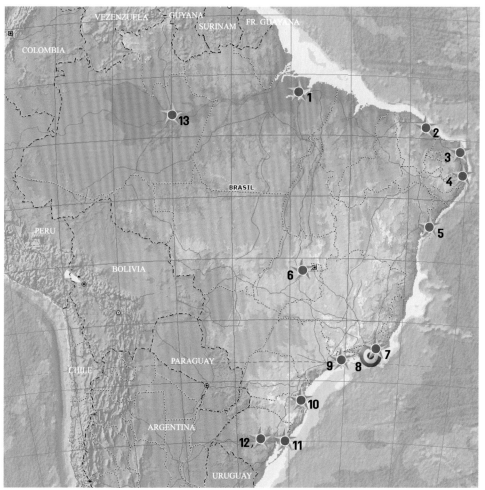

1. Belém (BABE)
2. Base Aérea Fortaleza (BAFO)
3. Base Aére Natal (BANT)
4. Base Aérea Recife (BARF)
5. Base Aérea de Salvador (BASV)
6. Base Aérea Annapolis (BAAN)
7. Base Aérea Santa Cruz (BASC)
8. Sao Pedro de Aldeida (SBES)
9. Sao José dos Campos (EMBRAER)
10. Base Aérea Florianópolis (BAFL)
11. Base Aérea Canoas (BACO)
12. Base Aérea Santa María (BASM)
13. Base Aérea Manaus (BAMN)

Chapter 4

CHILE

Chile entered the jet age in 1954 with the delivery of a score of British-built fighter trainers. These were soon joined by the usual mix of trainers and obsolete fighters offered by the US Government to almost every Latin America country, the Lockheed F-80/T-33 combo. The jet fleet was kept relatively small, at only two squadrons up until the mid-1960s, when the air force selected a new multi-role fighter to expand its capabilities – the British-built Hawker Hunter.

The US and the UK continued as its mains suppliers in the early and mid-1970s, acquiring its first supersonic fighters from the first in 1975. A regional dispute over three archipelagos in the Beagle Channel almost turned into full scale war with Argentina during December 1978 and the Fuerza Aérea de Chile (FACH, Chile Air Force) found itself in an inadequate position to fight the modern Argentine Air Force. The dispute was mediated and settled by the Vatican, but tensions continued for several more years.

Chile's right-wing government found itself without many friends, especially as the Pinochet dictatorship was constantly accused of human rights abuses. Isolation meant that spare parts for its jet fighters were hard to come by. Availability was mainly dependent on the mood of the British or American administrations. This eventually helped to set up an acquisition policy based on diverse sources that would not compromise the effectiveness of the combat fleet to a single model or supplier.

France became a one-time supplier of jet fighters to Chile in the late 1970s and these were considerably upgraded to allow their operation well into the 21st Century. A Brazilian effort during the 1980s to supply light attack jets proved unsuccessful.

Israel was approached to provide a variety of systems, from air to air missiles, to Mirage IIICJ interceptors to Kfir multi-role fighters, but Israel's main contribution to Chilean military power came in the form of upgrade packages for to its combat fleet. The Israeli knowledge and technology transfer were a big boost to the local developing aerospace industry. Spain also became an important source for technology transfer during this decade.

The FACH upgraded most of its fighter fleet to extremely competent standards during the 1990s, with modern avionics and advanced munitions. Although it invested heavily in the development of combat support assets, such as the IAI Phalcon AEW and Tanquero tanker conversion, its jet fighter acquisition programmes were limited to a squadron of second hand fighters from Belgium.

The advent of democracy, an all time high international copper price, and a very competent economy brought a surplus in financial resources to the Chilean armed forces by the early 2000s. In fact, the copper law that dates from 1958 assigns 10 per cent of all copper export income for armed forces procurement. This allowed the military to procure enough funds for the acquisition of advanced F-16C/Ds in 2002. This buy is a historical achievement as these F-16s were the first newly-built fighters acquired by a Latin American air force from the United States since 1983. The fleet was ingeniously expanded with second-hand F-16s from the Netherlands. By the early 21st century the FACH had the best equipped fighter force in the region and is planning on acquiring a next generation fighter for around 2012–2015 If the FACH decides to acquire additional F-16s this will mark a change in its current procurement policy towards a more efficient, yet politically dependant single-source policy.

De Havilland Vampire (1954–1980)

De Havilland Vampire T.Mk.55 (J-01) has been the first ever jet entering FACH in 1954. (via Eduardo Ahumada)

Eager to join rival neighbour Argentina in the fighter-jet club, the Chilean Government began negotiations with the US for the supply of modern equipment during the early 1950s. A negative from this source prompted it to speedy negotiations with the United Kingdom who was at the time enjoying an export-boom to the region. The De Havilland Vampire was selected to become Chile's first operational jet fighter and on 22 October 1953 a contract for five two-seat Vampire T.Mk.55 fighter-trainers was signed.

The fighter-trainers were assigned the serial numbers J-01 to J-05 and they were delivered to Grupo 7 at Los Cerillos Air Base in May 1954. The first accident claimed J-04 in November that same year during an aerobatic-training manoeuvre. In 1956 the FACH bought a replacement Vampire, applying the serial number J-04 of the lost aircraft.

The Vampire served as an excellent entry-level fighter for the FACH pilots, operating as escorts for the sister-based Grupo 8, which was equipped with B-25 Mitchell bombers in the newly established Ala 1 (1 Wing).

In 1958 the Vampires were supplemented by the F-80 Shooting Star and later replaced by the T-33s in the fighter training role. The fleet was also placed on reserve status. A re-organization during 1961 brought about a change in their serial numbers, the fleet being renumbered in the J-301 to J-305 range. They were re-activated in 1963 and transferred to Grupo Aereo 8 at Cerro Moreno Air Base, where they served again in the fighter-trainer role until 1971, when all but J-302 was retired.

By December 1972 the remaining T-33, J-302 was renumbered as J-301 and joined by ten former RAF and former Royal Navy aircraft, comprising four Vampire T.Mk.11s, and six Sea Vampire T.Mk.22 trainers. These second-hand Vampires had been retired from UK military service from 1967 and were acquired via Hawker Siddley Ltd, as they were required to serve as lead-in fighter trainers for the new Hawker Siddley Hunter fleet. They were numbered from J-302 to J-311. The replenished fleet was painted in a desert camouflage pattern and transferred to Grupo Aereo 4 at Iquique were they operated in the advanced trainer role until 1980.

Manufacturer	Aircraft Type	Delivered	Number	Serial Numbers	Remarks
De Havilland	Vampire T.Mk.55	1954	5	J-01 to J-05	J-301 to J-305 from 1961
De Havilland	Vampire T.Mk.55	1956	1	J-04	attrition replacement; J-304 in 1961
De Havilland	Vampire T.Mk.11	1972	4	J-302 to J-305	ex-RAF
De Havilland	Sea Vampire T.Mk.22	1972	6	J-306 to J-311	ex-RN

Lockheed T-33 (1956–1977)

Lockheed T-33 (J-324) has been delivered at part of the second batch in 1959 as armed trainer. Today is exhibited inside Cerro Moreno Air Base.
(Andrés Contador Krüger)

The first four Lockheed T-33-1-LO armed trainers arrived in Chile during October 1956. They joined the five Vampire fighter-trainers in service with Grupo 7 at Los Cerillos Air Base. They had serial numbers J-314 to J-317 assigned to the aircraft.

With the delivery of a second batch made up of nine aircraft (serial numbers J-318 to J-326) in 1959, all the T-33s were transferred to Grupo 9 at El Tepual. A pair of reconnaissance configured RT-33A examples was also acquired at the time, comprising serial numbers of J-327 and J-328. This second batch comprised former USAF aircraft, most of them built around 1949 and were acquired via the US sponsored Military Assistance Program.

In 1967 the T-33 fleet was transferred to Grupo 12, together with the F-80s and Vampires. This unit was based at Punta Arenas, and was responsible for air defence and ground attack in the south of the country. The T-33s were converted into AT-33A close air-support versions and painted in a new four colour camouflage pattern. One AT-33A was lost on 19 September 1968.

The fleet started to wind down operations by 1974 and all of them were placed in storage by 1977. They were replaced by the A-37B Dragonfly.

Manufacturer	Aircraft Type	Delivered	Number	Serial Numbers	Remarks
Lockheed	T-33A-1-LO	1956	4	J-314 to J-317	
Lockheed	T-33A	1959-1964	9	J-318 to J-326	ex-USAF
Lockheed	RT-33A	1959-1964	2	J-327 & J-328	ex-USAF

Lockheed F-80 Shooting Star (1957–1974)

Chile replaced its WW-II vintage P-47 Thunderbolt fighter-bombers with Lockheed F-80C-10-LO Shooting Star jet fighters acquired through the US sponsored Military Assistance Program (MAP). Eighteen refurbished former USAF F-80Cs (serial numbers J-330 to J-347) were delivered between December 1957 and June 1958. The aircraft had been built between the years of 1947 to 1949.

A total of 18 F-80 Shooting Stars served from 1957–1974 as jet fighter within FACH. (via Santiago Rivas)

The Shooting Stars were delivered to Los Cerillos Air Base and pressed into service with Grupo 7 alongside the Vampire fighter-trainers. By late 1958 the unit had replaced the older Vampire with their newer mounts. The first F-80C loss occurred in April 1959 when serial number J-337 crashed. It was followed shortly by the crash of J-341 a few months later.

Grupo 7 was tasked to participate in an international training operation during 1960. The FACH sent five fighters, supported by two C-47 transports to take part in operation 'Banyan Tree II', together with Brazilian, Colombian, Panamanian, Peruvian, and USAF units. The exercise was supposed to bring 'allied' forces to protect the Panama Canal in case the Cold War turned hot. Another crash claimed J-344 in November 1960.

During 1964 the remaining 15 aircraft, plus the armed T-33 trainers were used to form a new unit, to Grupo 9 based at El Tepual Air Base. In 1967 a few of the Shooting Stars were transferred to create Grupo 12 at Punta Arenas.

By 1969 the entire fleet had been reduced to seven flying aircraft and these were concentrated in the later unit, following the delivery of Hawker Hunters to Grupo 9. The last two operational F-80s were retired in 1974.

Manufacturer	Aircraft Type	Delivered	Number	Serial Numbers	Remarks
Lockheed	F-80C-10-LO Shooting Star	1957	18	J-330 to J-347	ex-USAF

Hawker Siddley Hunter (1967–1995)

When negotiations with the US for the transfer of up to 25 North American F-86F Sabre jet fighters through the Military Assistance Program failed, Chile began to shop around international markets for a new fighter. Several types were evaluated and the preferred choice was at that moment the new Northrop F-5A/B Freedom Fighter. The U.S. Government's negative to sell the F-5 in Latin America led Chile to a re-evaluation of all types.

In October 1966 a Chilean commission signed a contract (HSAL/66/C/066) with British company Hawker Siddley to buy 21 Hawker Siddley Hunter fighter-bombers. The fleet was made up by 15 single-seat Hunter FGA.Mk.71A (serial numbers J-700 to J-714), 3 reconnaissance configured Hunter FR.Mk.71A (J-715 to J-717), and 3 Hunter T.Mk.72 conversion trainers (J-718 to J-720). The Hunters were actually second-hand aircraft, most of them F.4 or F.6 versions completely refurbished by Hawker and up-graded to Mk.71A standard (similar to the RAF's FGA.9, FR.10, and T.Mk.66 standards respectively).

The first four single-seat fighters (J-700 to J-703) had been in service with the Belgian Air Force from 1955 to 1962, the next ten aircraft (J-704 to J-713) had served the Royal Netherlands Air Force from 1956 to 1964. The last aircraft was a former RAF aircraft (XG232). The reconnaissance versions were all former RAF aircraft, while the two of the trainer versions were former Dutch aircraft. The first two-seater, J-718 had an even more exotic career, having served with the Iraqi and Lebanese air forces before being returned to Hawker. Deliveries were made by ship to Valparaiso a year after contract signature and the aircraft were subsequently assembled by a team of Hawker

Hawker Hunter FGA Mk.71A
(J-725) on exhibit with a full
assortment of weaponry during
the early 1970s.
(Horacio Gareiso)

Siddley technicians. The Hunters were assigned to the 7th Air Group, replacing the mixed fleet of F-80C fighters and T-33 armed trainers at Los Cerillos Air Base.

A follow on contract (HSAL/69/C/84) was signed in 1969. This involved 11 single-seat Hunter FGA.Mk.71As (J-722 to J-732) and 1 two-seat T.Mk.72 (J-721) conversion trainer. The Hunter designated J-721 was one of the original two-seat prototypes (P.1101). Deliveries of this second batch started in March 1970 to Grupo 9 at El Tepual Air Base in Puerto Montt.

Hunters were some of the most visible assets to be used in the coup d'état against left-wing President Salvador Allende. On 11 September 1973 Hunters from Grupo 7 were used to attack radio stations loyal to Allende and the Presidential Palace (La Moneda) as well as the Presidential Residence.

A major re-organization of the FACH started after Pinochet took power, and the Hunter fleet was earmarked for expansion. A dozen fighter-bombers were transferred from Grupo 7 to Grupo 8, at Cerro Moreno, near Antofagasta, replacing its tired B-26 Invaders. A further six Hunters, comprising two fighter-bombers (J-733 and J-737), three reconnaissance versions (J-734, J-735 and J-738), and one trainer (J-736) were acquired in late 1973. Their delivery would be difficult, as the new right-wing dictatorship was about to be embargoed by the western powers. The FACH sent a group of Hunter pilots in a C-130 Hercules transport to the UK, from where they flew the 'authorized'

This Hawker Hunter FGA Mk.71A
(727) although long retired is
keep in perfect condition by
Grupo 8
(Andrés Contador Krüger)

Hawker Hunter FGA Mk.71A
(715) during a mission close to
Chilean coast.
(via Santiago Rivas)

Hunters, crossing the Atlantic, from Africa to Brazil. This feat was to become the first air-delivery of British aircraft to South America.

The three groups operated the type until 1976, when the Hunters from Grupo 9 were transferred to Grupo 8, as new F-5Es arrived from the US. Hunters were submitted to a minor upgrade that included fitting of the Shafrir AAM by IAI technicians.

As political differences with neighbouring Argentina turned into a territorial dispute over three islands in the Beagle Channel, Hunters from Grupos 7 and 8 were deployed to Punta Arenas. They would face Mirage IIIEAs fighters of the Argentine Air Force on their own, as the newly delivered F-5s were not available due to a spare parts embargo. An emergency plan to obtain some 100 operational Hunters prompted negotiations with India for the procurement of its Hunter FGA.56 fleet. As the potential conflict was resolved through diplomacy these negotiations were eventually cancelled.

On 26 March 1980 Hunter J-721 was lost. By late 1981 some 18 Hunters were operational, and they were all concentrated in Grupo 8. As a reward for their 'collaboration' with British intelligence services during the Falklands campaign, the FACH began to receive arms shipments from the UK that included Hunter fighters and Canberra bombers. These comprised 12 former RAF Hunter FGA.Mk.9 (serial numbers J-743 to J-754) and 2 former Kuwaiti Air Force Hunters –T.Mk.67 (serial numbers J-741 and J-742). In 1983 a Hunter F.6A was delivered from RAF stocks as a spare parts source. They were all assigned to Grupo 8, although only about five of them were put in operational service, as most of them were used as a spare parts source for the Shafrir-capable fleet.

A major upgrade of the fleet under project *Aguila* began in 1983 that included the re-design into a more ergonomic cockpit by the FACH's logistics command. Chilean company ENAER developed a self-protection suite that included Caiquen 2 RWR and Eclipse chaff/flare dispensers. The upgraded Hunters were from then on known as Aguilas (Eagles).

The Aguila programme ended in 1989 and apparently was comprised of ten aircraft (serial numbers J-702, J-718, J-722, J-724, J-727, J-728, J-732, J-733, J-736, and J-740). This last aircraft was built by the FACH using parts from J-700 and J-707.

By the early 1990s the Hunter fleet was down to 20 flying aircraft, out of a total of 53 aircraft delivered over some 15 years earlier. Their operation was becoming expensive and their age was showing. Hunters with the serial numbers J-729 and J-732 were retired in 1990, while J-724 was lost on 23 March 1991. The FACH soon began to look for a replacement and eventually opted for an interim buy of former Belgian Mirage 5 fighter-bombers. The last Hunter was retired from service in 1995 after some 28 years of service in Chilean skies.

Manufacturer	Aircraft Type	Delivered	Number	Serial Numbers	Remarks
Hawker Siddley	Hunter FGA.Mk.71A	1967	15	J-700 to J-714	second hand; refurbished
Hawker Siddley	Hunter FR.Mk.71A	1967	3	J-715 to J-717	second hand; refurbished
Hawker Siddley	Hunter FGA.Mk.72	1967	3	J-718 to J-720	second hand; refurbished
Hawker Siddley	Hunter FGA.Mk.71A	1970	11	J-722 to J-732	second hand; refurbished
Hawker Siddley	Hunter T.Mk.72	1970	1	J-721	second hand; refurbished
Hawker Siddley	Hunter FGA.Mk.71A	1974	2	J-733 & J-737	second hand; refurbished
Hawker Siddley	Hunter FR.Mk.71A	1974	3	J-734, J-735, J-738	second hand; refurbished
Hawker Siddley	Hunter T.Mk.72	1974	1	J-736	second hand; refurbished
Hawker Siddley	Hunter FGA.Mk.9	1982	12	J-743 to J-754	ex-RAF
Hawker Siddley	Hunter T.Mk.67	1982	2	J-741 & J-742	ex-KAF
Hawker Siddley	Hunter F.Mk.6A	1983	1	Not assigned	ex-RAF

Cessna A-37B Dragonfly (1975–)

The FACH selected the Cessna T-37B Tweety Bird (or just 'Tweet') as its next generation basic/advanced jet trainer in the early 1960s and received four T-37s in 1963. They soon became the standard jet trainer at the air academy in El Bosque Air Base, becoming a familiar type to most Chilean pilots.

With the development of the basic T-37 into the COIN-oriented A-37B Dragonfly, the FACH selected the type to equip a combat squadron in 1972. Negotiations with the US were affected by the September 1973 coup, but deliveries of 1974-built aircraft began in 1975. The first batch of 16 Dragonflies was assigned the serial numbers J-600 to J-615 and equipped Grupo 1 at Los Condores Air Base in Iquique.

Delivery of a second batch of 18 Dragonflies (serial numbers J-616 to J-633) to Grupo 4 started in January 1977, during a short period in which US arms sales to Chile resumed. In May 1978 the first Dragonfly was lost, followed by another accident in late November 1980. By 1980 Grupo 4 had ceased A-37 operations, as its pilots were

One of the A-37 (605) delivered with first batch in 1975. Note the impressive six under-wing fuel tanks.
(Andrés Contador Krüger)

converting to fly the more powerful Mirage 50. Grupo 12 received the A-37Bs replacing the recently retired T-bird/Shooting Star fleet at Punta Arenas.

On 10 July 1986 two more A-37Bs were lost in a mid-air collision over Santa Isabel Island, while on a training mission. The next known accident occurred during 1991, when a Dragonfly crashed into the sea. With this, the FACH had lost some ten aircraft since their delivery, serial numbers J-604, J-606, J-610, J-612, J-613, J-618, J-622, J-626, J-628, and J-631.

Initial plans had called for the new ENAER-developed A-36 Halcon light fighter to replace the A-37 from the early 1990s, but the A-37B's performance record allowed it's career to be extended. In 1991 the US Government offered ten former Illinois Air National Guard (ANG) OA-37Bs at bargain prices. Operation *Norte-Sur* saw Chilean pilots fly their second hand mounts in a transcontinental journey from Illinois to San-

This OA-37B (644) has been delivered in 1992 as part of ten AO-37B from ex-USAF stocks to Grupo 3.
(via Santiago Rivas)

tiago in Chile. The aircraft were assigned serial numbers J-635 to J-644 (J-600 was re-assigned as J-634) and delivered to Grupo 3 from May 1992.

On 28 November 2001, one of the oldest serving Dragonflies (J-601) was unable to deploy its landing gear. Its pilot performed one of the most incredible landings, using the aircraft's four under wing fuel tanks as landing gear. The aircraft was repaired and put back into service.

A group of 14 surviving aircraft were returned to the US in 2001, these included J-602, J-607, J-614, J-619, J-620, J-621, J-635, J-637, and J-642 where they were refurbished and put in storage. The former Chilean aircraft were then offered to Colombia, who declined the 27-year old aircraft.

By 2003 the FACH had some 17 aircraft in strength, although only about 12 were in operational conditions. The FACH had selected the F-16 Fighting Falcon as its replacement, yet they remain on and the F-16 has replaced the entire Mirage fleet.

Manufacturer	Aircraft Type	Delivered	Number	Serial Numbers	Remarks
Cessna	A-37B Dragonfly	1975	16	J-600 to J-615	J-600 latter re-serial J-634
Cessna	A-37B Dragonfly	1977	18	J-616 to J-633	
Cessna	OA-37B Dragonfly	1992	10	J-635 to J-644	ex-USAF

Northrop F-5 Tiger II (1974–)

The FACH had shown interest in the F-5A/B Freedom Fighter-series since 1967, but US strict export controls prevented negotiation from taking place. With left-wing Salvador Allende's democratic election as president in late 1970, the Soviet Union reportedly offered MiG-21s during the early 1970s. The US finally agreed to provide a squadron

F-5E Tigre III with full weaponry: Mk.82 & Mk.82SE bombs, AIM-9 & Magic missiles. (via Eduardo Ahumada)

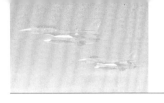

One FACh F-5E lines up behind a FAB C-130 to pick up some fuel during CRUCEX IV.
(Cees-Jan van der Ende/alfokilo.nl)

of F-5E/F tactical fighters after the overthrow of Allende. The new anti-communist Pinochet Regime began receiving the first of 15 F-5E and 3 F-5F fighters in March 1974 acquired through an USD 55 million FMS contract that also included AIM-9 Sidewinders. Deliveries were paused, due to Pinochet's human rights record, only to resume from 1976.

The Tigers were delivered to Grupo 7 at Cerro Moreno Air Base and assigned serial numbers J-800 to J-814 (F-5Es) and J-815 to J-817 (F-5Fs). This allowed the older Hunters to concentrate in Grupo 8 and 9. Further scandals of human rights abuses by the Pinochet dictatorship brought about a US embargo on military hardware that grounded more than half of the fleet.

By the mid-1980s the F-5 fleet had been earmarked for a serious upgrade and the FACH began to study several proposals, ranging from their replacement with second

This good lateral view shows the external changes of the F-5E Tigre III upgrade programme.
(Andrés Contador Krüger)

This F-5F (817) landing at El Bosque Air Base was also upgraded to Tigre III standard. (Andrés Contador Krüger)

hand aircraft such as the IAI Kfir to their complete overhaul and upgrade. This second option proved to be the most attractive.

Under project *Tiffany* the FACH awarded the Israeli Aircraft Industries (IAI) an USD 200 million contract for the upgrade of its F-5s to the F-5 'Plus' configuration in 1988. Two F-5Es (805 and 809) were upgraded in Israel during 1993 and IAI worked with local aerospace company ENAER on upgrading the remaining aircraft in-country. A further 12 single-seat and 2 two-seaters (serial numbers J-816 and 817) were upgraded with new avionics, central computer, MFDs, HOTAS, and GPS, but the heart of the program was its new radar. The standard Emerson Electric AN/APQ-159 lightweight radar was replaced with the powerful Elta EL/M-2032B multi-mode pulse-doppler radar, increasing detection range from 37 km to over 100 km.

In 1997 the FACH further enhanced the fleet's capabilities fitting a flight refuelling probe to 12 single-seat fighters, now known as F-5 Tigre III (note the designation change to Spanish).

During 2003 the Tigre III fleet received another upgrade, comprising a new (more advanced) MFD, and wiring to fire the Python IV dogfight and Derby long-range missiles. They have since been referred to as Tigre III Plus. These are undoubtedly the most capable F-5s flying in the world today.

Manufacturer	Aircraft Type	Delivered	Number	Serial Numbers	Remarks
Northrop	F-5E Tiger II	1974	15	J-800 to J-814	
Northrop	F-5F Tiger II	1974	3	J-815 to J-817	

ENAER A-36 Halcón (1980–)

The A-37B Dragonfly, coupled to the T-37 Tweet trainer proved to be an excellent addition to the FACH. However, several factors including political stability and US embargos proved hard on the type's serviceability. In the late 1970s the FACH began to

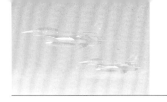

A-36CCs like the one shown
(430) will most probably soldier
on for many more years due to
financial constrains.
(Claudio Lucchesi)

look for an aircraft that could complement and eventually replace its A-/T-37 fleet in dual light strike/training capabilities. The selected aircraft was to be produced under license in Chile by ENAER.

Negotiations with Spain's Construcciones Aeronáuticas S.A. (CASA) in 1979 led to the development of the standard C-101 in service with the Ejército del Aire (Spanish Air Force) into the C-101BB. As an offset, Spain agreed to purchase some 40 aircraft of the ENAER T-35 Pillan primary trainer for its own air arm.

CASA supplied four C-101BBs (serial numbers 401, 402, 403, and 405), known locally as the T-36BB Halcón (Falcon) during 1980 and these were followed by eight aircraft assembled by ENAER from kits supplied by CASA (serial numbers 404, 406 to 412). The T-36BBs entered service with Grupo 1 at Los Condores Air Base, Iquique. During March 1984 the FACH suffered its first Halcón fatality when number 405 crashed during an exhibition near El Bosque Air Base, destroying eight houses and killing three civilians.

A fifth CASA-built number 413 was delivered during February 1984 and it served as a prototype for the A-36 programme. The emerging A-36CC light fighter has an increased weapons-carrying capability, upgraded engine, a DEFA-553 30-mm centre-line cannon pod, and enhanced avionics. Deliveries began in 1986 with three aircraft (numbers J-414 to J-416) in service by 1988. Production then paused with work concentrating on the development of the A-36M attack fighter. This model featured new Ferranti INS, HUD, and the capability to carry two Sea Eagle anti-ship missiles. The A-36M was offered for export, with the Venezuelan Navy expressed interest in obtaining eight aircraft but, this lagged and never developed into an order.

Production of the BB/CC versions resumed and ENAER delivered two T-36BB trainers and an A-36CC in June 1991, these being serial numbers J-417 to J-419. Aircraft numbered J-417 and J-418 were the last two-seat trainers to be built and construction switched to A-36CC models for the next few years. An order for a further 18 light fighters was placed with ENAER and deliveries started in 1994 until to 1998. They were designated the serial numbers J-420 to J-437 and assigned to Grupo 3 at Temuco.

ENAER A-36CC Halcón (437) at FIDAE in 2008. It served as prototype for Halcón II upgrade. (Andrés Contador Krüger)

Having gained considerable experience in the upgrade business, ENAER offered the Halcón II programme, which comprised a SAGEM avionics suite, HOTAS, HUD, GPS, and Rafael Shafrir II air-air missiles. Further plans called for the fitting of a locally developed RWR as well as in-flight refuelling capability. The aircraft numbered J-437 served as prototype and the FACH earmarked 12 aircraft to be upgraded. Halcon IIs were all assigned to Grupo 3.

In June 1999 the fleet suffered a major blow when two of its recently delivered A-36CCs (serial numbers J-435 and J-436) collided in a mid-air collision. Their crews were unharmed. This was followed by the loss of an A-36CC attached to Grupo 1 that crashed while performing a bombing training mission in northern Chile, some 60 km from Iquique. Grupo 3 stood down Halcón operations in 2003 and its aircraft were concentrated at Grupo 1.

Plans to keep the Halcón II fleet in service until 2015 were put in doubt during 2004, when the FACH expressed interest in replacing them with 19 former Swiss Air Force Hawk Mk.65 advanced trainers. However, this fell through and the fleet will therefore continue in service for several years to come.

Manufacturer	Aircraft Type	Delivered	Number	Serial Numbers	Remarks
CASA	C-10BB Aviojet	1980	4	J-401 to J-403, J-405	
CASA	T-36B Halcón	1980	8	J-404; J-406 to J-412	Assembled by ENAER
CASA	C-10BB Aviojet	1984	1	J-413	
ENAER	A-36CC Halcón	1986	3	J-414 to J-416	
ENAER	T-36B Halcón	1991	2	J-417 & J-418	
ENAER	A-36CC Halcón	1991	1	J-419	
ENAER	A-36CC Halcón	1994	18	J-420 to J-437	

Aviation Marcel Dassault–Breguet Aviation Mirage 50 Pantera (1980–2007)

By the mid-1970s the FACH's combat capabilities had been upgraded with the delivery of a squadron of F-5E/F Tiger II tactical fighters. Yet it found itself deploying 20-year old Hawker Hunters to the south of the country when a major crisis with Argentina over a small number of islands in the Beagle Channel threatened to escalate into conventional warfare. US sanctions over the Pinochet regime's human rights abuse issues effectively grounded the new F-5s. The Hunters would have to fight it out against recently delivered supersonic Mirage IIIEAs!

A deal to buy some 30 Mirage IIICJ interceptors from Israel did not proceed for political reasons, and Chile kept searching for a new high-end supersonic fighter supplier. France had been a traditional supplier of high-quality, high-price weapons to Latin America, and Chile would be no exception. In 1979, the FACH ordered the AMD-BA Mirage 50. The delta-winged fighter powered by the more efficient Atar 9K-50 was determined as superior to anything in Argentina's inventory. Once contract negotiations were settled, a group of Chilean fighter pilots were sent to France to receive conversion training.

The contract with Dassault comprised a first batch of eight former French Air Force fighters, Mirage 5F, refurbished to Mirage 50F standard. These aircraft were delivered from 1980 to Grupo 4 at Comodoro Arturo Merino Airport in Santiago, and were assigned the serial numbers 501 to 508. They were second-hand aircraft, ordered by Israel in 1967 and impounded by France and pressed into Armée de l' Air service as the Mirage 5F. These fighters lacked radar.

A second batch of eight new build fighters comprised six single seat Mirage 50C (serial numbers 509 to 514) and two twin-seat Mirage 50D fighters (serial numbers 515 and 516). They were delivered from 1982 and all were in service by late 1983. The single-seat aircraft were the 'full' Mirage 50 version with Agave multi-mode radar. On the other hand, the Mirage 50Ds were intended as conversion trainers. They were powered by the earlier Atar 9C engine and lacked radar, so, in essence, they were Mirage 5s.

One of the two-seat Mirages (number 516) was lost in an accident during 1983 and replaced by a former French Air Force Mirage IIIBE. The new aircraft received the same 516 serial number and was refurbished by Dassault before delivery in 1984. The

Mirage 50 Pantera 514 acted as prototype for the last Mirage 50CN Pantera upgrade. (Andrés Contador Krüger)

Mirage 50DN Pantera 515 is
configured as conversion trainer,
lacking radar and is equipped
with earlier engine.
(Andrés Contador Krüger)

responsibility of providing air defence for the southern part of the country, Grupo 4 moved to its new base at Punta Arenas during March 1986.

In order to keep up with the constant modernization of Argentina's Mirage fleet (which was mostly carried out by IAI), Chile also approached Israel. Work on the Chilean fleet started in November 1985 under project 'Bracket'. This was based on IAI's Mirage upgrade kit and included new canards, communication and self-defence equipment. The programme was managed by local company ENAER.

By 1988 the programme had matured into a thorough upgrade program that also included the Elta EL/M-2001B radar, a new HUD, laser-guided weapons, and new air-to-air missiles. FACH serial number 514 was used to create a prototype and this was followed by the number 510 as the first Pantera version. Deliveries started again in 1993, and the type has since been known as the Mirage 50CN Pantera.

In 2003 there were reports that the FACH acquired a large spares package from the South African Air Force (SAAF) to support its Pantera squadron. Some sources incorrectly suggested that the FACH had acquired a batch of 12 former SAAF Cheetahs to replace or augment the Pantera fleet. The last nine Panteras were retired from service from mid-2007 onwards and replaced with F-16s. The final ceremony took place on 28 December 2007.

Manufacturer	Aircraft Type	Delivered	Number	Serial Numbers	Remarks
AMD-BA	Mirage 50F	1980	8	J-501 to J-508	ex-ALA; refurbished
AMD-BA	Mirage 50C	1983	6	J-509 to J-514	
AMD-BA	Mirage 50D	1982	2	J-515 & J-516	
AMD-BA	Mirage IIIBE	1984	1	J-516	ex-ALA

SABCA Mirage 5 Elkan (1995–2006)

As the Chilean Hawker Hunter fleet reached the end of their service lives in the late 1980s, the FACH began to study their possible replacement. Several options were analyzed, starting with former USAF F-16s, which were at the time, still out of the equation for political reasons. Former Israeli Kfirs were also considered, and due to the good business relationship between IAI and ENAER, these seemed to be the preferred choice, but the deal fell through. Former RAF Jaguars or Spanish Mirage IIIEEs were

Mirage 5MA (715) with AIM-9 missile
(Santiago Rivas)

other alternatives, but they were dropped in favour of recently upgraded former Belgian Air Force Mirage 5s.

The Belgian Air Force operated over 100 Mirage 5 fighter-bombers from the early 1970s and had recently submitted 20 surviving aircraft to SABCA's MirSIP upgrade program. MirSIP (Mirage Systems Improvement Program) included new navigation and attack systems, HOTAS and GPS in order to boost the Mirage 5's life up to 2010. The upgraded aircraft were known as Mirage 5MA and MDs.

After several months of negotiations, which brought final price down from USD100 million to USD54 million, an order was finally signed in July 1994 for 15 single-seat Mirage 5MAs and 5 two-seat Mirage 5MDs, as well as 5 attrition replacement airframes. The replacements included four reconnaissance optimized Mirage 5BR and one two-seat Mirage 5BD.

After a year-long conversion training program hosted by the Belgian Air Force at St. Truiden, a group of 45 instructors, pilots, and mechanics returned to Chile in March 1995. Mirage deliveries, by now designated as the Mirage 5M 'Elkan' (Guardian in Mapuche, a local indigenous dialect) started that same month. They formed Grupo 8 flying out of Cerro Moreno Air Base, Antofagasta, and assigned serial numbers J-701 to J-715 for the 5MAs and J-716 to J-720 for the 5MDs.

Surprisingly, the five attrition replacements were put into operational service, as the Mirage 5BR replaced the remaining Hunter FR.71 reconnaissance fighters. The Mirage

Mirage 5MA (710) taxing home in front of a second Mirage, armed with a Sidewinder missile.
(Chris Lofting)

Mirage 5MA (710)
(Andrés Contador Krüger)

5BR used the same Vinten reconnaissance cameras as the Hunters, so the dedicated reconnaissance crew did not suffer many transition pains. The 5BRs were assigned the serial numbers J-721 to J-724 and the two-seat 5BDs was used for conversion training from the Hunter to the 5BR. It was re-assigned the serial number J-725.

The first accident occurred in November 1999, when an Elkan crashed during its approach to Presidente Ibañez Airport in Punta Arenas. By late 2001 another three aircraft had been retired, including a 5BR (J-722) and the 5BD (J-725). These two were put on display at the Aerospace Museum and Cerro Moreno gate respectively. On 14 January 2003, another Elkan was lost while on a training flight north of Cerro Moreno. A limited upgrade of the fleet started in 2004, with the type receiving a flight refuelling probe similar to that fitted to the Panteras. Their main armament was the AIM-9L/P Sidewinder AAM.

Elkan operations stood down on 27 December 2006 after accumulating some 14,000 flight hours. They were replaced by the arriving F-16C/D Pumas. Seventeen of the Mirage 5BDs and BRs survived but, only eight were still airworthy!

Manufacturer	Aircraft Type	Delivered	Number	Serial Numbers	Remarks
SABCA	Mirage 5MA	1995	15	J-701 to J-715	
SABCA	Mirage 5MD	1995	5	J-716 to J-720	
SABCA	Mirage 5BR	1995	4	J-721 to J-724	
SABCA	Mirage 5BD	1995	1	J-725	

Lockheed-Martin F-16 Fighting Falcon (2006–)

In 1995 the FACH began 'CAZA 2000' (Fighter 2000) in order to acquire a new generation fighter-bomber that could replace the aging fleet of A-37B Dragonfly light-attack fighters. The introduction of MiG-29 fighters in neighbouring Peru required that CAZA 2000 provide a superior multi-role fighter, and it would be a new-built aircraft.

CAZA 2000 called for a first buy of 20 fighters, to be followed by a second batch of 40 to replace the entire combat fleet. Candidates were narrowed down to four: the Lockheed-Martin F-16C, Dassault Mirage 2000-5, Saab JAS-39 Gripen, and Boeing F/A-18C. In 1998 production of the F/A-18C version was terminated by Boeing and this

F-16 CJ (856) prior to delivery
at Ft. Worth in Texas.
(Jonathan Derden)

effectively took it out of the competition. Since the FACH operated both the Mirage 50 and Mirage 5 in updated versions, the 2000-5 was a clear favourite. Some sources even went so far as to announce an order for seven Mirage 2000s in the late 1990s. But by the end of 1998 CAZA 2000 suffered from a severe cut in funding by about 50 per cent promting the second hand fighter option back into the consideration process.

The programme was re-launched in 1999, under a new name, NAC (Nuevo Avión de Combate, New Combat Aircraft) and with a revised requirement for 10 to 12 new fighters. The FACH selected the F-16C/D as the favourite and began to lobby for the release of this aircraft-type to Chile. FACH wanted to acquire the late model F-16 equipped with the APG-68(V) radar, CFT and armed with AMRAAMs and Mavericks. The first negotiations also included two refurbished KC-135R tankers. The clear 'offensive' nature of this arms package brought the deal into the limelight and produced an international controversy. Peru announced that it would need to acquire extra MiG-29s and bring in a BVR capability.

One of four F-16DJs (858) pairs
with one F-16CJ.
(Santiago Rivas)

F-16DJ (859) with Magic Mk.2 missiles underwing and AIM-9 Sidewinder air combat pod. (Andrés Contador Krüger)

After a couple of years of negotiations, the FACH signed a contract with Lockheed-Martin on 20 May 2003 for the supply of six F-16C Block 50Ms single-seat and four F-16D Block 50Ms two-seat fighters. The contract was codenamed '*Peace Puma*' and Chile chose the FMS track to acquire the aircraft. Scheduled delivery to the FACH's Grupo 12 was to start in February and end in December 2006. The F-16C is locally known as Puma and has the serial numbers in the 851 to 860 range. These F-16s have been the first new-built fighters delivered to Chile since 1983, and equipped Grupo 3 at Iquique, replacing the recently retired Mirage Elkans.

Chilean Pumas are equipped with Lightening II designator pods (four of which were ordered in 2004), armed with Python IV, Derby air-to-air missiles, JDAMs, SPICE glide-bombs, and Griffin LGBs.

In September 2005, the FACH finished negotiations with the Netherlands for the acquisition of 18 second hand F-16AM/BM fighters. The USD 185 million deal was followed by an USD 7 million contract with Lockheed-Martin for the upgrade and modifi-

One of the ex-KLu F-16AM (727) touches down after a display at FIDAE. (Santiago Rivas)

One of seven ex-KLu F-16BMs which has been upgraded to MLU standard before delivery to Chile in 2006.
(Erik Katerberg)

cation of some systems. As a NATO ally, the Dutch F-16s were wired to fire the HARM and Shrike anti-radar missile. This capability was deleted by Lockheed-Martin (as an expressed desire by the United States Government), before the aircraft could be delivered to Chile. The former Dutch batch comprised 11 F-16AM single-seat and 7 F-16BM two-seat fighters. Training of Chilean instructors in the Netherlands commenced in early 2006 and these replaced the Mirage 50 Panteras with Grupo 8 at Cerro Moreno. During May 2009, the Chilean Minister of Defence announced the acquisition of a second batch of 18 F-16s from the Netherlands, which would bring total Chilean F-16 numbers up to 46. The USD 270 million deal is expected to also comprise upgraded F-16AM/BM examples. These will replace the remaining F-5s in service and standardize FACH fighter assets on the F-16.

Manufacturer	Aircraft Type	Delivered	Number	Serial Numbers	Remarks
Lockheed-Martin	F-16C Block 50	2006	6	J-851 to J-856	
Lockheed-Martin	F-16D Block 50	2006	4	J-857 to J-860	
Fokker	F-16AM	2006–2007	11	J-721 to J-731	ex-KLu; upgraded to MLU
Fokker	F-16BM	2006–2007	7	J-732 to J-738	ex-KLu; upgraded to MLU
Fokker	F-16AM	2010–2011	18		ex-KLu; upgraded to MLU

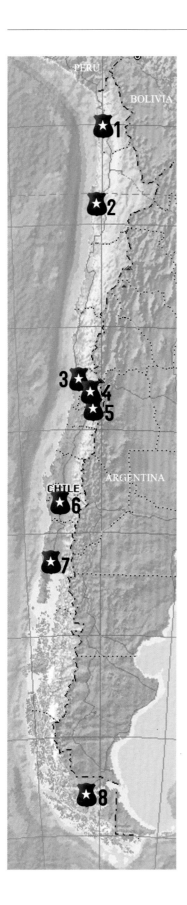

1. Los Cóndores Air Base,
   Iquique
2. Cerro Moreno Air Base,
   Antofagasta
3. Arturo Merino IAP, Santiago
4. Los Cerillos Air Base,
   Santiago
5. El Bosque Air Base, Santiago
6. Maquehue Air Base, Temuco
7. El Tepual Air Base,
   Puerto Montt
8. Chabunco Air Base,
   Punta Arenas

Chapter 5

COLOMBIA

Colombia contributed heavily to UN forces during the 1950-53 Korean War, providing a total of some 6,200 troops that served with four infantry battalions attached of the US Army's 24th Division and later the 7th Division. Colombian casualties amounted to 639, most of which were suffered by the 3rd Infantry Battalion, when it was overrun by a full Chinese Division during March 1953. The Colombian Navy provided six vessels during this war. This contribution made Colombia a close ally of the United States and as such, was the first Latin American country to obtain US-built jets.

This fleet of armed jet trainers was followed shortly by Canadian-built fighters, also the first ever Non-NATO/Non-Commonwealth contract involving Canadian jets. The US-designed fighter fleet defended Colombian skies until the early 1970s, when American refusal to sell modern fighters vectored Colombia, as many of its neighbours, towards the Mirage club.

A new generation of counter-insurgency (COIN) jets, especially designed for the role and tested in Vietnam, entered service with the Fuerza Aérea Colombiana (FAC, Colombian Air Force) in the early 1980s. US influence during this period was only shadowed by Israeli companies, which moved in and obtained most of the upgrade contracts. Along with the upgrades came a squadron of Israeli fighter jets which have formed the main national defence sector since then.

By the late 1990s the Colombian fleet was old and tired. A refurbishment and upgrade program injected a few more years and more effectiveness into the ageing fleet. New precision-guided munitions became an addition to the fighter force, as the supersonic jets were now employed as ground-attack fighters, effectively converting into counter-insurgency machines.

During the early 2000s the FAC developed a requirement for up to two dozen light jet fighters to replace its ageing fleet, with the Argentine AT-63 and the Brazilian AMX considered among other types, however, this was one instance in which jets fell victim to turboprops and the Super Tucano was eventually selected for the role. A Spanish offer to donate eight former Qatari Mirage F1s was discarded, causing a major diplomatic incident during 2003. It was not until late 2007 and early 2008 that the intented upgrade and expansion of the conventional combat fleet was finally addressed. The Kfir C-10 was selected to become the FAC's standard jet fighter with a requirement for 24 aircraft.

Lockheed T-33 (1954–1999)

FAC-2033 was one of 18 AT-33As obtained in 1958. These aircraft were not only jet trainers, but also equipped with machine-guns and weapons pylons.
(Gregg Megs Collection)

Right after the Korean War, and in large part due to Colombia's contribution to the allied war effort, the US Congress authorized the sale of up to 18 Lockheed T-33A armed jet trainers at a reduced USD 1.16 million. The package included substantial spares and maintenance equipment. Colombian pilots attended conversion training at Lackland AFB in Texas where one pilot was killed in an accident.

The first batch of six aircraft arrived in 1954 at Palanquero Air Base displaying the serial numbers FAC-2001 to FAC-2006. They were soon followed by another 12 aircraft numbered FAC-2007 to FAC-2018. An US offer for a further 18 Lockheed T-33A-5-LOs surplus to USAF requirements was taken up by the FAC and their delivery started in 1958. Most of these were almost new aircraft, being issued to the USAF in 1957. They were modified to the armed AT-33A version with fixed 0.50-cal machine guns and weapons pylons. They were assigned serial numbers up to FAC-2044, although an AT-33 with the number FAC-2067 has also been reported. These former USAF aircraft formed the 2do Grupo de Combate (2nd Combat Group).

T-birds were first used in combat during Operation *Marquetalia*, a US-backed counter insurgency operation aimed at re-taking the town of Marquetalia from communist peasant control. The 1964 operation also involved OH-23 helicopters, special COIN groups and seven infantry battalions. A lack of reconnaissance assets was solved with the delivery of four RT-33A variants (serial numbers FAC-2071 to FAC-2074) that same year. The RT-33s formed a reconnaissance unit at El Dorado International Airport.

With the arrival of the Mirage supersonic fighters, the remaining T/AT/RT-33 fleet was concentrated at the 2do Grupo de Combate in 1972 at Apiay Air Base. They were quite active in COIN operations as well as advanced/combat training missions through the 1970s. One of the RT-33s (FAC-2072) was lost in November 1976. In 1977 the T-birds were transferred to the 3er Grupo de Combate at Barranquilla and used mainly on border patrol duties.

In February 1978 the USAF delivered a further 12 aircraft to the FAC. By the early 1980s the fleet which totalled 52, had been reduced to 31 flying aircraft, used in the training role alongside the Cessna T-37s. The reconnaissance-configured RT-33s were retired in 1981.

Like most of other AT-33As obtained in 1958, FAC-2027 served with 2do Grupo de Combate.
(via AMMA)

FAC-2005 was lost on 17 December 1989, leaving only 13 flying aircraft at that time. The EMB-312 Tucano turboprop trainer was selected in 1990 to replace them and 14 aircraft were delivered starting in 1992. The remaining T-33s were placed on reserve status, with most of them being retired during October 1996. The final T-33 sortie was performed in late 1999, after 45 years of service.

Manufacturer	Aircraft Type	Delivered	Number	Serial Numbers	Remarks
Lockheed	T-33A-1-LO	1954	18	FAC-2001 to FAC-2018	
Lockheed	AT-33A	1958	18	FAC-2019 & FAC-2020; FAC-2031 to FAC-2044; FAC-2067	
Lockheed	RT-33A	1964	4	FAC-2071 to FAC-2074	
Lockheed	T-33A-5-LO	1978	12		

Lockheed F-80 Shooting Star (1955–1966)

The FAC received 15 single-seat F-80 fighter-bombers in 1955 as part of the US Military Assistance Program to its South American allies. The fighters joined the Sabres in the 1er Grupo de Combate at Palanquero Air Base, forming the 10th Fighter-Bomber Squadron. These fighters were destined to replace the older P-47D Thunderbolt fighter-bombers in service since 1946. The Thunderbolts were retired in 1956, after the F-80C squadron reached initial operational capability (IOC).

The aircraft were applied the serial numbers FAC-2051 to FAC-2065. These aircraft were mostly refurbished former USAF Korean War veterans, built around 1947–49.

The P-80 in FAC service had with only 11 years a much shorter operational life than the T-33s. 2061 seen here is exhibited at Base Aérea "Brigadier General (H) Camilo Daza" in Bogota. (Santiago Rivas)

There are reports that a further ten former USAF aircraft were delivered from 1963 and had serial numbers of FAC-2330 to FAC-2339. However, there is no photographic evidence to support this, and that number range has been reported as applied to Beech T-34A Mentor basic trainers.

By 1966 all of the Shooting Stars had been withdrawn from service. The Shooting Star performed poorly in Colombian service with up to nine aircraft having been written off (60 per cent of the force) by the time they were retired. Most of the survivors were preserved as monuments and at least one, number FAC-2058 was sent to the Alaska Air National Guard.

Manufacturer	Aircraft Type	Delivered	Number	Serial Numbers	Remarks
Lockheed	F-80C Shooting Star	1955	15	FAC-2051 to FAC-2065	ex-USAF

Canadair Sabre Mk.6 (1956–1968)

The FAC began negotiations with Canadian companies during late 1955 in order to obtain modern jet fighters as well a modern navigation and an air control system. Canadair was approached with the idea of producing 24 Sabre Mk.6 jet fighters for the Colombian Air Force. This was the first sale of Canadian-built jets to a Latin American country.

The contract was valued at USD 8 million and followed by a separate agreement with Canadair to establish a service and maintenance facility for jet aircraft, whereby Canadair technicians would stay for at least two years training Colombian technicians. This facility would also service the country's recently acquired T-33 trainers.

By March 1956 Canadair was issued an export license for six Sabre Mk.6 fighters, which was the first non-NATO or non-Commonwealth contract for Canadian-built jet fighters. Further Canadian plans to sell Avro CF-100 fighters to Bogotá were unsuccessful, mainly because the US held a veto option on the deal. In late April 1956 it started to receive six brand new Sabre 6 (F-86F) jet fighters. The new fighters were assigned the serial numbers FAC-2021 to FAC-2026 and put in service with Grupo de Combate at Palanquero Air Base.

In 1956 Colombia received as first non NATO and Commonwealth country six Canadian CL-13B Sabres. In this shot dated late 50s/ early 60s FAC-2023 prepares for another mission.
(via AAMA)

The first write-off (FAC-2025) came in June 1956, while the unit was still working on its initial operational capability. It was followed by the loss FAC-2026 on 18 September 1956.

By 1963 only two aircraft remained in operation, after FAC-2022 was lost on 22 June 1960 and FAC-2021 in June 1961, so attrition replacement aircraft were acquired through MAP. Four aircraft were requested, these being former Spanish Air Force F-86F-25-NH Sabres (serial numbers FAC-2027 to FAC-2030) transferred via the USAF. Maybe a further two F-86Fs were acquired as attrition replacement aircraft, but information on this is scarce.

The Sabres began to be withdrawn from use in 1966 and all were retired by 1968. Their intended replacements however, did not come until 1972, when the Mirage 5 entered full operational service.

Manufacturer	Aircraft Type	Delivered	Number	Serial Numbers	Remarks
Canadair Ltd	CL-13B Sabre 6	1956	6	FAC-2021 to FAC-2026	
North American	F-86F-25-NH	1963	4	FAC-2027 to FAC-2030	ex-Spanish AF

One (FAC 2024) of the six Canadair CL-13B Sabres survived as exhibition piece at Marco Fidel Suarez Air Base.
(Carlos Narvaez)

Cessna T-37 Tweet (1969-)

T-37C (2104) from Escuela Militar de Aviación takes off for a trainings mission. (Banco de Fotos Movifotos via AAMA)

In order to replace its North American T-6 Texan trainers, the Colombian Air Force acquired ten brand new Cessna T-37C Tweet armed trainers in 1968. They were initially delivered to the Escuela Militar de Aviación (military flight school) in 1969, displaying serial numbers FAC-2101 to FAC-2110. On 25 May 1971 FAC-2110 was lost in an accident. The T-37 became the standard Colombian advanced trainer during the 1970s and into the 1980s. By the late 1980s the T-37C fleet had been reduced to seven flying aircraft. The aircraft designated FAC-2101 was retired and FAC-2104 was stored and stripped for spare parts. T-37 FAC-2110 was lost in an accident. In the early 1990s the FAC began negotiations for the acquisition of some replacements aircraft.

In 1992 the Fuerza Aérea Colombiana obtained a major anti-narcotics package that included a dozen T-37B Tweet trainers as well as OA-37B attack and C-130 transport aircraft. Deliveries began in 1993 and comprised four former Chilean and eight former USAF Tweets. The Chilean machines were applied with the serial numbers FAC-2111 to FAC-2114, while the former USAF aircraft received FAC-2115 to FAC-2122 range.

By the mid-1990s the remaining T-37s were grouped into the 215th Combat Squadron, part of the 1st Combat Command and pressed into service as COIN platforms. The unit was assigned to German Olano Air Base in Palanquero. Their place in the training syllabus at the Escuela Militar de Aviación was taken over by 14 Embraer EMB-312 Tucano trainers. On 25 June 2002, one aircraft, reported as FAC-2128 (actually it was FAC-2118) was lost, while on a training flight. Several replacement aircraft have been mentioned, but this type of aircraft went to retirement in 2003 without a proper replacement air-

In the later part of their career FAC's T-37s received a two-tone colour scheme and were used in COIN role as training role has been taken over by EMB-312 Tucano. (Fuerza Aerea Colombiana)

FAC 2126 is one of the latest T-37 batch obtained from USA. Seen here during delivery in November 2008.
(Tomas Cubero)

craft in sight. Most of this air fleet was placed in open storage at Base Aerea Militar 4 in Barranquilla. In 2008 FAC decided to re-activate its T-37 training syllabus. One of the stored aircraft was put back into service and the government acquired eight former USAF examples that had been stored at Davis Monthan AFB. In November 2008, the first batch of four T-37Bs, comprising FAC-2123 to 2126 arrived in Colombia. In January 2009, three further examples were transferred to the FAC, these were allocated serial numbers 2127 to 2129 and finally, FAC-2130 was transferred in March 2009.

Manufacturer	Aircraft Type	Delivered	Number	Serial Numbers	Remarks
Cessna	T-37C Tweet	1969	10	FAC-2101 to FAC-2110	
Cessna	T-37B Tweet	1992	8	FAC-2115 to FAC-2122	ex-USAF
Cessna	T-37B Tweet	1992	4	FAC-2111 to FAC-2114	ex-FACH
Cessna	T-37B Tweet	2008	8	FAC-2123 to FAC-2130	ex-USAF

Dassault Mirage 5 (1972–)

As Colombia's fighter fleet was growing older and increasingly more expensive to operate, the FAC High Command began to look for a replacement to its venerable Sabre in the late 1960s. The process was actually a long and an overdue one. The F-80C Shooting Stars had been retired in 1966 and the last operational Sabre was retired by 1968, leaving the country without a front-line fighter force!

The supersonic Mirage 5 was selected as Colombia's next generation fighter and a contract for 18 aircraft was signed with Dassault in 1970. The contract included a USD 31 million first payment for the first three aircraft. One can stipulate that the total value was for around USD 160–180 million. The Mirage selected by Colombia was to be operated in the dual interceptor and fighter-ground-attack (FGA) role.

Deliveries began in March 1972 and included 2 twin-seat Mirage 5COD conversion trainers (serial numbers FAC-3001 and FAC-3002), 2 5COR reconnaissance models (numbers FAC-3011 and FAC-3012) and, 14 single-seat 5COA (numbers FAC-3021 to

After several years without any frontline jet fighter, FAC received in 1972 14 Mirage 5COAs, operating as fighter & fighter-bomber.
(Javier Franco 'Topper' archive)

FAC-3034). They were a welcome addition to the 1st Combat Group at German Olano Military Air Base in Palanquero. Sadly, one of the single-seat fighters, FAC-3025, was lost a few weeks after delivery, on 21 August. One of the reconnaissance configured aircraft, the Mirage FAC-3012 was lost in an accident during November 1973, reducing the fleet to 16 flying aircraft.

Mirages that remained were the only supersonic fighters in the service of the Fuerza Aérea Colombiana through the 1970s and well into the 1980s. A requirement for a dozen Kfir fighter-bombers to complement the ground-attack role was outlined in the early 1980s, with the Kfirs to join the FAC by 1982, but this deal was delayed. Aircraft designated FAC-3032 was written-off in June 1985.

US indecision about the sale of IAI Kfirs to Colombia by 1987 prompted a major upgrade of the Mirage fleet. From 1988 IAI engineers arrived at Madrid Air Base and began to work close with the FAC's Maintenance Command (CAMAN) on a comprehensive upgrade to the fleet. The upgrade was to include structural modifications in the form of new (Kfir-style) canards, in-flight refuelling probes, a HUD, and a new fire-control system.

The loss of FAC-3023 in June 1990 further reduced the fleet, only to be hit with another loss of number FAC-308 by 1994. In October 1996 the remaining 5COR (FAC-3011)

Mirage 5COA (3027) in special paint scheme representing the national colours armed with two Mk.82 bombs and long range drop tanks.
(Fuerza Aerea Colombiana)

Mirage 5COA (FAC 3035) in grey overall colour scheme.
(Fuerza Aerea Colombiana)

The FAC Mirage fleet received an overhaul & upgrade from 1988 onwards, including canards, HUD and IFR.
(Javier Franco 'Topper')

was converted into a standard 5COA, after having its original OMERA reconnaissance cameras removed. The loss of the last reconnaissance fighter did not impact the FAC's operational capabilities as the US-sponsored *Plan Colombia* furnished a variety of intelligence gathering assets. The aircraft was designated FAC-3035.

FAC-3029 was written-off in November 1997 and on 29 September 1998, a Mirage 5 (FAC-3026) crashed near San Vicentedel Caguan in Caqueta province, killing the pilot.

The remaining 11 aircraft were further upgraded during 2001 to include night vision systems, Python III air-to-air missiles, and laser-guided bombs. The resulting aircraft has been designated 5COAM. The Mirage 5COD received a CLDS (Cockpit Laser Designator System) which allowed the aircraft to become a control and attack designator for the LGB-armed Mirage 5COAMs and Kfirs.

Manufacturer	Aircraft Type	Delivered	Number	Serial Numbers	Remarks
Dassault	Mirage 5COA	1972	14	FAC-3021 & FAC-3034	
Dassault	Mirage 5COD	1972	2	FAC-3001 & FAC-3002	
Dassault	Mirage 5COA	1972	2	FAC-3011 & FAC-3012	FAC-3011; later FAC-3035

Cessna A-37B Dragonfly (1978–2008)

The FAC accepted the US-proposed A-37B Dragonfly in order to replace its remaining A-26 Invader attack-bombers in 1977. An expected first batch of 6 aircraft was expanded to 12 by 1980. They began delivery in 1978, and assigned serial numbers FAC-2151 to FAC-2162, to Marco Fidel Suarez Air Base at Cali. The delivery was complete by 1981 and allowed the last bomber –an A-26 Invader to be phased out of service by 1982. The first loss of an A-37B (probably FAC-2154) occurred in 1981. Based at Cali, they formed the Escuadrón de Combate 411, a part of the Grupo de Apoyo Táctico (Tactical Support Group) operating alongside a dozen UH-1H Iroquois helicopter gunships mainly on COIN and anti-narcotic operations. The GAT took over the name of the 3rd Combat Air Command (CACOM).

Their excellent use in COIN operations led the FAC to order an additional 12 aircraft in April 1984. By that year end, nine aircraft had been delivered and the order was completed by 1985. These Dragonflies were assigned the serial numbers in the FAC-2163 to FAC-2174 range. Instead of forming a new unit, the 411th Squadron absorbed the aircraft and deployed a detachment of four Dragones (as they were locally known) to the San Andres, Providencia, and Santa Catalina Archipelagos. These islands were being threatened by Sandinista forces at the time, as they are a strategic post to block the Panama Canal.

A third batch of OA-37Bs was transferred from the USAF in 1989, receiving the serial numbers FAC-2175 to FAC-2182. They allowed the strengthening of a further two detachments at Palanquero (with the 1st CACOM) and Apiay (with the 2nd CACOM).

By 1996 several Dragons, including serial numbers FAC-2152, FAC-2156, FAC-2158, FAC-2162, FAC-2164, FAC-2166, FAC-2168, and FAC-2170 had been withdrawn from service, placed in storage or, preserved as museum pieces. On 28 June 1996 number FAC-2169 was written-off because of an accident. By the late 1990s the Dragonfly fleet was completely commited to anti-drug operations, during 1998 alone, Colombian A-37Bs shot down at least four drug-running light aircraft, another three from Febrary to August 1999 and one in June 2000. By 1999 the fleet's strength had fallen to some

One of the early A-37B (2162) in a new colour scheme including dragon markings. (Andrés Ramirez)

A-37B FAC-2168, armed with
Mk.81 bombs.
(Martin Hornlimann, Exavia/Milpix)

14 operational aircraft, with some sources rumoring that only 5 aircraft were in flying condition. The US State Department authorized a USD 14 million grant for a life extension program destined to keep the aircraft in service until 2010. This grant came through the 'Western Hemispheric Drug Elimination Act' and included upgrades and further training of Colombia personnel on the type.

The upgraded aircraft began to reach Colombia in 2002 and by 2004 the FAC had some 14 aircraft in strength, out of a possible 17. The 411th Squadron continued to provide a permanent detachment to the recently created GACAR (Grupo Aereo del Caribe, Caribbean Air Group) at the San Andres Airfield, recently upgraded to air base status, and the Dragons will continue to fly counter-drug interdiction patrols in this major drug route. FAC-2181 was lost on 3 August 2005 in a landing accident.

The Dragonfly was replaced in 2008, together with the OV-10s, with up to 25 new EMB-314 Super Tucano turbo-prop light attack fighters. However, as of early 2009, there were reports of a small number of A-37Bs still in operation.

Manufacturer	Aircraft Type	Delivered	Number	Serial Numbers	Remarks
Cessna	A-37B Dragonfly	1980	12	FAC-2151 to FAC-2162	
Cessna	A-37B Dragonfly	1985	12	FAC-2163 to FAC-2174	
Cessna	OA-37B Dragonfly	1989	8	FAC-2175 to FAC-2182	ex-USAF

Israel Aircraft Industries Kfir (1989–)

During the early 1980s the FAC developed a requirement for a second squadron of supersonic fighters to be used in mainly in ground attack missions. A failed attempt to buy a squadron of F-5E/F Tigers from the US, led Colombia to enter negotiations with Israel for the supply of Kfir fighter-bombers.

A very nice view of Kfir FAC-3034. See also the Mirage 5CO picture on p.103 to compare the two optically similar types. (Javier Franco 'Topper')

Once a crisis with Venezuela heated up in the summer of 1987, Colombia speeded negotiations and signed an Economic Cooperation Treaty with Israel that August. A USD 200 million order with Israel Aircraft Industries included 14 Kfirs with an option for a further 12, as well as an upgrade of the existing Mirage fleet to a near Kfir standard. U.S. Congress approved the deal that same year.

Deliveries began in 1989 but only 13 were delivered, comprising 12 second-hand former IDF/AF Kfir C.2 (serial numbers FAC-3040 to FAC-3051) and one brand new Kfir TC.7 that displayed the number FAC-3003. The final Kfir, supposed to be TC.7 number FAC-3004 was not delivered, some sources claim it was lost during training flights in Israel or may have been written off from the deal. The single-seat Kfirs were refurbished and upgraded to the C.7 standard with assistance from IAI technicians at the Comando Aereo de Mantenimiento in Madrid Air Base from 1990. The upgrade included HOTAS, Elta EL/M-2021B pulse-Doppler radar, chaff/flare dispensers, and a flight refuelling probe.

The first Kfir to be lost was number FAC-3042 on 2 May 1995, when it crashed into a mountain on its return to Palanquero Air Base from a night attack training sortie. A further upgrade performed with IAI kits in 1996 had made at least seven remaining Kfirs compatible with Python III air-to-air missiles and Griffin laser-guided bombs.

The Kfirs have been constantly used to attack rebel positions deep inside FARC-controlled territory. FAC-3046 crashed in June 2003 due to a bird strike that shut the engine over the Rio Magdalena area, the pilot, Juan Manuel Grisales, ejected and was later picked up by fishermen. On 14 August 2004, one Kfir was hit by a Stinger SAM while it was bombing FARC positions, but it managed to get back to base where it was repaired.

The excellent performance of the Kfir in Colombian hands led the FAC to select the Kfir C.10 over former USAF F-16s as its 21st Century multi-role fighter. On 7 February 2008 the FAC signed a USD 260 million contract with IAI for the acquisition of 13 former ISAF Kfir C-7s and a complete upgrade of the 24 aircraft fleet The ten Colombian single seat Kfirs will be upgraded to the C.10 (Kfir 2000) version, comprising the EL/M-

2032 radar, Derby BVRAAMs, new glass cockpit, HOTAS and EW capabilities, while the remaining ten former Israeli Kfirs and four two seat versions (comprising the Colombian and three former Israeli) will be upgraded to the C.12 version, which features the same enhancements as the C.10 version minus the EL/M-2032 radar and BVRAAM capability. This last version is dubbed the Kfir COA in Colombia.

Manufacturer	Aircraft Type	Delivered	Number	Serial Numbers	Remarks
IAI	Kfir C.2	1989	13	FAC-3040 to FAC-3051	only 12 delivered; upgraded to C.7 standard
IAI	Kfir TC.7	1990	1	FAC-3003	
IAI	Kfir C.10	2009	13	FAC-3052 to FAC-3061	ex-Israeli AF; upgraded to C.12 standard

Due to its performance Kfir C.2 will be FAC's prime fighter for 21st century. FAC-3044 seen here in CAP configuration with 2 Python Mk.3 missiles and 2 fuel tanks. Note second aircraft at left bottom. (Fuerza Aerea Colombiana)

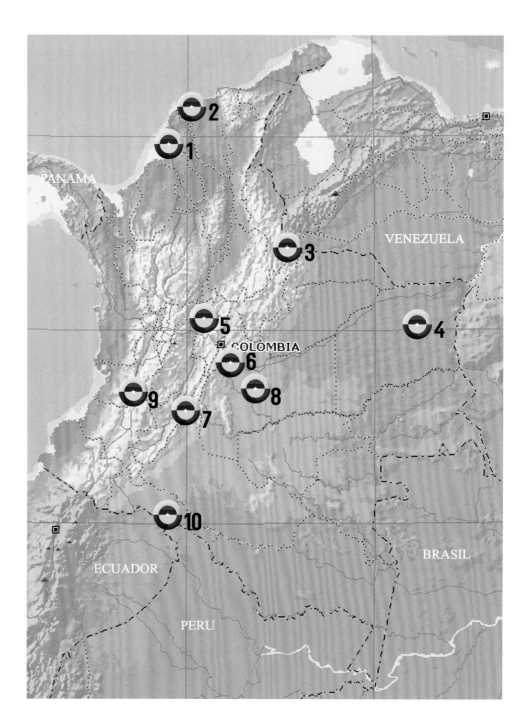

1. Cartagena
2. Barranquilla
3. Yopal
4. Marandúa
5. Palanquero
6. El Dorado, Bogotá
7. Melgar
8. Apiay
9. Cali
10. Tres Esquinas

Chapter 6

CUBA

President Batista had several plans for the Fuerza Aérea del Ejército Cubano (FAEC, Air Force of the Cuban Army) in the early 1950s and sent a number of pilots for conversion training in the United States. Lockheed T-33 trainers, F-80C Shooting Star fighter-bombers, and F-86 Sabre fighters were to form the backbone of this pro-American Caribbean state. The revolution changed the outcome of Batista's and the FAEC's plans. The new government quickly looked for an alternative source for modern jet fighters and contacted the British government in an attempt to exchange its Sea Fury fighter-bombers for an equal number of Hawker Hunter fighter jets during October 1959. The British government considered the deal, but soon caved-in under US pressure not to supply any modern combat equipment to the pro-Marxist Cuba. This turned modernization plans towards the Soviet Union mainly in the form of the Mikoyan i Gurevich design bureau.

With a new ally just some 145km south of the United States, the Soviet Union intended to place an offensive nuclear contingent made up of MRBMs and IRBMs on the island. They were to be protected by a regiment of Soviet Air Force MiG-21F fighters, a regiment of Ilyushin Il-28 tactical bombers and an air defence division with S-75 Dvina (ASCC Code SA-2) SAM batteries. This plan caused what is known in history as the Cuban Missile Crisis.

The world was at the brink of nuclear war during that crisis but diplomacy was able to intercede. As part of the 'cool down' agreements, the US guaranteed that the island would not be invaded. For their part, the Soviets agreed not to provide or base any 'strategic offensive' systems in Cuba. These negotiations pretty much dictated the types of aircraft that the Cuban Revolutionary Air Force and Air Defense (DAAFAR) would have access to during the next decades: The Ilyushin Il-28 (ASCC code Beagle) jet bombers were withdrawn from the island but the air defence MiGs stayed.

Cuban instructors, advisors, and observers from about every military service were sent to North Vietnam to learn from American combat tactics employed in the war and to train North Vietnamese in the use and application of Soviet hardware.

During the 1970s Cuban pilots were present in several parts of Africa, as part of Cuban expeditionary forces sent to support friendly governments. The first offensive fighter bombers reached Cuban squadrons by the end of that decade, being capable of striking US bases and strategic installations.

By the early 1980s the Cuban DAAFAR was the largest and best equipped air arm in the Caribbean, fielding some 100 combat jet aircraft, mainly MiGs. They formed a credible defense to any US invasion attempt and a real threat to US strategic assets in the Continental South East.

Force levels began to suffer after 1990, when Soviet assistance started to decline. The new Russian masters were not as eager to arm Castro with state-of-the-art fighters in exchange for ideological communion and sugar canes (Cuba's No.1 export). The DAAFAR found itself waiting for spares and struggling to get kerosene on the black market. Most of the older aircraft were stored in prime condition and kept in reserve status.

Since Cuba established the death penalty in 1999 for narcotic-related crimes, its air force has become one of the most active combat forces in the Caribbean. Cuban MiGs are instructed to shoot down any suspected narcotic (or subversive) aircraft that does not immediately respond or cooperate with landing instructions once they have entered Cuban airspace.

By the early 21st Century the Cuban Revolutionary Air Force was but a shadow of its former self, with some 30 fighter aircraft in operational condition, about 10 per cent its size from the 1980s.

Lockheed T-33 (1954–1968)

The Cuban Army Air Force (FAEC) began a notable expansion after Cuba signed the 1947 Rio Treaty of Mutual Defense, with surplus examples of North American P-51D Mustang fighters, P-47D Thunderbolt fighter-bombers and B-25J Mitchel bombers reaching Cuban squadrons. In May 1953 a group of Cuban pilots was sent to the US in order to receive several courses, including jet conversion training on T-33A trainers and F-84 Thunderjet fighters. By this time the Lockheed T-33A was selected to be the country's first jet aircraft, and a Lend-Lease Agreement under the MAP was finalized by 1954. Deliveries began in June with four aircraft in service by 1955. They were designated serial numbers 701, 703, 705, and 707.

A group of Cuban pilots was selected during 1954 and sent to receive training on the F-84 Thunderjet and F-86 Sabre fighters at Moody AFB in Georgia. A further four T-33As had been delivered by August 1956, these wearing the serial numbers 709, 711, 713, and 715. In this year the USAF mission in Cuba offered to provide up to 13 refurbished F-80C Shooting Stars to replace the old P-47D Thunderbolt fighter-bombers. The aircraft were to start deliveries in 1957, but this was cancelled.

Cuban T-33As were pressed into action against insurgent forces, together with P-47D Thunderbolts, B-26 Invaders and C-47 Skytrains. They were armed with locally

This T-33 (709) was from the second batch delivered to FAEC before the Communist revolution stopped access to Western aircraft.
(via AAMA)

During the Bay of Pigs affair this particular T-33 (711) shot down three B-26C Invader piloted by CIA personnel.
(via AAMA)

developed 250-kg bombs. The only T-33A to be lost during the revolution was serial number 705, when one of its 250-kg bombs exploded in flight during late 1958. The aircraft was attacking a rebel position near Camaguey.

The seven surviving T-33As were put into service in the new Fuerza Aérea Revolucionaria (FAR, Revolutionary Air Force). During its formative years, the FAR was, in essence, a re-named (and re-aligned FAEC). Cuban T-33As formed the basis of air defense, as the country found its new place in the world.

In March 1961, thousands of Cuban exiles, backed by the CIA began an amphibious operation in Girón Beach. Cuban T-33s raced to the air in minutes, as their pilots had been sleeping on the runway at San Antonio de los Baños in anticipation of a counter-revolution attack. During what became known as the Bay of Pigs fiasco, T-33 'serial number 711' shot down three B-26C Invader bombers piloted by CIA personnel.

Although spares were quite difficult to obtain for the T-33 fleet, there are reports that state that the last Cuban T-33 was retired until 1968, operating as a fighter-trainer for the new MiG fleet.

Manufacturer	Aircraft Type	Delivered	Number	Serial Numbers	Remarks
Lockheed	T-33A	1954	4	701, 703, 705, 707	
Lockheed	T-33A	1955	4	709, 711, 713, 715	

Mikoyan i Gurevich MiG-15 (ASCC code Fagot) (1961–1982)

Castro initiated secret arms deals with the Soviet bloc in 1960, sending several officers to evaluate and eventually train on different aircraft. The MiG-15bis was selected to be Cuba's first jet fighter, and Nikita Krushov agreed to provide several aircraft after a visit from Raul Castro to Moscow during June 1960.

With MiG-15 the new DAAFAR started its inventory of Soviet types. Interesting to note that Raul Castro signed this deal in June 1960 with Nikita Kruzhov. Since 2006 Raul Castro is Cuba's president.
(via AAMA)

A small group of experienced pilots, most of them T-33 veterans, was selected for conversion training in the Soviet Union and Czechoslovakia. The first Soviet jet fighters arrived in Cuba during May 1961 in the form of 20 MiG-15s. They were accompanied by four two-seat MiG-15UTI (ASCC code Midget) tactical trainers. The MiGs were delivered by ship and assembled at San Antonio de los Baños Air Base by Soviet technicians.

A group of Soviet instructor pilots began flying the fighters in June while a training program was hastily assembled to produce Cuban MiG pilots. By November, Cuban officers assumed control of the first MiG squadron, the Carlos Ulloa squadron.

Another group of pilots was sent to China to receive basic jet training. Once the Chinese and Czech-trained Cuban pilots returned to Cuba another two fighter squadrons were established. These were identified as 'Chinos' and 'Checos' according to where they received their training. Delivery of further MiG-15bis, as well as reconnaissance-configured MiG-15SR continued.

When the Cuban Missile Crisis erupted, the FAR had some 36 MiG-15bis/Rbis and they were all deployed to remote landing strips to avoid destruction on the ground. They were to provide point air defense and anti-shipping attack missions in the event war broke out with the US. Once MiG-15s were operational the FAR could intercept the constant flights of USAF RF-101 Voodoo and USN RF-8 Crusader reconnaissance aircraft.

The Santa Clara-based MiG-15 squadron was replaced with a new MiG-17 unit in 1964 and transferred to Holgin Air Base. Further deliveries of MiG-15s to Cuba were limited to the two-seat MiG-15UTI converted trainer version. As modern MiGs began to join the Cuban squadrons, MiG-15bis were deemed obsolete and placed in reserve status. MiG-15UTIs were also reportedly then sent to Angola in 1975 to support a squadron of MiG-17 (ASCC code Fresco) fighter-bombers.

MiG-15UTIs was the trainer for most generations of Cuban airmen up until 1982, when they were replaced by the Czech-built Aero L-39C advanced trainers. However there are reports of the MiG-15UTI being in service at least until 1988, before being placed in open storage on 'reserve' status.

Manufacturer	Aircraft Type	Delivered	Number	Serial Numbers	Remarks
Mikoyan Gurevich	MiG-15bis	1961	36	07, 18, 20, 32, 36, 50, 53, 103	ex-VVS
Mikoyan Gurevich	MiG-15UTI	1961	4		ex-VVS
Mikoyan Gurevich	MiG-15UTI	1963	6		ex-VVS
Mikoyan Gurevich	MiG-15UTI	1966	20		

Mikoyan i Gurevich MiG-17 (ASCC code Fresco) (1962–1998?)

Deliveries of the MiG-17 fighter-bomber started in 1962. These MiGs were of the S.104 (MiG-17AS) version and came actually straight from the Aero Vodochody production line in Czechoslovakia. Although armed with early air-to-air missiles, they supplemented a squadron of MiG-15s at Santa Clara AB on ground-attack duties. Soviet-built MiG-17Fs (ASCC code Fresco-C) were used mainly as interceptors instead. Cuban pilots slanted to fly MiGs were trained at Krasnodar, in the USSR, together with hundreds of pilots from other friendly countries.

Immediately upon becoming operational, Cubans intensively trained anti-invasion operations, foremost dedicated maritime strikes, but also strikes in support of coastal defence troops. Anti-ship operations were trained to a degree where within only a few years Cuban were regarded as the best anti-ship MiG-17 pilots between all Soviet-friendly states. Consequently, several Cubans were sent to North Vietnam to train a group of ten North Vietnamese MiG-17 pilots in anti-ship attack techniques. The results of their work became obvious when the North Vietnamese attacked several USN warships off their coast and damaged a USN destroyer, in 1972.

Additionally, MiG-17 proved not only as successful and popular in Cuban service, but also resistant to any sorts of electronic countermeasures, so that the DAAFAR requested the Soviets to provide an additional regiment of MiG-17Fs instead of planned

MiG-17AS (232) is optimised as fighter-bomber. (DoD)

Two MiG-17s with S-24 unguided rockets. (Mario Martinez collection)

MiG-21PFMs. Since the delivery of the later type was already in the process, this decision could not be reverted any more.

There was some dissent between the crews too, though, and on 5 October 1969 a Cuban pilot defected with his MiG-17A (232) to Homestead AFB in Florida. While the pilot was granted political asylum, following careful inspection, his aircraft was returned to Cuba.

In 1975, the DAAFAR was organized to establish a small contingent for deployment in Angola. A total of nine MiG-17AS and MiG-17Fs and at least one MiG-15UTI were shipped to Luanda in December 1975. Adorned with Angolan markings though flown exclusively by Cuban pilots, they flew a large number of combat sorties in the campaign against FLEC (Cabinda Enclave Liberation Front), in northern Angola. As soon as FLEC was defeated, in April 1976, the MiG-17 unit was deployed against UNITA in the south as well. Overall, MiG-17 did not meet expected success during this campaign, foremost due to its short range and poor payload. Correspondingly, the type was soon relegated to training duties and all surviving aircraft sold to Angola.

Meanwhile, in late 1977, a group of Cuban MiG-17 pilots was deployed to Ethiopia to support a supposedly "Marxist" government in its struggle against Somali invasion of the Ogaden region. In Ethiopia Cuban pilots flew MiG-15UTIs and MiG-17Fs delivered from South Yemen, however, and no aircraft provided by Cuba or USSR, as usually reported. This stems from the fact that some of Cuban advisors were present in South Yemen already since 1970. Similarly, reports about deliveries of MiG-17PFs to Cuba in 1982 proved false as well.

Exact number of MIG-17s delivered to Cuba over the time remains unknown. Even though some sources put their numbers as high as 100, it is unlikely that the DAAFAR ever received more than 40. The type was eventually replaced by MiG-23BNs in the early and mid-1980s.

Manufacturer	Aircraft Type	Delivered	Number	Serial Numbers	Remarks
Aero Vodochody	S-104	1962	12 – 18	230, 232, 237	
Mikoyan i Gurevich	MiG-17F Fresco	1964	20	212, 215, 216	

Mikoyan i Gurevich MiG-19 (ASCC code Farmer) (1961–1964)

Cuba has been no exception in operating the MiG-19: due to bad handling just for very few years.
(via Santiago Rivas)

The FAR received a total of nine of ex-Soviet Air Force MiG-19Ps supersonic fighters already in June 1951, but none were assembled before autumn 1962, when several Soviet Air Force units deployed in the country as well.

Assigned serial numbers between (at least) 82 and 89, Cuban MiG-19s began flying operations in November 1962. The type did not prove a success, regardless if flown by Soviet or Cuban pilots. Already on the second day of operations, one of MiG-19s crashed, even though pilot ejected safely. Two additional MiGs crashed soon after, one of them killing a Soviet instructor. With the fleet almost halved, and disliked for its poor handling and mechanical reliability, remaining Cuban MiG-19s were soon stored and the unit that was in the process of converting to them equipped with MiG-21PFMs to reach Cuba instead.

Manufacturer	Aircraft Type	Delivered	Number	Serial Numbers	Remarks
Mikoyan i Gurevich	MiG-19P	1961	9	82, 85, 88, 89	ex-VVS

Mikoyan i Gurevich MiG-21 (ASCC code Fishbed) (1963–?)

The first MiG-21s supersonic interceptors arrived in Cuba already in September 1962, but were originally not intended to serve with DAAFAR. Instead, they were the mounts of the Soviet Air Force's 213 IAP. They were originally stationed at Kubinka AB and part of the 12th Air Defence Division. This unit was deployed to Cuba together with one division equipped with SAMs in order to protect the island, but also the planned deployment of Soviet short-range ballistic missiles and nuclear-bombs armed Ilushin Il-28 bombers.

How many MiG-21s exactly arrived with 213 IAP at Santa Clara AB remains unknown, but most of available accounts indicate between 36 and 42, including at least two MiG-21Fs from the original "0-series", organized in three squadrons. Although

A line-up of MiG-21s: a row of ex-Soviet MiG-21s in Cuba, in 1962. Note the first aircraft is one of few early MiG-21Fs while last three aircraft are MiG-21PFMs.
(via AAMA)

wearing Cuban insignia they were exclusively Soviet-flown and soon became involved in several incidents with USAF and USN reconnaissance fighters and their escorts underway over Cuba, including at least one clash that involved some violent manoeuvring against a pair of Lockheed F-104C Starfighters and almost ended with both sides opening fire.

The US government immediately protested at the presence of Soviet squadrons so close to its borders and the subsequent discovery of Soviet short-range ballistic missiles eventually caused the Cuban Crisis of 1962. In the course of increasing tensions, on 5 November 1962, two Soviet-flown MiG-21s intercepted a pair of USN Vought RF-8 Crusaders underway on a reconnaissance sortie within the frame of the Operation Blue Moon, but did not manage to open fire at them.

Following the withdrawal of practically all the other Soviet units from Cuba, in 1963 V-VS' MiG-21s were "nationalized" and Soviets began training Cuban pilots to fly them. The first Cuban pilot soloed on a MiG-21F already during the early summer, and by August 1963 the first squadron was declared operational.

Following extensive problems with MiG-19s, and in order to enable the DAAFAR to form a night-interception unit, in 1964 the Soviets provided the first batch of MiG-21PFS'. Equipped with R1L radar, RS-2 (AA-1 Alkali) and R-3S (AA-2 Atoll) missiles, these fighters roved a significant improvement over the earlier MiG-21F-13s, even though lacking its 30mm cannon and Cubans decided to follow up with a batch of MiG-21PFMs, delivered already the following year.

The often reported deliveries of "MiG-21PFMA" variant in 1966 were probably related to Cuban orders for even more advanced MiG-21Ms (equipped to carry four R-3S missiles and a built-in 23mm cannon), MiG-21Rs and also first four MiG-21U two-seat conversion trainers. Arriving from 1968, these enabled the DAAFAR to re-equip two interceptor squadrons based at San Antonio de los Banos, while two newly-established

A seven ship formation consisting of two MiG-21Us and five MiG-21PFMs. (Mario Martinez collection)

units took over surviving MiG-21F-13s and operated them from Frank Pais IAP, near Holguin. Together with MiG-17s, this sizeable MiG-21 fleet turned the Cuban Air Force into one of the most potent Latin American air forces of the late 1960s, and through the 1970s the DAAFAR began to flex it muscles in various incidents with neighbouring countries.

In 1970, several MiG-21s thundered high over Bahamas, "delivering a message" to the local government after this arrested a number of Cuban fishermen inside its territorial waters. Although several USN F-4s arrived to counter this demonstration, the fishers were subsequently released.

By 1974 old MiG-21F-13s were in demand of replacement. Correspondingly, the DAAFAR requested delivery of MiG-21MF fighters and MiG-21UM trainers. The Soviets reacted only after Cuban decision to deploy its troops in support of what the leadership in Havana considered "another Marxist" movement in Angola. In January 1976, giant Soviet Air Force Antonov An-22 transports flew 12 MiG-21MFs directly to Luanda, via Ethiopia. There, the new MiGs entered service with a DAAFAR unit assigned to the emerging Angolan Air Force. Flown by a group of experienced and highly capable pilots, Cuban MiG-21s proved their mettle during the following months. In several dozens of strike sorties, they delivered decisive blows against UNITA rebels, and certainly had a role in that movement agreeing to a ceasefire, later the same year.

Instead of MiG-21MFs, Soviets began deliveries of MiG-21bis' to Cuba, and these officially entered service in October 1976, again flown by an interceptor unit based at

MiG-21MF (511) with standard armament of four R-3S missiles over Florida Straits. (Cory McDonald, Florida Memory)

MiG-21bis (672) after defection to NAS Key West on 18 September 1993. (DoD)

San Antonio de Los Banos AB. Cuba thus had a number of pilots experienced on this variant when Havana decided to send some of them to aid Ethiopian Air Force in its conversion to MiG-21bis and MiG-21R, as well as in the last phase of the Ogaden War, in the early 1978.

Meanwhile, DAAFAR MiG-21Ms and new MiG-21bis were involved in another international stand off, this time with the Dominican Republic, in 1977, after a Cuban merchant vessel had been detained inside the local territorial waters. The few remaining vintage North American P-51D Mustang fighters of the Dominican Air Force attempted to react, but were humiliated by the modern Mach 2 fighters, and the Dominicans eventually released the Cuban ship.

Large Peruvian orders for Sukhoi Su-22 fighters, later in the 1970s, caused the spread of rumours that Cuba might deploy a squadron of its MiG-21s to this country as well, but something of this kind never happened.

The 1980s proved to be some of most challenging times for the Cuban MiG-21 force, but also times of some of wildest rumours surrounding it. The contingent deployed in Angola was meanwhile reinforced by deliveries of additional MiG-21MFs and MiG-21PFMs (all of them paid for by the Angolan government and therefore Angolan possession), but it suffered repeated losses. At least five Cuban-flown Angolan MiG-21MFs and MiG-21bis' were shot down by improved anti-aircraft armament of the UNITA, in 1981 and 1982, and two in air combats with South African Mirage F.1s. Five more MiGs were lost and several damaged in 1983. Due to these and additional losses in subsequent years, by 1987 most of MiG-21 operations in Angola were relegated to Angolans, and the type replaced by MiG-23 within Cuban units.

Attempts to link various losses of Angolan transport aircraft (particularly those that occurred in "blue-on-blue" incidents), or claimed downings of transports underway with supplies for UNITA with Cuban-flown Angolan MiG-21s – published by various Cuban and Russian sources – are unrealistic. Similarly, corroboration for claims that a squadron of Cuban MiG-21s formed with Nicaraguan (Sandinista) pilots and trained in Cuba and Bulgaria was deployed in Nicaragua for several months, but then returned to avoid an international scandal, is not forthcoming.

Cuba

The position of the MiG-21 fleet was not much better in Cuba either, particularly since the 1980s saw increasing traffic of light aircraft, often involved in drugs trafficking, around – and often through – the Cuban airspace. One of early attempts to intercept one such intruder resulted in a crash of a DAAFAR MiG-21, on 21 February 1982. Similarly, during the US interventions in Grenada, in 1983, and in Panama, in 1989, Cuban MiG-21s could do little more but shadow many of USAF transport aircraft underway in the area.

Although the DAAFAR MiG-21bis' fleet was eventually reinforced to something like 30 aircraft by the late 1980s, it was to encounter even more significant problems. Once the USSR stopped providing spare parts, technical support and fuel to Cuba, the Cuban Air Force was practically grounded. Colossal plans for replacement of the entire MiG-21 fleet by "200" MiG-29s were abandoned, and remaining MiG-21PFMs – used solely for training purposes in the last few years of their career – soon stored. Majority of MiG-21Ms and MiG-21bis' was to follow: theoretically stored and "held in reserve", most of them never flew again. Furthermore, Moscow's announcements at its will to refurbish a large part of Cuban MiG-21-fleet, from 2001, proved an empty promise and as of 2005, the DAAFAR was left with barely six operational MiG-21s distributed between two units based in San Antonio de los Banos and Holguin.

The last role the once mighty and omni-present Cuban MiG-21-fleet was to play therefore appears to be a "semi-documentary" about their involvement in Angolan war, shot two years ago. For this opportunity, several surviving MiG-21 airframes were painted in Angolan markings.

Manufacturer	Aircraft Type	Delivered	Number	Serial Numbers	Remarks
Mikoyan i Gurevich	MiG-21F	1963		01, 04	ex-VVS
Mikoyan i Gurevich	MiG-21F-13	1963	36	10, 11, 16, 25, 26, 29, 31, 34, 36, 38–40, 43, 66	ex-VVS w/o camouflage
				006, 007, 411, 430	with camouflage
Mikoyan i Gurevich	MiG-21PFM	1966	12	361, 362, 365, 367, 368, 371, 374, 377–380, 384	
Mikoyan i Gurevich	MiG-21U	1966			
Mikoyan i Gurevich	MiG-21R	1968	4	103, 108, 111	
Mikoyan i Gurevich	MiG-21M/MF	1974	12+12	510, 511, 513, 514, 515, 516, 517, 518, 520	
Mikoyan i Gurevich	MiG-21UM	1974	6	405 (505?), 502, 503	
Mikoyan i Gurevich	MiG-21bis	1976	36	600, 602, 614, 622, 632, 642 (542?), 647 (547?), 650, 656, 660, 663, 664, 665, 672, 780	

Mikoyan i Gurevich MiG-23 (ASCC code Flogger) (1978–)

Experiences from Cuban intervention in Angola, in late 1975 and early 1976, as well as requirements of the Cuban involvement in Ethiopia, which started in late 1977, have shown that the FAR is in need of a more potent fighter-bomber, foremost one capable of carrying higher payloads over longer ranges than available MiG-17s and MiG-21s. With production and exports of early marks of MiG-23 reaching their peak, but also financial support of countries hosting Cuban contingents in Africa, the USSR was also capable of delivering several batches of such fighters at a relatively low price.

When the first corresponding order was issued remains unknown, but a group of Cuban pilots spent most of 1977 with training on MiG-23BNs (ASCC code Flogger-H) in the USSR, and several of them arrived in Ethiopia in March 1978, together with first examples of this type delivered to that country.

Only a few weeks later the first batch of eight MiG-23BN (serialled 710 to 723) and two MiG-23UBs (ASCC code Flogger-C; serialled 700 and 701) were delivered by Soviet merchant ships to Cuba. They entered service with the strike unit UM2661, based at San Antonio de Los Banos AB, officially declared operational by December 1978, when this unit participated in a major naval exercise with the Soviet Navy.

The arrival of MiG-23BNs in Cuba increased the levels of alertness in the southern USA then these fighter-bombers possessed the capability to hit several strategic bases in Florida, including McDill AFB, Homestead AFB, or the nuclear reactor at Turkey Point. They also became the reason for Washington opening negotiations with Venezuela for sale of F-16 fighters.

By 1982, with older variants of MiG-21 due for retirement or relegated to training duties, Cuba received another batch of eight MiG-23BNs, but also its first MiG-23MFs (ASCC code Flogger-B; serial numbers between 810 and 823), as well as three additional MiG-23UM conversion trainers (702 to 704). This second batch of MiG-23BNs entered service with Squadron UM1890 based at Santa Clara, while all MiG-23MFs were concentrated within an unknown Interceptor Squadron of the UM1779 Regiment,

A line-up of different MiG-23 versions: in front a MiG-23UB followed by MiG-23BNs (DoD)

MiG-23BN 722 dcparts Kcy West after US returned the defected aircraft back to Cuba. (Dale McDonald, Florida Memory)

based at San Antonio de los Banos AB (note: reports about stationing of any MiG-23s in San Julian are definitely wrong).

Increased numbers of MiG-23s enabled training of additional crews. Coupled with meanwhile improved capabilities of the Angolan air force – the operations of which were closely coordinated with the DAAFAR contingent deployed in that country – this resulted in agreement to re-equip the Cuban units detached to that country with MiG-23ML interceptors. Ordered and paid for by Angolans, the first eight MiG-23MLs and one MiG-23UM arrived in Angola in the early 1984, and entered service with the local air force, although they were flown and maintained exclusively by Cubans. Their first unit became operational by the summer of the same year but suffered a very unpleasant loss of two MiG-23MLs and one MiG-23UM in emergency landings due to bad weather early on.

Deliveries of replacement- as well as additional Floggers to Angola enabled the Cubans to establish their second squadron and by 1985 as at least for short periods of time as many as 24 MiG-23MLs were operational. However, combat attrition and operational losses were extensive and by 1988 no less but eleven Cuban-flown MiG-23MLs and MiG-23UMs were shot down and several heavily damaged by ground fire – in addition to the three examples mentioned above. It was apparently for this reason that during the same year seven Cuban MiG-23BN were shipped to Angola, together with their crews. Although assembled and prepared for operations they never flew a single combat sortie, though. On the contrary, during the Cuban withdrawal Angolans agreed to supply seven of their MiG-23MLs to Cuba, and these aircraft (serials 223, 232, 240, 241, 242, 243 and 245) officially entered service with the San Antonio de los Banos-based unit already equipped with MiG-23MFs and assigned to Regiment UM1779, in late 1988. All seven MiG-23BNs were quietly returned as well.

In 1990, following introduction of MiG-29s, remaining 13 MIG-23BNs and one MiG-23UB were transferred to Santa Clara AB, from where one of their pilots defected with his aircraft to the NAS Key West, Florida, USA, on 20 March 1991, where he asked for political asylum. This MiG-23BN (serial 722) was returned to Cuba, nevertheless.

In subsequent years the DAAFAR went through the crisis caused by the poor economic condition of the entire country and cancellation of Soviet material and financial aid. Flying was minimized due to a permanent shortage of fuel, and there were also frequent shortages of spares. It was probably a technical malfunction caused by such circumstances that lead to the crash of one MiG-23UM (708) near Frank Pais IAP, Holgin, in 1993. Nevertheless, a diminishing number of Cuban MiG-23s remained operational and in 1996 one of the MiG-23UMs was involved in downing of two Cessna light planes flown by "Hermaos al Rescate" ("Brothers to the Rescue"), a Florida-based organisation of Cuban exiles, while operating outside the Cuban airspace as SAR aids for Cuban refugees attempting to flee the island. In that case, the MiG-23UM served as a command platform for a MiG-29UB, while a flight of three MiG-23MLs vainly attempted to intercept a third Cessna.

By 2002, the remaining MiG-23 inventory was reduced to less than 20 intact airframes, including 8 MiG-23MFs, 7 MiG-23MLs, and between 3 and 5 MiG-23UB/UMs. But, in essence, like most of MiG-23BNs, these aircraft are practically withdrawn from active service and placed in storage.

Manufacturer	Aircraft Type	Delivered	Number	Serial Numbers	Remarks
Mikoyan i Gurevich	MiG-23BN	1978	8	710 to 723	not in sequence
Mikoyan i Gurevich	MiG-23UB	1978	2	700 & 701	not in sequence
Mikoyan i Gurevich	MiG-23BN	1982	8	724 to 737	
Mikoyan i Gurevich	MiG-23MF	1982	12	810 to 823	not in sequence
Mikoyan i Gurevich	MiG-23UB	1982	2	702 to 704	
Mikoyan i Gurevich	MiG-23ML	1984	36		only flown by Cuban pilots, but owned and operated by Angolan AF, 7 re-delivered to Cuba.
Mikoyan i Gurevich	MiG-23UM	1985	3	705 to 707	
Mikoyan i Gurevich	MiG-23ML	1985	18		

Aero L-39 Albatros (1982–?)

Like most Communist air forces of the time, Cuban fighter pilots received most of their formal training in the USSR. Indeed, Cuba was one of the most dependent members of the Soviet training establishment, having sent close to 3,400 aviators for training in Soviet skies. However, a token training organization was created in Cuba as the Escuela Militar de Aviación (Military Aviation School).

By the late 1970s it was clear that the basic MiG-15UTI fighter-trainer was outdated, and the Cuban High Command selected the Czechoslovakian Aero L-39 Albatross as its next advanced trainer. The first batch of 15 aircraft, L-39C advanced trainers, arrived in April 1982. They were assigned serial numbers 01 to 15.

A rare view: a L-39 armed with R-60Mk missiles and an unguided rocket pod. (Luis Dominguez collection)

The second batch arrived in late 1982 and comprised six aircraft, serial numbers 16 to 21. This was followed by a third and final delivery of nine aircraft that received the numbers 22 to 30.

Cuban L-39s formed two training squadrons of the Escuela Militar para Pilotos Aéreos (EMPA, Air Pilot Military School) at La Coloma Air Base. These squadrons formed UM 1660. Student pilots would receive basic and advanced jet training on the type, before moving on to the MiG-21UM, MiG-21MF, or MiG-21PFMAs of UM 1650. UM 1660 was to provide CAS and anti-ship attack in a case of war. They were armed with 57-mm rocket launchers and gun pods.

In the early 21st Century the eight to ten remaining aircraft were distributed among units based in Holguin, Ciudad Libertad and San Antonio de Los Baños. By 2007 there were only about five aircraft in operational condition.

Manufacturer	Aircraft Type	Delivered	Number	Serial Numbers	Remarks
Aero Vodochody	L-39C Albatross	1982	21	01 to 21	
Aero Vodochody	L-39C Albatross	1983	9	22 to 30	

Mikoyan i Gurevich MiG-29 (ASCC code Fulcrum) (1989–?)

As most Communist-bloc air arms, the Cuban Air Force selected the MiG-29 (ASCC code Fulcrum) as its next generation air superiority fighter in the 1980s. Cuban Generals (and Castro) showed interest in the type as early as 1985, and had an eventual requirement for up to 200 MiG-29s to replace the MiG-21 fleet by the mid-1990s.

The initial requirement called for a full regiment with 40 MiG-29s in service by 1991. The first order covered half the initial requirement, including 20 MiG-29s, compris-

MiG-29 UB (900)
(Lopez Miera via Luis
Dominguez)

ing 18 single-seat MiG-29 (9.12B) versions and 2 two-seat MiG-29UB (9.51). Deliveries started in October 1989 to the 231° Fighter Squadron at San Antonio de Los Baños and were cut short by the disintegration of the Soviet Union. Only eight aircraft were delivered including the two conversion trainers (serial numbers 900 and 901) and six single-seat fighters (serial numbers 910-915).

The 231° Fighter Squadron participated in the combined exercise 'Escudo Cubano' (Cuban Shield) during May 1990, showing-off its R-60MK (AA-8 Aphid) and R-27 (AA-10 Alamo) air-to-air missiles.

Anti-narcotic operations were not strange to the FAR, and after a MiG-21PFMA crashed while manoeuvering to intercept a slow flying narco plane, the FAR began training against a PZL-104 Wilga light aircraft. MiG-29 pilots had received a lot of practice in this kind of operations and were quite prepared to take part in the 1996 operation against exiled-operated light aircraft.

On 24 February 1996, a MiG-29UB (900) interceptor took off, with a MiG-23UB tasked as a communications-relay platform. The MiG-29 intercepted a flight of three Cessna 337 light planes (US Civil registrations N2456S, N2506, and N5485S) that belonged to Hermanos al Rescate. Brothers to the Rescue was an exiled organization that provided SAR cover to fleeing Cuban 'boat people' (by way of the Florida Straits), constantly penetrating Cuban airspace. The Cuban MiG-29 shot down two of the Cessnas (N2456S and N5485S) using R-60MK (ASCC code AA-8 Aphid C) missiles. The two crews, consisting of four US citizens (Cuban-Americans) were killed.

By 2006 there were reports that only three MiG-29s remained in strength, and that another three had been completely cannibalized for spare parts.

Manufacturer	Aircraft Type	Delivered	Number	Serial Numbers	Remarks
Mikoyan i Gurevich	MiG-29 (9.12B)	1989	6	910 to 915	
Mikoyan i Gurevich	MiG-29UB (9.51)	1989	2	900 & 901	

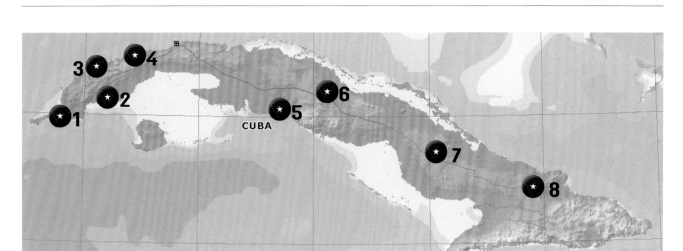

1. San Julián
2. La Coloma
3. San Antonio de los Baños
4. Playa Baracoa
5. Cienfuegos
6. Santa Clara
7. Camaguey
8. Holguín

Chapter 7

DOMINICAN REPUBLIC

By the early 1950s President Trujillo's right-wing government boosted the largest and best equipped air force in the Caribbean. As most of his equipment comprised WW-2 era fighters and bombers, a major modernization programme centered on obtaining surplus equipment including its first jet fighters. As such, the Dominican Republic became the first Caribbean country to operate jet fighters when it acquired a squadron from Sweden.

Attempts to buy up to 25 North American F-86 Sabre fighters from the US in 1955 were frustrated by the US Congress, which vetoed another attempt to acquire a similar quantity of Sabre fighters from the Japan Air Self Defense Force. In deference, a second batch of jets was acquired from Sweden during 1956, forming a second jet fighter unit.

A US military mission delivered a handful of second hand armed jet trainers in 1957, but these were quickly withdrawn by the US after Trujillo broke diplomatic relations. A contact with France provided Trujillo's armed forces with new equipment, including helicopters and tanks, but negotiations for a squadron of Dassault Mystère jet fighters did not prosper, although a group of Dominican pilots had been trained on the type.

After Trujillo's death, the Fuerza Aérea Dominicana's (FAD, Dominican Air Force) operational levels fell victim to budget constraints. Vampires continued to provide the country with the first line of defense during the 1960s and throughout the 1970s. Attempts to acquire more modern aircraft were frustrated by lack of funds or political instability. In 1974 the remaining jets were withdrawn, as their ground personnel could not guarantee their operation and the country's defenses relied on WW-2 era propeller fighters for the next few years.

After Cuban MiGs humiliated the Dominican Air Force, playing and taunting with the old Mustangs off the Dominican coast, the government asked the US for assistance. Supersonic fighters, in the Northrop F-5 class were required, but the US only offered to provide a squadron of light attack jets. They were eventually accepted and entered service in the mid 1980s. These remained in service until 2001, when the last surviving aircraft were put in storage, effectively ending jet operations in the country.

De Havilland Vampire (1953–1974)

Up to 25 De Havilland (actually English Electric built) Vampire F.Mk.1 fighter jets were acquired by Trujillo's agents following a deal which included some 22 North American P-51D Mustangs from the Royal Swedish Air Force in 1952. These Vampires joined the Mustangs in the Escuadrón de Caza Ramfis (Ramfis Fighter Squadron, named after his

FAD received their first fighter jets – Vampire F.Mk.1 – already in 1952. These were based at Trujillo Air Base with Ramfis Fighter Squadron. Note the unusual paint scheme. (via Santiago Rivas)

son Ramfis Trujillo) at Trujillo Air Base (San Isidro) and received serial numbers 2701 to 2725. The jets were accompanied by a group of Swedish personnel, contracted by Trujillo to train his pilots and maintain his new Vamps.

In August 1957 they were joined by a further 17 Vampires, this time the FB.50 fighter-bomber version, obtained from the same source. They were assigned serial numbers ranging from 2726 to 2742 and joined the fighter-bomber squadron, known as Escuadrón Leónidas (named after Rafael 'Leonidas' Trujillo).

In 1960 the Swedish instructors left, and the fleet soon began to suffer from poor serviceability. Half the fleet was cannibalized for spare parts, in order to keep the other half of the aircraft in flying condition. Once Trujillo was assassinated in May 1961, the operational situation of the fleet turned to worse.

Some remaining Vampires were activated in the summer of 1965, when rebel forces known as the Constitucionalistas tried to take power. They operated alongside Mustangs and armed T-6 Texans, attacking rebel positions in Santo Domingo. The air force was re-organized in 1966, and the remaining 15 airworthy aircraft were grouped with Mustangs and Texans to form the Dragones Verdes (Green Dragons), a USAF-trained outfit designed for COIN work.

The Hawker Hunter was selected as a Vampire replacement in the early 1970s, however attempts to purchase up to 25 failed and the last 12 Vampires were retired in 1974.

Manufacturer	Aircraft Type	Delivered	Number	Serial Numbers	Remarks
De Haviland	Vampire F.Mk.1	1953	25	2701 to 2725	
De Haviland	Vampire FB.Mk.50	1957	17	2726 to 2742	

Lockheed T-33 (1956–1968)

The Dominica Republic received four refurbished AT-33-LO-5 armed jet trainers in 1956 as part of a US funded military assistance programme to modernize the air force. They received FAD serial numbers 3301 to 3304 and they joined the Vampires and Mustangs

The T-33s were also integrated in Ramfis Fighter Squadron alongside P-51 Mustangs and Vampires.
(via Gary Kuhn)

in the Escuadrón Ramfis. They were withdrawn in June 1958 by the Military mission, as relations between the US government and the Dominican Republic worsened, to the point of breaking off diplomatic relations. These armed trainers wound up in Brazil.

In 1967 the re-formed Fuerza Aérea Dominicana obtained a pair of ex-USAF T-33As in an attempt to replace its ageing fleet of Vampires and Mustangs with the popular armed jet trainer. These were applied the serial numbers 3305 and 3306 and supplied by the US via the MAP.

Following suit with the previous T-33 fiasco, these were withdrawn by the US, after the Dominican Republic failed to accept a larger fleet by 1969. They were instead supplied to Uruguay.

Manufacturer	Aircraft Type	Delivered	Number	Serial Numbers	Remarks
Lockheed	AT-33A-5-LO	1956	4	3301 to 3304	
Lockheed	T-33A-1-LO	1967	1	3305	
Lockheed	T-33A-5-LO	1967	1	3306	

Cessna A-37B Dragonfly (1984–2001)

The retirement of the old Vampire fleet left a handful of WW-2 vintage North American P-51D Mustangs left to defend Dominican skies. After an embarrassing episode off the Dominican coast, in which Cuban MiG-21s played with the tired Mustangs, the Dominican Air Force quickly turned to the United States for assistance. The United States offered to supply some 16 Cessna A-37B Dragonfly attack aircraft. They were not ideally interceptor aircraft, such as the more suitable Northrop F-5E, but they were still several generations ahead of the current Mustangs.

The first batch of eight aircraft (serial numbers FAD 3701 to 3708) joined the FAD during 1984, and allowed the sale of the Mustang fleet to international collectors. They joined the Escuadrón de Combate 'Dragones' (Dragons Combat Squadron) at San Isidro. Dominican Dragonflies had their first operational intercept in 1985, when one shot down a Beechcraft D-18 during an anti-narcotic operation. These were former USAF aircraft, most of them built between 1969 and 1971.

One A-37 (3707) near its home base of San Isidro AB in 1997, just a few years before retirement.
(Rafael Marti)

The second batch of Dragonflies never arrived. Instead the FAD received 8 Cessna O-2 light observation aircraft, which were used for coastal patrol, border surveillance and reconnaissance. In 1986 the US suspended its military assistance program to the Dominican Republic, eventually cancelling it altogether by 1988, ending any hopes of further A-37B deliveries. After a numbers of accidents, including two (FAD3706 and 3708) in 1996, one in 1998 (FAD 3705) and one in 2000 (FAD 3704), plus two write-offs, the A-37B attack-fighter fleet was reduced to two flying aircraft. The unit responsible for operating them since 1984, the Dragones Squadron was de-activated in March 2001. The main reason behind the deactivation was the high cost of only having a two-aircraft fleet in service. This ended jet operations in the Dominican Republic.

Manufacturer	Aircraft Type	Delivered	Number	Serial Numbers	Remarks
Cessna	A-37B Dragonfly	1984	8	3701 to 3708	ex–USAF

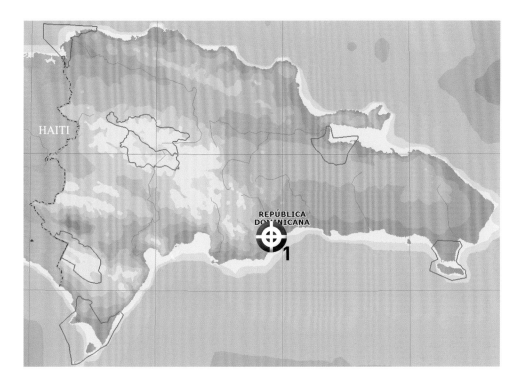

1. San Isidro Air Base (Trujillo)

Chapter 8

ECUADOR

Ecuador lost over half its territory after a humiliating defeat in a 1941 war with Peru. Since then, Ecuadorian governments have been interested in having modern and capable armed forces, as not to be overpowered again.

The Fuerza Aérea Ecuatoriana (FAE, Ecuadorian Air Force) has focused on the quality of its hardware and the training of its pilots, to defend its skies from its neighbour's larger forces. Most of the financial resources assigned to the military during the 1950s were destined to create a strong enough air arm. Close contact with the RAF saw its officers receiving conversion training in the UK, while the FAE received two squadrons of first generation Meteor jet fighters and Canberra bombers.

The FAE soon found that a modern jet fleet was not enough and encountered serious infrastructure problems as it did not have the appropriate installations for jet operations. Salinas and Mariscal Sucre (Quito's International Airport) proved unsuitable for its new jet fleet, so in August 1955 a local company started construction of a new jet base in Taura, near Guayalquil. Considered as Fightertown Ecuador, Taura began operations in late 1956 and since then has been the centre for the country's combat jet operations. US influence translated into a squadron of first generation F-80 fighter jets and AT-33 armed trainers by the late 1950s.

During the 1960s the FAE introduced mainly transports and helicopters, as defense spending shifted towards the Navy. After the discovery of large oil reserves in the late 1960s the FAE obtained British Strikemaster and American-built A-37B close air support fighters aimed mainly at providing the bulk of counter-insurgency operations.

But focus shifted again towards Europe, as the Military Junta that ruled the country from 1976 to 1979 wanted nothing but the best, something the US was not in a (political) position to provide. British and French-built front-line fighters and fighter-bombers (Mirage F-1s and Jaguars) soon equipped two squadrons, placing the FAE at the forefront of South American air forces.

In early 1981 Ecuador was again plugged into full scale operations against its southern rival, but this time, it had a much stronger air force to prevent an overwhelming Peruvian invasion. Its new hardware was put to test with mostly positive psychological results. After this brief conflict, the FAE reorganized and expanded with another squadron of high-performance fighters, this time coming from Israel.

By the early 1990s the FAE's numbers had dwelled, but continued to provide an effective air-defense umbrella. A renewed conflict with Peru during the mid-1990s brought about an efficient modernization program. All its front-line fighters were upgraded with new avionics and defense aids, however, much needed modern force multipliers, such as AEW and tanker services for the fighter fleet were not even con-

templated. Peru's MiG-29 acquisition prompted Ecuador to consider a Russian order for up to 18 MiG-29M late generation fighters for a reported USD 600 million. However, signature of a peace treaty with Peru in 1998 ended this as well as negotiations with Sukhoi. Rumors that the FAE was to replace its varied fighter fleet with up to 50 F-16C Fighting Falcons were no more than a pipedream, as such a purchase would had clearly alter the military balance in the region as well as put a long term financial stress on the armed forces.

Gloster Meteor (1954–1972)

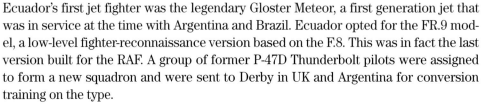

Ecuador's first jet fighter was the legendary Gloster Meteor, a first generation jet that was in service at the time with Argentina and Brazil. Ecuador opted for the FR.9 model, a low-level fighter-reconnaissance version based on the F.8. This was in fact the last version built for the RAF. A group of former P-47D Thunderbolt pilots were assigned to form a new squadron and were sent to Derby in UK and Argentina for conversion training on the type.

The FAE selected 12 former RAF fighters in 1954, these being VZ597, WH547, VW366, WB136, VZ610, WH540, WH543, WH549, WH550, WH553, WH554, and WH555. They had the Rolls-Royce Derwent RD8 engines and weapons fit that included 51-mm rockets, although the reconnaissance equipment was removed and replaced by 20-mm cannons. The Meteors were refurbished at Tarrant Rushton before delivery.

They arrived by ship and their offloading took some creativity, as La Libertad port did not have the proper equipment. They were offloaded at the Anglo, a British oil company rig and transported by truck to Salinas Air Base near Guayalquil. The white-painted aircraft were assembled by FAE personnel under the supervision of Gloster technicians. They were assigned the serial numbers 701 to 712, and formed the first Ecuadorian jet unit in late 1955.

In January 1957 the unit moved to the newly constructed Taura Air Base where they formed the 13th Tactical Squadron. The Meteors were armed with up to eight 51-mm rockets and tasked with performing border patrol on the Peruvian border. They joined the newly delivered T-33s.

In 1966 the recently organized 2111th Squadron re-activated the remaining Meteors and in mid-1967 they formed the short-lived aerobatic display team Aguilas (Eagles). The team was dissolved by 1968. By this time the Meteors had been re-numbered to FF-111 to FF-122.

Pilots from short-lived (1967–68) aerobatic team Aguilas pose in front of one Meteor FR.9 with special colourscheme.
(via Guido Chavez)

One Gloster Meteor FR.9 (FF-114) receives some outdoor engine maintenance sometime after 1968.
(via Guido Chavez)

In 1972 the FAE decided to replace its ageing first generation Meteors with newer fighter-bombers. British-built equipment was clearly favoured by FAE commanders. An attempt to acquire former Belgian Air Force Hawker Hunters failed and the 2111th eventually received the Jaguar International strike fighter as a replacement. Two Meteors crashed during their service life in Ecuador. Not much official information about these accidents due to the secrecy of the Ecuadorian military at that time. The last accident occurred in 1972, when a Meteor crashed on approach to Quito International Airport, the pilot was apparently not sober and crashed into a residential area. The engine had penetrated a house and stopped a few yards away from a baby's crib. The baby was miraculously not harmed!

Manufacturer	Aircraft Type	Delivered	Number	Serial Numbers	Remarks
Gloster Ltd.	Meteor FR.Mk.9	1954	12	701 to 712	ex-RAF; FF-111 to FF-122

Lockheed T-33 (1956–1996)

Ecuador acquired three Lockheed T-33A jet trainers in November 1956 and began operations out of Guayaquil airport. They were joined by four F-80C Shooting Star jet fighters in 1957 and the mixed fleet, by now known as Escuadrón Táctico 14 (EA14, Tactical Squadron 14) moved to newly constructed Taura Air Base. A further two T-33A-1-LO and three T-33A-5-LO joined the squadron that same year.

Once enough F-80s had been delivered to EA14, the T-33s were transferred to form a new unit Escuadrón Táctico 12 (EA12). A further nine aircraft were acquired in 1965. These were of the armed AT-33A-20-LO configuration, especially suited for COIN operations. The remaining aircraft were moved to Eloy Alfaro Air Base in Manta during October 1978, and were sent to receive a major overhaul in Colombia. Ecuadorian T-33s received a new Vietnam-style camouflage scheme and some artwork in the form

T-33 FAE 502 is one of the upgraded T-33s to AT-33 standard.
(Erik Katerberg)

A line-up of retired FAE T-33s with FAE 606 as first aircraft. Note the machine gun in nose. (Anno Gravemaker)

of shark mouths on the nose. The remaining aircraft were assigned to CAS duties and upon arrival were christened as Tiburones (Sharks). Their unit, by now known as the Escuadrón de Combate 2312 (Combat Squadron, being the same 12th Squadron now under command of the 23rd Combat Wing) was known as the Tiburón squadron from 1983.

By the early 1980s the air force had a new generation of European fighters and fighter-bombers in frontline service. However the Tiburones still provided a powerful punch, and Ecuador signed a USD 25 million contract with the Sabreliner Aircraft Corporation for the upgrade of 25 T-33s to its proposed subsonic attack aircraft configuration. Ecuador's 6 remaining A/T-33s together with 19 former USAF aircraft received new nose-mounted 0.50-cal. guns, re-enforced structure, communication, and navigation equipment. Some of the former USAF T-33s had belonged to the Republic of China's Air Force (Taiwan) where they had been replaced by the new AIDC AT-3. Delivery of the refurbished AT-33s began in mid-1987 and concluded by 1989.

AT-33A FAE799 was written off on 8 May 1991, and was one of at least five accidents of the type. Another crashed near Eloy Alfaro Air Base during the 1995 Cenepa conflict.

After the 1995 conflict with Peru, the FAE High Command decided to retire its remaining AT-33s at a ceremony in Eloy Alfaro Air Base during November 1995, although the last AT-33s were put in storage until 1996. The 20 or so remaining aircraft were to be replaced by 16 upgraded former USMC A-4M Skyhawks, in a similar deal to that offered to Argentina at the time. This deal was eventually cancelled. The transfer to Bolivia of eight Skyhawks to be used for spare parts but, in 2001 the negotiations stalled and eventually also was cancelled.

Manufacturer	Aircraft Type	Delivered	Number	Serial Numbers	Remarks
Lockheed	T-33A-1-LO	1956	3		
Lockheed	T-33A-1-LO	1957	2		
Lockheed	T-33A-5-LO	1957	3		
Lockheed	AT-33-20-LO	1965	9		
Lockheed	AT-33	1987	19		upgraded by Sabreliner

Lockheed F-80 Shooting Star (1957–1974)

The US Government designated the Lockheed F-80C Shooting Star as the official replacement for Latin American P-47D Thunderbolt users. Ecuador accepted the aircraft to replace its 20 Thunderbolt fighter-bombers which it had originally received following signature of the 1947 Rio Treaty of Mutual Defense. A group of Ecuadorian pilots, most of them former Thunderbolt drivers, were sent to the United States for conversion training, although some training was also conducted in Panama. Ground crews were trained in Ecuador by an US mission.

The first four aircraft reached Ecuador in January 1957 and wore the serial numbers 720 to 723. Deliveries to Taura Air Base where most of the fighter assets had been concentrated continued until 1960, at which time the FAE had received 18 fighters. Two of them were apparently used as a spare parts source, with operational aircraft wearing the serial numbers 720 to 735. They formed the Escuadrón Táctico 14 (ET 14) operating alongside the recently received T-33s and next to the Meteors of ET 13.

In about 1964 the FAE applied new serial numbers to its aircraft and the F-80C fleet was re-numbered using the prefix 'FT' and random numbers from FT-184 to FT-884. Known numbers are FT-184, FT-394, FT-714, FT-769, FT-808, FT-809, FT-810, FT-851, FT-867, FT-872 and FT-884.

Six aircraft were returned to the US in July 1965 as the type was by then qualified as obsolescent by the Ecuadorian military. The remaining Shooting Stars (nine aircraft, with probably only seven airworthy) were used to equip the 2112th Fighter Squadron in 1966. These were grouped with the new 2111th Squadron (equipped with Meteors) to form the 21st Fighter Wing. The unit operated Shooting Stars until 1974, when they were completely retired.

Manufacturer	Aircraft Type	Delivered	Number	Serial Numbers	Remarks
Lockheed	F-80C Shooting Star	1957	18	720 to 735	2 used for spares

P-80 (FT-714) nicely restored before being mounted as gate guard.
(Erik Katerberg)

BAC 167 Strikemaster (1972–)

With a growing British tradition inherited from the Meteor-trained officers, the FAE's High Command ordered the armed version of the BAC Jet Provost advanced trainer, the strike-oriented BAC 167 Strikemaster Mk.89 in early the early 1970s. A first batch of eight aircraft was delivered in October 1972, receiving serial numbers FAE-243 to FAE-250. The aircraft were initially used for advanced training at the Escuela de Aviación Militar (Military Flight School) at Salinas Air Base.

On 20 September 1973 the FAE lost its first Strikemaster, FAE245 and was followed by FAE 249 in November. In late 1973 the Strikemasters had logged up close to 1,500 flight hours. In 1974 a follow-up batch of eight improved Strikemaster Mk.89As (serial numbers FAE-251 to FAE-258) was delivered to complete the squadron. These mostly served as replacements, since attrition of this type had been high. The newly delivered aircraft joined the survivors of the original batch at Taura Air Base, they equipped the 2113th Squadron. In 1975 numbers FAE 250 and FAE 248 were lost during June and November respectively, followed by FAE 253 on 27 December 1976 and FAE 258 on 18 October 1977.

By late 1979 the number of available aircraft was down to the original eight, as FAE 255 and FAE 256 were lost during January and November of that same year. By this year they had been re-located to Manta. Further attrition followed, as FAE 247 was lost on 4 August 1980 and FAE 243 was written-off on 14 October 1981.

In 1987 the FAE acquired another batch of (by now British Aerospace) Strikemasters. Six complete aircraft had been put in storage after production ended pending future sales. The USD 10 million contract comprised delivery of the six Strikemaster Mk.90s (serial numbers FAE 259 to FAE 264) between November 1987 and October 1988. One of the aircraft from the last batch (FAE 261) was lost during 1997, and another (FAE 259) crashed on 11 March 2001. By mid-2006 there were seven Strikemasters on strength with a further three stored. A further two former Botswana Defence Force Strikemaster Mk.83s (in turn former Kuwaiti aircraft) were acquired in late 2006 from Global Aviation Ltd. a UK-based company. Both were delivered during early 2007 and put into service, raising the total operational number to nine Strikemasters.

BAC 167 (263) with Matra 155
rocket pod
(Jorge Delgado)

A formation of two BAC 167s: FAE 266 is a Mk.83 from Botswana, FAE 246 is a Mk.89A from original batch. (Anno Gravemaker)

Manufacturer	Aircraft Type	Delivered	Number	Serial Numbers	Remarks
BAC	Strikemaster Mk.89A	1972	8	243 to 250	
BAC	Strikemaster Mk.89A	1974	8	251 to 258	
British Aerospace	Strikemaster Mk.90	1987	6	259 to 264	
BAC	Strikemaster Mk.83	2007	2	265 & 266	ex-Botswana AF

Cessna A-37B Dragonfly (1975–)

A-37 and its full range of weaponry. In the background you can see the same with a BAC 167 Strikemaster. (Jorge Delgado)

The negotiations for a first batch of 13 A-37B Dragonfly COIN jet fighters were concluded with the United States in 1975. These light fighters were to equip the 2112th Squadron of the 21st Combat Wing at Taura Air Base. They wore serial numbers FAE-374 to FAE-386.

With the pending arrival of the Mirage F.1 interceptors, the Ecuadorian Dragonflies were re-assigned to the 231st Group, 23rd Combat Wing at Eloy Alfaro Air Base in Manta, where they formed the 2311th Dragones Squadron in July 1979. There are reports that state that only ten aircraft were available at this time, with the other three probably stored due to lack of spares.

During the 1981 war with Peru, the Dragones squadron was instructed to perform CAP over Ecuadorian airspace. In the early afternoon of 28 January, a pair of A-37Bs (FAE-381 and FAE-384) took to perform a reconnaissance flight over the Paquisha area. They encountered a pair of Peruvian A-37Bs and engaged them. Far from being an effective air-to-air platform, both pairs of Dragonflies fought it out. The Peruvian

OA-37B (390) taxing towards take-off for another mission. (Erik Katerberg)

aircraft returned home after damaging FAE-381's left wing with 7.62-mm gunfire and forcing it to land without further incident. FAE-381 was repaired and returned to service. No further Dragonfly engagements were recorded.

According to several sources, by the late 1980s the number of operational Dragonflies had dwindled to five aircraft.

Reinforcements arrived in September 1994, when FAE-387 was delivered, as attrition replacement for an aircraft lost (unknown serial number) on 11 February 1994. It was followed by another aircraft, in February 1995. During the 1995 war with Peru, the A-37B fleet was again committed to front-line operations. Between 11 and 13 February the Dragones, escorted by Kfirs, were heavily involved in bombing Peruvian land forces that were to overrun the Ecuadorian base at Tiwinza. On 12 February FAE-392 piloted by Capt. Rojas and Lt. Camacho was hit by a Peruvian SA-7 or SA-16 SAM but managed to land at the airstrip at Macas. The aircraft was hastily repaired and nicknamed 'Tiwinza'. According to Peruvian claims, an Ecuadorian A-37B was shot down by an Igla SAM one day later.

After the conflict, the surviving fleet received a comprehensive upgrade that included flight refuelling capability and the ability to fire Shafrir air-to-air missiles. A batch of 14 former USAF OA-37Bs began to be delivered in February 1997. These aircraft were applied serial numbers FAE-368 to FAE-373, FAE-388 to FAE-391, and FAE-393 to FAE-395. One of the 1997 delivered aircraft displays an unidentified serial number.

An unidentified Dragonfly was lost on 1 June 2000. The Dragones continued to provide the FAE with an effective CAS aircraft during the early years of the 21st Century, with over 20 aircraft still in service by 2009. These are operated by the 2311th Squadron at Manta. Several aircraft are constantly deployed to the 31st Combat Wing to fly CAPs over the Ecuadorian Amazon.

Manufacturer	Aircraft Type	Delivered	Number	Serial Numbers	Remarks
Cessna	A-37B Dragonfly	1975	13	374 to 386	
Cessna	A-37B Dragonfly	1994	1	387	ex-USAF
Cessna	A-37B Dragonfly	1995	1	392	ex-USAF
Cessna	OA-37B Dragonfly	1997	14	368 to 373, 388 to 391, 393 to 395	ex-USAF

SEPECAT Jaguar (1977–2003)

By the early 1970s the Peruvian Air Force was going through an expensive modernization and expansion program that included brand new Mirage and Sukhoi fighter-bombers. Ecuador's jet fighter fleet on the other hand, was limited to subsonic armed jet trainers and COIN aircraft. So, the task to find a new high performance fighter was a critical point in Ecuador's defence plans.

The United Kingdom had become the nation's main arms supplier, with the RAF providing a comprehensive influence in its organization, training and structure. Ecuador looked at the best 'exportable' material and selected the English Electric Lightning as its next fighter as apparently US export controls prevented the acquisition of ex-British F-4K Phantoms. The FAE was to acquire former RAF Lightinings to replace its Meteor-equipped squadrons. After negotiations stalled again, the FAE approached the Belgian Air Force with an order for a dozen Hawker Hunter F.6 fighters and a T.7 conversion trainer. Final decision was for a brand new model that could perform both air defence and interdiction missions, although focusing mainly on the latter. France reportedly offered Mirage 5 fighter-bombers, however during 1974 the FAE selected the SEPECAT Jaguar International fighter-bomber. An order worth BPD20 million included ten Jaguar ES and two Jaguar BS fighter-bombers. A group of veteran pilots, mainly former Meteor drivers, were chosen to undergo a conversion training program in Scotland which started in 1974.

Deliveries started in January 1977 and Jaguars became Ecuador's first supersonic jet fighters. They equipped the 2111th Jaguares Squadron of the 211th Combat Group/21st Wing at Taura Air Base. The single-seat fighter-bombers were received the serial numbers 289, 302, 309, 318, 327, 329, 339, 340, 348, and 349. The two-seat versions were assigned the serial numbers 283 and 305. The delivery flight included several stops in West Africa, Asuncion Island and Brazil.

The first accident occurred in August 1988, when serial number 316 crashed. This was followed by number 340 in October 1989 and, number 289 in 1990. A fourth Jaguar, (probably number 349) was lost in 1991. The fleet was then subjected to an extensive overhaul.

Jaguar 329 during delivery flight from Toulouse in August 1977. (Collection Martin Hornlimann / MILPIX)

Jaguar (339) with Matra rocket pods.
(Anno Gravemaker)

The FAE contracted for three former RAF airframes, stored at Shawburry in UK, to be used as a spare parts source. The fleet was also subjected to a brief enhancement programme, which included a new self-defense suite, comprising a new chaff/flare dispensing system, SPS-20 RWR, an avionics upgrade that included GPS, a new INS, and radios.

During the 1995 war, the available Jaguars (some sources state up to six) were split into pairs and dispersed to highways that became emergency runways. They acted as a strategic reserve designated to attack sensible economic assets in northern Peru in case the conflict escalated. By 2003 Jaguars serial numbers 339 and 348 were inoperable and the remaining six Jaguars (four single-seats and two twin-seats) were placed in reserve status.

Manufacturer	Aircraft Type	Delivered	Number	Serial Numbers	Remarks
SEPECAT	Jaguar ES	1977	10	289, 302, 309, 318, 327, 329, 339, 340, 348, 349	
SEPECAT	Jaguar EB	1977	2	283 & 305	

Dassault Breguet Mirage F.1 (1979–)

With a squadron of brand new Jaguar fighter-bombers in place, the FAE began to search for an adequate air-defence fighter. Negotiations for a squadron of ten Northrop F-5E and two F-5F Tiger II tactical fighters with the U.S. failed miserably, and further attempts to buy up to two squadrons of IAI Kfir multi-role fighters from Israel encountered similar export restrictions. This prompted Ecuador to go shopping to Europe once again.

Mirage F.1 (FAE 812) with
captive R.550 missile
(Erik Katerberg)

The French-made Dassault Mirage F.1 was considered by the FAE to be superior to the Kfir and the French Government placed no restrictions in its sale. Of course the price tag was much higher, and the FAE found itself paying much more than it expected.

The USD 260 million contract for a multi-role interceptor/attack version included 16 single-seat and 2 two-seat fighters. The contract included training for a group of Ecuadorian pilots and ground technicians in France starting in 1978. Delivery of the single seat version, designated Mirage F.1JA, started in May 1979 and had serial numbers FAE-801 to FAE-816 applied. The two seat conversion trainer versions (F.1JBs) were delivered in June 1980 with numbers FAE-817 and FAE-818 (latter numbers 830 and 831).

Mirages originally formed a fighter flight at Mariscal Sucre IAP to defend Quito. Once deliveries had concluded and IOC was attained, they formed the 2112th Fighter Squadron, nicknamed Aguilas (Eagles), as part of the Taura-based 21st Combat Wing. The first accident occurred in June 1980, involving FAE-804. Another fatality struck the

Probably the most famous
Ecuadorian Mirage F.1 (806)
parking at its drive-through
shelter. Note the black Su-22
kill marking below the cockpit
and R.550 Mk.1 missiles left of
aircraft.
(Anno Gravemaker)

squadron again in 1985 when FAE-810 and FAE-815 had accidents and were written off. The last two-seater to be delivered (FAE-818) was lost on 25 January 1988.

During the border war of 1981, two Mirage F.1s engaged a pair of Peruvian Su-22s (11th Fighter Squadron 'Tigers') that had penetrated Ecuador's airspace. One of the Mirages fired an R.550 Magic I AAM at its maximum range, but the Sukhois made a fast dash back home in afterburner as the Magic missile missed.

The Aguila Squadron was again in combat during the 1995 Condor War with Peru. After the Peruvian Air Force mounted several CAS sorties over the battle zone, the 21st Combat Wing was tasked with providing air cover for Ecuadorian posts. On 10 February a pair of Mirages (FAE 806 and 807) piloted by Mayor Raul Banderas (leader) and Captain Carlos Uscategui (wingman), call sign Conejos (Rabbits) where scrambled together with a pair of Kfirs to intercept an incoming Peruvian flight of five intruder aircraft (two Su-22 and three A-37B Dragonflies).

The Ecuadorian fighters got at visual range of the Peruvian intruders and had a field day. The Mirages went after the Sukhois and this time the Magic missiles killed their targets. One of the Kfirs also shot down a Dragonfly. The remaining two Dragonflies managed to escape the killing. This intercept prevented further Peruvian flights over the battlefield.

The FAE took this into consideration and highlighted a number of requirements to enhance its ability to counter its enemy in a future scenario. Rumours that the FAE had plans to replace its entire fighter fleet with up to 50 brand-new F-16C/D Fighting Falcons proved to be just that, rumours. Once funds originally destined to buy a squadron of brand new MiG-29SE had been re-assigned, the Mirage fleet was earmarked for a much needed upgrade. The program included new communications, a mission planning computer, combat management system and a new GPS-navigation system. New armament includes Python III and Magic II air-air missiles. If current plans continue, the Mirage F.1JA will be Ecuador's main interceptor at least until the year 2012, providing a much needed air defence deterrent together with the new Kfir CE.

Manufacturer	Aircraft Type	Delivered	Number	Serial Numbers	Remarks
Dassault	Mirage F.1JA	1979	16	801 to 816	
Dassault	Mirage F.1JE	1979	2	817 & 818	

Israel Aircraft Industries Kfir (1981–)

The General Supreme Council which governed Ecuador started negotiations with Israel for the supply of 24 Kfir fighters in 1977. However, the Carter Administration was quite strict in its export licenses (which it had to approve, as the Kfir's power-plant is an American-built J-79 engine) and Ecuador opted for a squadron of French-built Mirages.

The Regan Administration was not as strict as Carter's, and the Kfir deal was approved. In May 1981 the Ecuadorian Government signed an USD 80 million contract with Israel for the supply of 10 single seat Kfir C.2 (serial numbers FAE 901 to 910) and 2 two-seat TC.2 conversion trainers (serial numbers 930 and 931). The contract included two training courses for Ecuadorian pilots, maintenance equipment, spares and

Kfir CE (909) with Python Mk.3
(left) and Python Mk.4 (right)
missiles.
(Erik Katerberg)

a flight simulator. The Kfirs formed a new squadron, the 2113th *Leones* (Lions) based at Taura Air Base, Guayaquil, on 10 March 1982.

There are reports that the Kfirs were upgraded to C.7 standard during the late 1980s, after which they were painted in a light gray scheme. However this was not the case, they remained in the original C.2 standard. By 1994 the FAE had lost two Kfirs in accidents (numbers 903 and 910).

Kfirs were at the front lines during the 1995 war with Peru. The mission was to provide air superiority for Ecuadorian ground troops fighting in the Alto Cenepa region. On 10 February 1995, two Kfirs where scrambled together with two Mirages to intercept a Peruvian attack package composed of two Sukhoi Su-22 and three A-37B Dragonflies. The Kfir pair, call sign Bronco took off after the Mirage flight, with Captain Mauricio Mata (leader) at the controls of FAE 905 and Captain Guido Moya (wingman) flying FAE 909. Kfir number 905 shot down an A-37B using a Shafrir AAM, while the Mirages destroyed both Su-22s.

In 1996 the FAE started negotiations to acquire another eight Kfir fighters from IDF/IAF stocks in an USD 40 million contract. The contract provided for the delivery of three refurbished Kfir C.2 fighters (serial numbers 911 to 913) and one TC.2 fighter-trainer (FAE 932) which took place in September 1997. The remaining four aircraft

Kfir C2 (907)
(Erik Katerberg)

were to have been upgraded to the latest Kfir C.10 or Kfir 2000 standard and delivered by 2000. The contract also included new missiles and the modification of some of the FAE's fighter fleet to carry them. Ecuador became the launch customer for the Kfir 2000, marketed as Kfir CE, which includes new Elta EL/M-2032 multi-mode radar, FLIR, color MFDs, HOTAS, flight-refueling capability and the provision to carry advanced Python IV and Derby missiles as well as PGMs.

The FAE only received two Kfir CEs, modifying its contract and starting a program to upgrade at least six of its remaining Kfirs with IAI supplied kits at the Latacunga maintenance centre through an USD 60 million contract that included Python III and IV missiles. By 2002, the FAE had upgraded at least three fighters (numbers 901, 902 and, 908) to the CE standard. A two-seat Kfir (either numbers 931 or 932) crashed on 23 October 2004 while on a ceremony flight near Taura Air Base.

Manufacturer	Aircraft Type	Delivered	Number	Serial Numbers	Remarks
IAI	Kfir C.2	1981	10	901 to 910	
IAI	Kfir TC.2	1981	2	930 & 931	
IAI	Kfir C.2	1996	3	911 to 913	
IAI	Kfir TC.2	1996	1	932	
IAI	Kfir CE	1996	2	914 to 915	

A three ship formation of Kfir C.2s high over Ecuador. (FAE)

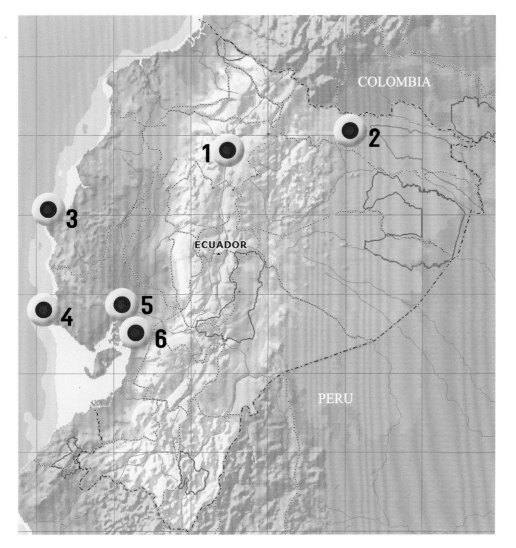

1. Mariscal Sucre Air Base, Quito
2. Lago Agrio Air Base
3. Eloy Alfaro Air Base, Manta
4. Ulpiano Paez Air Base, Salinas
5. Simon Bolivar Air Base, Guayaquil
6. Taura Air Base

EL SALVADOR

After fighting with WW-2 vintage Mustangs and Corsairs against the Honduran Air Force in the 100-Hour War (also referred to as the Soccer War) of 1969, the Fuerza Aérea Salvadoreña (FAS, Salvador Air Force) began an ambitious re-equipment program. Strong political support for Israel in the early 1970s meant that this country would get very involved in the Salvadorian defence expansion. In 1973 Israel agreed to re-build the FAS and outlined a plan to supply over 50 aircraft for the fledging air arm. These comprised a number of retired IDF/IAF jets and new Arava STOL transports.

Delivery of the Ouragan and Magisters helped bring an 'edge' back to Salvadorian pilots and increased moral. The second-hand aircraft formed the basis of the FAS combat fleet during the 1970s and early 1980s. The deal however, prompted a major arms race with neighbouring Honduras, who also sought Israeli products to equip its air force. The delivery of Super Mystere jet fighters to Honduras was misinterpreted in some sources and wrongfully attributed to El Salvador. No Super Mysteres ever served in Salvadorian colours. A top-up batch of second hand Magisters was acquired from France in the late 1970s and assigned to the flight school.

In late 1979 a Military junta took control of the government, ousting General Carlos Humberto Romero. During the next 12 years the country was plugged into probably the worst revolution in Central America's modern history. A peace agreement signed with Honduras in 1980 allowed the FAS to concentrate on expanding its counter-insurgency capabilities.

US military aid began to reach the air force in 1981 in the form of tactical utility helicopters and obsolete transports, but these were soon followed by light attack jets. Several deliveries were recorded during the 12 year long revolution, with the A-37B Dragonfly becoming the mainstay of the combat fleet from the mid-1980s up to this date. US Military aid to El Salvador amounted to about USD 1 billion during the civil war. After the 1992 peace accords, the Salvadorian air force disengaged from COIN activities and US military aid also wound down.

A post-war re-organization created a new command scheme, in which each airbase (Ilopango and Comalapa) housed an Air Brigade. The entire jet fleet was designated to the fighter-bomber squadron and moved to the 2nd air brigade at Comalapa. The A-37B continues to provide the country with its first line of defence.

Fouga CM-170 Magister (1974–1991, 2001–2002)

As part of a major re-equipment programme, the Fuerza Aérea Salvadoreña acquired a group of 28 aircraft from Israel, including 20 MD-450 Ouragan fighter-bombers, 4 IAI Arava STOL transports and 4 CM-170 Magisters in 1973.

Israel Aircraft Industries (IAI) had obtained production rights for the Magister and began delivery of the type for use in the tactical support role. Israeli-built examples had fixed 7.62-mm machine guns in the nose and the Marbouré II engine. The former Israeli aircraft were to be used as advanced trainers as well as front-line attack aircraft. Salvadorian officers were dispatched from 1973 to receive appropriate training in Israel.

Delivery of the first three Magisters by ship took place on 10 Febraury 1974. A fourth was delivered on 15 June 1975. These aircraft received serial numbers 500, 503, 505, and 507. The first three Magisters (known locally as Torogoz) were used to form the Cuscatlán aerobatic display flight in 1978. The flight performed in international shows, attending the Guatemalan National Aviation Day on 10 December 1978. This led to conflicting rumours about Magisters in service with the FAG. That same year the FAS managed to obtain another three Magisters, this time from French Air Force stocks. The aircraft were delivered on 26 April 1979. The French Magisters had a more powerful Marboure VI engine but lacked the fixed 7.62-mm guns of the Israeli aircraft, so they were used for advanced training duties and applied the numbers 509 to 511.

FAS-503 was lost on 22 April 1980. The remaining aircraft were heavily involved in the 1980-1992 war, flying alongside UH-1 Huey helicopter gunships, Ouragan fighter-bombers and A-37B attack aircraft.

The fleet was de-activated in 1991 for financial reasons, although aircraft number FAS-511 is mentioned as lost in an accident on 26 May 1993. Two aircraft (FAS-509 and FAS-510) were returned to operational conditions during 2001, but number FAS-509 was lost on 16 September 2002, when it crashed during a demonstration training flight over Ilopango Air Base, killing its pilot, Colonel Milton Andrade, the FAS Commander.

Manufacturer	Aircraft Type	Delivered	Number	Serial Numbers	Remarks
IAI	CM-170 Tzukit	1974	3	500, 503, 505	ex-IDF/IAF
IAI	CM-170 Tzukit	1975	1	507	ex-IDF/IAF
Fouga	CM-170 Magister	1979	3	509 to 511	ex-ALA

FAS used its four CM-170 from Israeli stocks in tactical role thanks to the fixd mounted 7.62mm machine guns. 505 is today preserved at the Civil War Museum
(Iñigo Guevara y Moyano)

Dassault MD-450 Ouragan (1974–1998)

Quantity was clearly preferred over quality and the traditional US sources were completely closed for political and financial reasons after the 100-Hour War. Israel was keen in obtaining a market for its large fleet of second hand aircraft that were being withdrawn as new, more modern fighters took place in Israeli squadrons. The Ouragan had served with the IDF since 1955 and was replaced by new A-4 Skyhawk fighter-bombers from 1972. Israel offered former IDF/AF Dassault MD-450 Ouragan swept-wing fighter-bombers to the FAS as part of its re-equipment programme and El Salvador decided to procure 20 Ouragans.

A group of 19 Salvadorian maintenance personnel was sent to Israel to receive training on the Ouragan during May 1974. The first nine Ouragans arrived on 24 August 1974 and were designated the serial numbers FAS-700 to FAS-708. They formed the Escuadrilla de Caza y Bombardeo (Fighter and Bomber Flight) at Ilopango Air Base. Another 11 Ouragans were delivered by 1975, but only 18 aircraft were ever put in service, 2 were used as a source of spare parts. Ouragans replaced the old Mustangs in the fighter-bomber role from 1976, with the last Mustang operation flown in 1978. Plans were set to wire at least half of the fleet to fire the Shafrir air-to-air missile, although only one aircraft (FAS-712) is confirmed to have carried the weapon. An accident claimed the first Ouragan, FAS-708 on 18 August 1976 over San Vicente. This was followed by the loss of FAS-710 on 15 June 1978 over La Paz, while FAS-715 crashed on take-off at Ilopango on 23 April 1979.

Although considered as front-line fighters and not really COIN aircraft, the entire fleet was used in operations against guerrillas during the 1980-1992 war. The Ouragans were armed with quadruple 20-mm cannons, unguided rockets, and general purpose bombs. Israeli-built napalm bombs were also used, these being acquired from the late 1970s. They were used to intercept illegal flights, usually transporting weapons and supplies for the guerrillas, and at least in one such case, one Ouragan shot down an aircraft coming from Nicaragua on 25 January 1981.

The fleet was considerably depleted on 27 January 1982 after a sabotage operation disguised as a surprise guerrilla attack claimed five aircraft (FAS-700, 703, 707, 711, and 712) and damaged a sixth (FAS-706).

The Dassault MD-450 Ouragan was designed as fighter, but has been used by FAS for COIN operations during the war in 1980 onwards.
(via AAMA)

Replacements began to arrive immediately, but these came from the United States in the form of the somewhat younger A-37B Dragonfly. The remaining Ouragans were grouped into the Escuadrón de Caza y Bomberdeo (Fighter-Bomber Flight) alongside Dragons and Magisters. With the growing number of operational fighters, the FAS was re-organized in 1986 and the fighter-bomber squadron became the Grupo de Caza y Bombardeo (Fighter and Bomber Group), part of the Ala de Combate (Combat Wing).

By 1988 at least eight Ouragan fighters were still in service, and these moved together with the Dragons and Magisters to the new (and secure) Comalapa Air Base. Some eight aircraft were still in service by 1994, when the unit was re-designated as a squadron, however most of its 'combat' operations had been taken over by the Dragons since 1992. The last operational Ouragan was apparently retired until 1998.

Manufacturer	Aircraft Type	Delivered	Number	Serial Numbers	Remarks
Dassault	MD-450 Ouragan	1974	9	700 to 708	ex-IDF/AF
Dassault	MD-450 Ouragan	1975	11	709 to 717	ex-IDF/AF; two used for spare parts

Cessna A-37B Dragonfly (1982–)

After the 27 January 1982 air base sabotage which claimed the destruction of some 14 aircraft, including 5 Ouragan fighter-bombers, US aid for the FAS increased dramatically. An USD 235 million aid package began to arrive that summer in the form of UH-1H/M Iroquois helicopters, C-123K transports, O-2 observation, and A-37B light attack aircraft.

Two groups of pilots were trained on the A-37B by the USAF in Panama and pilots from the second group ferried the first six aircraft on 15 June 1982, along with four

OA-37 (427) is one of the many in Latin America acquired from ex-USAF stocks.
(via Milton Andrade)

Still today A-37 serves in first line of defence.
(André Du-Pont)

Cessna O-2As. These formed the Escuadrón de Caza y Bombardeo (Fighter-Bomber Squadron) on 4 December 1982. These were former USAF machines built in the early 1970s and still in good shape. The A-37Bs were nicknamed Dragones while the O-2As known as Martillos (Hammers).

The first write-off (serial number FAS-420) occurred on 18 March 1983. An attrition replacement (number FAS-426) arrived during 1984 and was followed by another three former USAF OA-37B aircraft in 1985. By this time training of Salvadorian pilots was performed at Laughlin AFB in Texas on the T-37 Tweet. During 1986 the FAS was re-organized, with the Combat Group becoming the Ala de Combate (Combat Wing), and the Fighter-Bomber Squadron becoming the Grupo de Caza y Bombardeo (Fighter-Bomber Group).

Construction of a new section of the Comalapa International Airport, at San Luis Talapa in La Paz, also began in 1986. An eleventh aircraft (FAS-430) entered service the same year, and was lost less than a year later, in March 1987. Counter-insurgency operations moved to the new Comalapa Air Base during April 1988 and with them the Combat Wing moved its nine operational A-37B Fighter-Bomber Group to the new base. FAS-426 was lost that July. Along with this came the re-activation of the Escuadrilla Cuscatlán, an aerobatic demonstration team that had been formed with Magisters some ten years earlier. Up to four Dragons were assigned to this demonstration team, while still employed in operational duties.

FAS-429 was shot down by enemy AA fire during the 'Ofensiva hasta el tope; Febe Elizabeth vive' (Febe Elizabeth lives, offensive to the max) offensive of late 1989. The aircraft was lost over San Miguel. Rapid reinforcements during 1989 included four former USAF OA-37B that received serial numbers FAS-431 to FAS-434.

As part of a major re-organization under the auspices of Plan ARCE 2000, the Fighter-Bomber Group was re-named as Fighter-Bomber Squadron in 1994. By this time

Roughly half of the Dragonfly fleet consists of A-37Bs like 422 shown here.
(George Trussell)

there were nine Dragons in service. The aircraft numbered FAS-431 was lost to an enemy SAM (probably an SA-7) in late 1990 and number FAS-423 in December 1992.

In 2001 the United States offered 12 former US Navy TA-4J Skyhawk fighter/trainers at a cost of USD15.6 million, which would replace the older A-37B Dragons. However, the FAS deemed this offer as not practical. As of 2009, the FAS continued to operate its nine strong A-37B equipped squadron as the country's first line of defence.

Manufacturer	Aircraft Type	Delivered	Number	Serial Numbers	Remarks
Cessna	A-37B Dragonfly	1982	6	420 to 425	ex-USAF
Cessna	A-37B Dragonfly	1984	1	426	ex-USAF
Cessna	OA-37B Dragonfly	1985	3	427 to 429	ex-USAF
Cessna	A-37B Dragonfly	1986	1	430	ex-USAF
Cessna	OA-37B Dragonfly	1989	4	431 to 434	ex-USAF

A line-up of AO-37 & A-37Bs.
(Santiago Rivas)

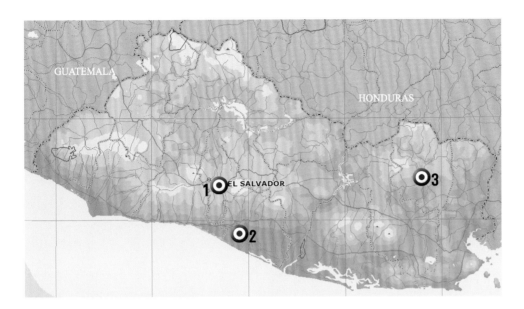

1. Ilopango
2. Comalapa
3. San Miguel

Chapter 10

GUATEMALA

The Fuerza Aérea Guatemalteca (FAG, Guatemala Air Force) received a score of Lockheed T-33 armed jet trainers in January 1963. This was as a preventive and defensive measure promoted by the United States against a possible retaliatory strike from Cuban forces for Guatemala's role in the 1961 Bay of Pigs attempted invasion. The T-33s remained Guatemala's first line of defense until the early 1970s, when the FAG received a squadron of COIN-optimized A-37B Dragonflies. Guatemala was the first country in Latin America to receive this later prolific type.

By the mid-1970s FAG planners attempted to acquire half a dozen Northrop F-5E Tiger II fighter jets, in an effort to form a supersonic interceptor squadron. However the FAG ran into the usual US refusal to supply such fighter jets to developing Latin American countries.

The U.S. stopped supplying military aid to Guatemala in 1977, and Guatemala turned to Israel as its main military supplier. Israel was eager to develop a market for its Kfir fighter-bombers in Latin America. The FAG outlined a requirement for up to 18 multi-role fighters. However, pressure from the US government apparently prevented negotiations from going any further.

With the build-up of forces in neighbouring Nicaragua and Honduras during the 1980s, a group of Guatemalan officers visited Jordan in July 1987 with the intention of acquiring up to 15 Northrop F-5As and 5 F-5Bs Freedom Fighters for an estimated USD 50 million. These negotiations also failed to proceed.

Interested in procuring a replacement for its tired A-37B fleet, by then pushing 33-years old, the Guatemalan Air Force evaluated several ideas in the early 21st Century. Among these was an offer for ten Belgian Air Component Alpha Jet armed/advanced jet trainers or the new Lockheed-Martin/KAI T-50 Golden Eagle. Other ideas include submitting the remaining A-37B fleet to a major upgrade program. Although it seems increasingly likely that Guatemala will revert to an all turbo-prop combat fleet.

Lockheed T-33 (1963–1997)

Guatemala received its first four jets in the form of Lockheed T-33A-1-LO armed trainers during January 1963, under the auspices of the US Military Assistance Program (MAP). These were former USAF aircraft built circa 1950. They operated in the Fighter-Bomber Squadron (Escuadrón de caza y bombardeo) alongside P-51D Mustangs out of La Aurora International Airport in Guatemala City. Their initial mission was to protect Guatemalan skies from possible Cuban retaliatory strikes to the Bay of Pigs disaster. The FAG allocated serial numbers 700, 707, 714, and 721 to these jets.

Long living T-33s faced only a short life in FAG as COIN trainer. They were also used for CAS. (via AAMA)

Hopes to replace its existing P-51D Mustangs with F-86 Sabre jets were not met by US approval. But pleased with the T-33's performance and encouraged by US advisors in the economy (spares and maintenance) of expanding its fleet versus acquiring another type, the FAG acquired an additional two aircraft, receiving numbers FAG 728 and 735. They were delivered in December 1964. MAP supplied another two aircraft in July 1965, comprising the COIN-oriented AT-33A-20-LO, with fixed armament and provision for rocket launchers and bombs. These last aircraft received FAG numbers 742 and 749.

Conversion training on the type was smooth, and US instructor pilots provided the proper COIN training for the Guatemalan crews. One US instructor died when FAG-707 suffered an accident. Guatemalan pilots, mostly former Mustang drivers learned to fly CAS missions pretty much as they had operated on their old mounts. The main drawback to the T-33s (locally known as Tango) was that they were very expensive (for the FAG) to operate.

In May 1966 the second casualty struck the young jet community, when one of the last pair of aircraft delivered (FAG-742) claimed the life of its crew. By the late 1960s the T-33s were completely committed to COIN missions, flying alongside P-51D Mustangs and A-26 Invaders.

In 1975 the US Military Mission in Guatemala announced that the T-33 fleet would not be supported further with US MAP funds. This caused an immediate grounding of the fleet and the sale of FAG-728 and FAG-735 to a private owner.

A line up of several FAG T-33s. First aircraft is the surviving AT-33A (749), which saw action against Nicaragua. (FAG archives via Mario Overall)

Parked today at a ramp at La Aurora IAP this T-33A (735) is the last survivor of the fleet. (Steve Homewood)

By 1982 the FAG had only one Tango remaining in operation (FAG-749), although some sources state that the aircraft was being used by 'friendly forces', operating in direct support for the Nicaraguan Contras, and apparently by a former Nicaraguan air force pilot that had escaped to Guatemala. These operations were apparently run and financed by the CIA.

The Republic of China (Taiwan) donated a score of ex-ROCAF T-33As in 1985. The aircraft were in fairly good condition but, the FAG had switched to operating the A-37B/PC-7 combination. They were scraped and never saw service.

Manufacturer	Aircraft Type	Delivered	Number	Serial Numbers	Remarks
Lockheed	T-33A-1-LO	1963	4	700, 707, 714, 721	ex-USAF
Lockheed	T-33A-1-LO	1964	2	728 & 735	ex-USAF
Lockheed	AT-33A-20-LO	1965	2	742 & 749	ex-USAF
Lockheed	T-33A-10-LO	1985	5		ex-ROCAF

Cessna A-37B Dragonfly (1971–?)

Plugged into counter-insurgency operations, the FAG asked the US Military Mission in Guatemala for assistance. At the time, US forces were experiencing heavily in COIN missions in South East Asia and had several aircraft specifically developed for tasks, such as the AC-47s Spooky, OV-10 Broncos, and A-37B Dragonflies. Considering it was based on a jet trainer, but with a large-enough pay-load to be considered a strike fighter, the A-37B was released for export to Guatemala.

Dragonflies first joined the FAG as a replacement for the retired A-26 Invaders in mid-1971. The Invaders had left the fleet some two years earlier. Eight factory-fresh aircraft joined the 4th Squadron, also known as the Escuadrón de Ataque (Attack Squadron). They displayed the standard South East Asian colors and serial numbers 400, 404, 408, 412, 416, 420, 424, and 428. Number 412 became the first casualty when it crashed near La Aurora Air Base on 26 June 1971 killing Lt. Col. Danilo Henry, at the time the FAG Deputy Commander.

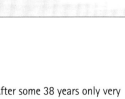
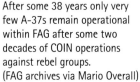

After some 38 years only very few A-37s remain operational within FAG after some two decades of COIN operations against rebel groups. (FAG archives via Mario Overall)

Ironically, the Dragonfly's first COIN mission was flown over El Salvador, when the FAG was asked in March 1972 by the Salvadorian government to help quell an attempted coup d'état. COIN operations against local guerrillas began in 1974 and soon occupied most of the A-37's flying time. The Alfas as they were known by their crews carried out continued CAS for army ground troops.

Another aircraft, number 420 was lost over the Pacific Coast during a training flight in 1974. The squadron received its full complement of Alfas by mid-1975, when another five aircraft, displaying serial numbers 432, 436, 440, 444, and 448 were delivered through the MAP.

In 1977 the US suspended military aid to Guatemala and stopped supplying all the needed parts as well as the required armament, this being napalm, rockets and GP bombs. A deal was struck with Argentina for the supply of the required ordinance, but Argentine 250-kg bombs were the only useful weapons for the Dragons. FAG-440 was lost over the Pacific Coast in 1978 killing its pilot and FAG-444 was cannibalized for spare parts after it suffered an irreparable landing accident at La Aurora Air Base.

The Alfas were used on COIN operations on a day-to-day basis throughout the 1980s. US support for the fleet had been withdrawn since 1977. Israel, by then Guatemala's main military supplier, refurbished the planes. In the early 1980s the Alfas began to train quite close with the armed PC-7s, becoming an interesting pair over the battlefield. In January 1985 FAG-408 was apparently shot down by rebel forces. Some sources state that it was brought down by an SA-7 MANPAD, however, small arms fire seems to be the true reason. There is no evidence that the Guatemalan insurgents ever obtained SAMs.

By the late 1980s only some three or four Alfas were kept in flying condition as most of the fleet was in dire need of a major overhaul. They were still heavily used in COIN operations up until 1991. The 1996 Peace Accords ended the 36 year long civil war, and this gave the FAG some space to breath. IAI was contracted to perform a structural refurbishment and a limited upgrade to five of the remaining Alfas.

By the early 21st century there were at least five Dragonflies in inventory, of which only two were operational, while the rest were being repaired with US Government funds once Military aid was resumed. Unfortunately, one of the operable Dragonflies, number 432 was lost in January of 2006, during an anti-narcotics operation.

Manufacturer	Aircraft Type	Delivered	Number	Serial Numbers	Remarks
Cessna	A-37B Dragonfly	1971	8	400, 404, 408, 412, 416, 420, 424, 428	
Cessna	A-37B Dragonfly	1974	5	432, 436, 440, 444, 448	

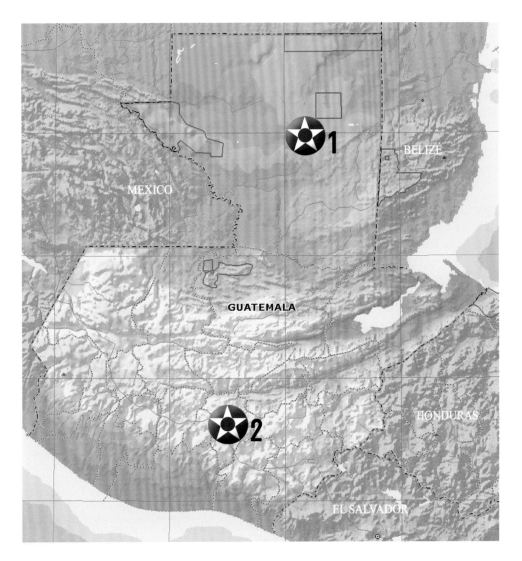

1. Teniente Coronel Danilo
   Eugenio Henry Sánchez
   Northern Air Command
2. La Aurora Air Base,
   Guatemala City

Chapter 11

HONDURAS

For most of the second part of the 20th Century, Honduras has been sandwiched by two aspiring regional military powers, El Salvador and Nicaragua. A short war with El Salvador in 1969 ended abruptly but with that country's clear military superiority. The Fuerza Aérea Hondureña (FAH, Honduran Air Force) was the only Honduran service capable of mounting offensive operations. The FAH has been at the forefront of Honduran armed services as it makes up for a weak army and an almost none-existent navy.

The 1969 war also known as the 100-Hour War or Soccer War triggered a local arms race with El Salvador. This arms race brought the first jet fighters into service during the 1970s. They were acquired from a wide variety of sources, quite unconventional sources to say the least: Israel, Venezuela and Yugoslavia.

By the early 1980s the FAH was Central America's most potent air force. It fielded a fighter squadron, two fighter-bomber squadrons, and an armed trainer flight, all of them jet-equipped units. Although obsolete, they still out-flew and out-performed anything else in the region. In the early 1980s an Israeli military mission visited Honduras and sketched out a plan to modernize the armed forces. The USD 200 million plan would bring the first supersonic fighters, in the form of the IAI Kfir, to Central America.

The plan was discarded due to lack of funds yet, in 1986 these plans re-surfaced as Israel offered to sell up to 20 Kfirs to replace the Super Mystère fighter-bombers. Just a few years later, the FAH became the first and so far only Central American country to field supersonic jets. American commitment and fear of a strong Nicaraguan (Sandinista) air force were the main reasons.

As peace overcame war after the Cold War and throughout the 1990s, the FAH switched to anti-narcotic operations. The elimination of Nicaragua as a major military threat and the demobilization of the strong Salvadorian Army also meant that the FAH could suspend its expansion and modernization process for a few years. Still, by the beginning of the 21st Century, Honduras boosts the best equipped air force in Central America.

North American F-86 Sabre (1970–1986)

The 1969 war prompted a rapid procurement and modernization program by the Honduran Air Force. Although the FAH had performed reasonably, it would need an urgent modernization to keep up with its rival's own expansion and modernization drive. The FAH was approached by a Belgian arms broker, who offered six Venezuelan F-86K

FAH 1101 is just one out of two from a total of six delivered F-86Ks that were brought into operational status.
(Mario Martinez Collection)

Sabres. A deal was struck and the aircraft were delivered in their original 1966 crates (as they were originally transferred from West Germany to Venezuela) to Honduras during 1970. They were not able to be put in operational condition, since the transfer was tagged as a 'black market' arms deal by the United States, who refused to provide any technical support for the fighters.

The Salvadorian response was swift and in 1973 it negotiated with Israel the transfer of close to 30 jet aircraft. This was comprised of Ouragan fighter bombers and Fouga Magister armed trainers. This new force would break the balance with the FAH and would seriously threaten Honduran capabilities in a renewed conflict.

Honduras obtained ten F-86E Mk.IV fighters from the Federal Yugoslav Air Force. The Sabres were Canadian-built aircraft that had originally served with the RAF in 1952. They had since then been transferred to the USAF in 1956 and on to Yugoslavia in 1958, so Honduras was actually the fourth official owner of these Canadian-built Sabres. The Sabres were refurbished by a US company in Florida and entered service designated as FAH-3001 to FAH-3010 from 1976 on.

Finally, in 1976 the FAH was able to put two of the stored F-86K Sabres into operation. These fighters were assigned the serial numbers FAH-1100 and FAH-1101. The Ks

FAH-1102, one of those six ex-FAV Sabres, never became operational. Today serialled as FAH 1100 it is preserved at Fundacion Museo del Aire de Honduras.
(Eduardo Cardenas)

FAH 3001 is one of the ten ex-Yugoslav AF Canadian-built Sabres.
(Mario Martinez Collection)

were the first radar-equipped fighters in Honduran service, they assigned a metal finish and had a shark mouth painted on the nose. These Sabres also had an unusual history. They had been built by Fiat in Italy, served with the German Luftwaffe from 1960 to 1966, and sold in 1966 to the Venezuelan Air Force. Two other F-86Ks (FAH-1102 and FAH-1103) were assembled, but never were flown. The last two aircraft (FAH-1104 and FAH-1105) were used as a source of spare parts. Rumors that the FAH was to receive four former Spanish Air Force F-86F Sabres through MAP in 1977 did not translate into a delivery. One Sabre Mk.IV was lost by 1978.

Venezuela provided maintenance support well into the 1980s, with Honduran Sabres being placed on sale in 1984. The asking price for the remaining aircraft (three Sabre Mk.4s and four F-86Ks) was USD 1 million. Although some African nations showed a remote interest in them, their career ended with the Honduras Air Force. They were operated until 1986, mainly in the close air support role. In 1987 they were sold to a local businessman for USD 600,000. However they remained in open storage on FAH grounds until 2007.

There are reports that a couple of Sabre Mk.IV fighters, flown by CIA pilots in September 1986, were used to attack a northern Nicaraguan airfield. They destroyed two

One of those CL.13 Sabres Mk.IV saw action against Nicaragua in September 1986. Today FAH 3006 is preserved at Fundacion Museo del Aire de Honduras.
(Eduardo Cardenas)

SF-260 Warrior light-attack aircraft and three Mi-8 assault helicopters. This was the last account in history of Sabres in combat. Following its original Cold War conception idea, F-86s ended its career of fighting Communist forces.

Manufacturer	Aircraft Type	Delivered	Number	Serial Numbers	Remarks
Fiat	F-86K Sabre	1970	6	1100 to 1105	ex-Venezuelan AF; ex-West German AF
Canadair Ltd	CL.13 Sabre Mk.IV	1976	10	3001 to 3010	ex-Yugoslav AF; ex-RAF; ex-USAF

Honduras operated a single T-33 (222) as trainer. Seen here still active during the late 1970s. (Eduardo Cardenas)

Lockheed T-33 (1975–1988)

The FAH obtained one Lockheed T-33-1-LO advanced trainer in order to help its pilot's transition from the old piston-engine F4U-4/5 Corsairs to the new A-37B Dragonfly attack and Sabre jet fighters.

The aircraft (number 51-6528) had originally been built for the USAF and then transferred in 1964 to the Royal Netherlands Air Force (KLu) where it received the serial number M-51. It was later placed in storage in December 1970, pending its sale. Honduras acquired the aircraft via US broker Consolidated Aero Export in 1975. The T-33 arrived in December 1975 and begun operations wearing the number FAH-222. A three-digit serial number was changed to FAH-1200 keeping with the standard practice of applying four-digit serial numbers to 'front-line' jet aircraft from 1977.

The T-33 was apparently placed in open storage in 1981. Some reports suggest that it was kept in service or at least in inventory up until 1988. There are reports about a T-33 performing reconnaissance missions during the 1969 war with El Salvador, as well as that the FAII acquired a trio of RT-33s before that date. All of this has proven to be false.

Manufacturer	Aircraft Type	Delivered	Number	Serial Numbers	Remarks
Lockheed	T-33A-1-LO	1975	1	222; 1200	ex-KLu

Today the sole T-33 (222) is in open storage at Fundacion Museo del Aire de Honduras since as early as 1981. (Eduardo Cardenas)

Cessna A-37B Dragonfly (1975-?)

With a growing insurgent movement in Central America during the 1970s, the US moved to offer much needed reinforcements to local armed forces. The Cessna A-37B Dragonfly was at the forefront of this policy, as it was a modern, inexpensive, light attack jet. Honduras received its first new-built jets in 1975, when half a dozen Dragonfly light-attack aircraft joined its ranks. They were assigned serial numbers FAH-1001 to FAH-1006 and formed the Escuadrilla de Ataque (Attack Flight) at Base Aérea Armando Escalón Espinal in San Pedro Sula. The Honduran Dragonflies differed from standard USAF birds in that they did not use the aerial refuelling probe, but the single point fuelling station. FAH-1003 was lost in the southern part of Honduras during 1977 due to a problem with its fuel indicator system.

With a growing Communist presence and the ever more threatening Sandinista armed forces receiving enormous amounts of aid from the Soviet Union and Cuba, the FAH received a follow-on batch of six A-37B Dragonflies from 1982. These had been constructed some ten years earlier and used by the USAF during the 1973–1982. They joined the attack flight at San Pedro Sula and were assigned the serial numbers FAH-1007 to FAH-1012. Along with this second batch of light attack-fighters, the USAF dispatched a pair of instructors to create a cadre of Honduran instructors that formed an A-37B syllabus in-country. The USAF officers left in late 1983.

An aircraft from the second batch, FAH-1010 was lost during February 1984. In September a top-up batch of former USAF aircraft, comprised of five OA-37Bs (re-designated as Observation-Attack by USAF) were delivered to La Ceiba Air Base. These older aircraft, some of which had been built in 1968, were generally, in good condition. They were assigned serial numbers FAH-1014 to FAH-1018.

On 12 November 1987, FAH-1002 and FAH-1005 were lost in an accident, reducing the fleet to 13 aircraft. In the summer of 1988 another aircraft was lost, this one being identified by the USAF serial number 68-7970. This aircraft might have been in operation with a USAF or even a CIA outfit. There are reports that state FAH-1013 as being

A-37B FAH-1006 during a joint exercise with USAF. Note the vintage US-made 100lbs bomb under starboard wing. (DoD)

A-37B FAH 1106 is from the first batch delivered and served in attack role.
(Collection Martin Hornlimann / MILPIX)

damaged in an accident on 14 May 1996. This number apparently was never applied to any of the delivered aircraft, as a mere speculation one would argue that the 'unlucky 13' was not applied due to superstition.

Manufacturer	Aircraft Type	Delivered	Number	Serial Numbers	Remarks
Cessna	A-37B Dragonfly	1975	6	1001 to 1006	
Cessna	A-37B Dragonfly	1982	6	1007 to 1012	ex-USAF
Cessna	OA-37B Dragonfly	1984	5	1014 to 1018	ex-USAF

Aviation Marcel Dassault Super Mystère B2 (1976–1996)

After the 1969 Soccer War, the Honduran Air Force quickly started an expansion and modernization program. Israel was keen to sell its used hardware and found an excellent market in both countries. El Salvador bought 18 Ouragan fighter-bombers and Honduras was quick to match this. It started negotiations with Israel for the delivery of up to 21 Aviation Marcel Dassault (AMD) Super Mystère B2 fighter-bombers.

The Israeli SMB.2 had been the subject of a profound modernization programme in Israel during the 1970s which included US-built Pratt & Whitney J-52 engines, upgraded avionics, two additional hard points for air-to-air missiles, and more fuel capacity. The resulting aircraft were re-named as Sa'ar (Storm). However, the US had not approved such sale, as it was allowed to veto the sale of American-made engines and it expressed its dissatisfaction in such deals.

This changed as the Cold War heated up and the first five aircraft were delivered from 1976, and were accompanied by an Israeli Lt. Col. The experienced Israeli SMB.2 pilot was in charge of training the Honduran pilots on the 'new' fighter-bombers. The remaining aircraft were delivered by 1978, with serial numbers ranging from FAH-2001 to FAH-2021. Super Mystères were taken by the Escuadrón de Caza at La Ceiba Air Base and tasked with air defence. One aircraft crashed into the Pacific Ocean during August 1981.

Super Mystere with rail for Shafir Mk.2 and unknown pod next to fuselage.
(Santiago Rivas)

Three unarmed Super Mystere during one of the exercises with USAF.
(Ratones de Hangar)

On 9 March 1983, a SMB.2 shot down a civilian registered DC-3 using its 30mm DEFA cannon, the illegal aircraft was performing a drug-running operation.

The FAH began to support Contra operations in northern Nicaragua during 1984 and by mid-1985 it was heavily involved in the fighting. In July 1985 the FAH dispatched Super Mystère fighters to support a 500-strong Contra unit attacking a Nicaraguan Army unit near Jalapa. One Super Mystère shot down an in-coming Sandinista Air Force Mi-8 helicopter with a Shafrir AAM. It also damaged a Sandinista Mi-24 during one such interdiction operations.

A complete engine overhaul was performed by an US-company in Texas and started in 1985, producing some 11 operational fighters by the late 1980s. During 1986 one Super Mystère was lost, followed by a second on 23 July 1987 designated (FAH-2010), a third (FAH-2002), a fourth (FAH-2011) and, a fifth (FAH-2013) was cannibalized for spare parts. By 1992 the fleet had been reduced to just six aircraft.

On 27 January 1996, the FAH deactivated its Super Mystère squadron, marking the event with a ceremony and a fly-by of four aircraft (numbers FAH-2004, FAH-2005, FAH-2007, and FAH-2014). The eight remaining operational aircraft were retired due to a lack of spare parts and placed in open storage, while awaiting a buyer. A lack of fighter assets led the FAH to re-activate six of its retired SMB.2s' in 1997. They were to

A nice close-up view of Super Mystere FAH 2003.
(Dennis Vink)

receive new ejection seats, navigation equipment, hydraulic system, and radar. However, lack of funds and proper suppliers ended the initiative.

Manufacturer	Aircraft Type	Delivered	Number	Serial Numbers	Remarks
AMD	Super Mystère B.2	1976	5	2001 to 2005	ex-IDF/AF
AMD	Super Mystère B.2	1977	8	2006 to 2013	ex-IDF/AF
AMD	Super Mystère B.2	1978	8	2014 to 2021	ex-IDF/AF

CASA C-101 Aviojet (1984–?)

In order to form a new, modern training syllabus, the Honduran Air Force began to evaluate several aircraft that could fulfill the basic and advanced training courses. Two types were selected in the early 1980s, the Brazilian Embraer EMB-312 Tucano and the Spanish CASA C-101 Aviojet.

Honduras signed an order for four C-101BB-03 advanced trainers in 1983. The contract included an option for another four to eight aircraft which was never exercised. The BB-03 was an armed export variant of the standard C-101EB ordered by the Spanish Air Force. The new Aviojets were delivered in 1984 to the Escuela de Aviación Militar 'Cap. Roberto Raúl Barahona Lagos', at its new base near Palmerola in Comayagua. They were assigned the serial numbers FAH-235 to FAH-238.

The Aviojets were also pressed into service in COIN missions, and also on anti-narcotic flights. On 9 March 1987 one C-101 scored the first air-to-air kill of the type in history, using its 30-mm centreline cannon to shoot down an Aeroexpress Douglas C-47 being used on an illegal narcotic flight.

Some reports indicate that all aircraft were returned to flight status during 2004 by Honduran personnel with the help of ENAER technicians. Further reports have also

C-101 (238) during exercise "Amigo South" with USAF's 425th Tactical Fighter Training Squadron in March 1989. (USAF)

stated that the FAH received an additional five former Chilean Air Force (FACH) T-36s (or maybe A-36s), but this did not take place.

Manufacturer	Aircraft Type	Delivered	Number	Serial Numbers	Remarks
CASA	C-101BB-03 Aviojet	1984	4	235 to 238	

Northrop F-5E Tiger II (1989–)

When Nicaragua threatened to build up a fighter force based around former Cuban MiG-21s and MiG-23s, the FAH sought to obtain a modern multi-role fighter. Honduras had been asking the US for F-5E/F tactical fighters since 1982 and had also approached Israel for up to 24 Kfir fighter-bombers. With Nicaraguan crews training on MiG-21s in Cuba and Bulgaria, the US Subcommittee for Hemispheric Affairs agreed to provide 10 single-seat and 2 two-seat F-5 fighters from USAF stocks through an FMS contract *Peace Bonito* worth USD 75 million (in December 1987). The F-5s would also be used by Honduras to intercept Cuban and Soviet aid flights into Nicaragua in case the Cold War heated-up.

Some of the F-5Es were former South Vietnam Air Force aircraft that managed to escape before Saigon fell some 12 years earlier. Deliveries ended in April 1989 and the aircraft wore the serial numbers FAH-4001 to 4012. They were flown in by USAF pilots from Williams AFB. Immediately after their delivery, the F-5s proved their worth by downing a Sandinista Mi-17 helicopter that had penetrated Honduran airspace. Since then at least one F-5 is kept on a 5-minute alert to provide national air defence.

Once the Escuadrilla de Caza obtained IOC with the F-5, the FAH retired most of its Super Mystères, with the final eight soldiering on until 1996. Honduran F-5s main armament was its two M39A2 20-mm cannons as they were never supplied any Sidewinder missiles.

F-5E (4005) is FAH's ongoing air defender.
(Tim Spearman)

Rumours about the transfer or sale of the Tigers to Chile during 1995 were false. In fact at least half a dozen Honduran F-5s were shipped to Valparaiso in Chile, where ENAER technicians wired them to fire Shafrir II air-to-air missiles after refurbishment in Lockheed-Martin's Palmdale facility. Although there is no evidence that Honduras has acquired such missiles. The first fatality struck the squadron on 3 June 1999, when F-5E FAH-4004 crashed into the Atlantic. Further rumours of the F-5 fleet being exchanged for up to eight new Chilean A-36 Halcón light fighters proved again false and the Tigers will continue to defend Honduran airspace for many years to come. In 2008, amid a controversy surrounding FAH's capabilities, Honduran President, Manuel Zelaya publicly offered to provide Nicaragua's air defense necessities with the FAH's F-5s. The offer was not accepted.

Manufacturer	Aircraft Type	Delivered	Number	Serial Numbers	Remarks
Northrop	F-5E Tiger II	1989	10	4003 to 4012	ex-USAF; some ex-SVAF
Northrop	F-5F Tiger II	1989	2	4001 & 4002	ex-USAF

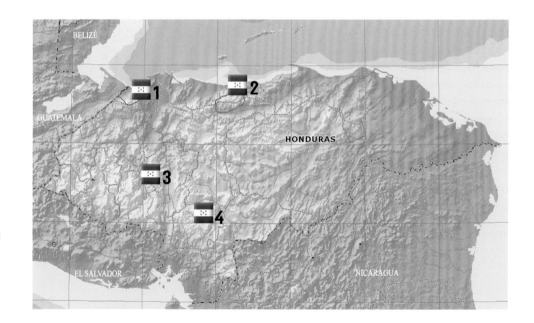

1. Coronel Armando Escalon Espinal Air Base, San Pedro Sula
2. Coronel Hector Caracciola Moncada Air Base, La Ceiba
3. Coronel Jose Enrique Soto Cano Air Base, Palmerola
4. Teniente Coronel Hernan Acosta Mejía, Tegucigalpa-Toncontin

Chapter 12

MEXICO

Being the southern neighbour to the huge military power of the United States certainly has its perks and also its difficulties. A modern and potent air force just south of the border has never been encouraged by any US administration. The absence of potential threats or any major military international participation has also curtailed Mexico's air-power doctrine to more traditional close air support and transport activities. However, plans for the acquisition of jet powered aircraft date back to 1946. These evolved and the first jet squadron was established in 1951. This was, however, a paper unit and it did not receive any jet equipment until after a decade.

It was in the early 1960s that the squadron received a number of former Canadian, first generation fighter jets. They were soon joined by another squadron of armed jet trainers, this time acquired from the USAF.

These former RCAF and USAF fighters formed the backbone of Mexican air defense through the 1960s. With the advent of massive oil reserves in the 1970s the air force developed a requirement for three tactical fighter squadrons equipped with a multi-role supersonic jet fighter. Several types were considered and the F-5 lightweight fighter eventually selected. The US agreed to provide but a dozen aircraft to form a single air defence squadron. Later in the 1980s the US agreed to provide a larger number of jet trainers to fulfill Mexican air defence requirements.

By the early 21st Century the Fuerza Aérea Mexicana (FAM, Mexican Air Force) jet fighters and armed jet trainers had dwindled considerably to less than 20 operational aircraft. With the advent of a new surveillance radar network, as well as a new air force and navy AEW force, both services sought to improve their capabilities.

The Mexican Navy announced a requirement for up to a dozen jet fighters. Several types were considered, from the L-39 and L-159 to the JAS-39 Gripen and Su-27. This last fighter was favored because of its speed, price and twin-engine characteristics. An order for five upgraded Su-27SMK and a single Su-30MK2 fighter was announced in 2006, however a new naval administration took office in late 2006 and announced the cancellation of the order.

The air force on its part decided to finally retire its long serving T-33 fleet in 2007, leaving the F-5 as its sole jet equipment until a proper replacement is obtained.

De Haviland Vampire (1961–1967)

It took FAM a decade between foundation of jet squadron and purchase of first jet fighter – a Vampire. That's why 200th Jet Fighter Squadron was also called Ghost Squadron.
(Mario Martinez collection)

Negotiations for the acquisition of a squadron of jet-powered aircraft initiated in the early 1950s and the unit in charge of operating them, the Escuadrón Jet de Pelea 200 (200th Jet Fighter squadron) was formed in 1951. This unit became known as the Escuadrón Fantasma (the Ghost Squadron), as it took almost a decade for the FAM to acquire its first jet fighters.

In 1960 the FAM managed to acquire a fleet of 15 former Royal Canadian Air Force (RCAF) Vampire F.Mk.3s through a Wisconsin-based company: Fliteways Inc. They had acquired 86 former RCAF Vampires in an effort to sell them to private individuals as executive transports. The aircraft had been built by the English Electric company. As they had been de-militarized for commercial sale, the FAM had to acquire a shipment of 20-mm cannons directly from the UK.

The aircraft were delivered to Mexico on 14 February 1961, 14 aircraft used to finally equip the 200th Jet Fighter Squadron. The FAM applied the serial numbers JP-01 to JP-14 (Jet Pelea – Fighter Jet). The fifteenth aircraft was used as a spare parts source. The 200th Squadron was assigned to the newly formed 7th Jet Fighter Group and was soon to be joined by the 202nd Jet Fighter Squadron and its AT-33's.

As there were no two-seat aircraft to perform conversion training, the FAM acquired a pair of Vampire T.Mk.11s from the Royal Air Force. These were former RAF (serial

Mexico operated one squadron of British built Vampires F.Mk.3. for just a few years before turning to much safer T-33.
(Mario Martinez collection)

numbers) XZ-414 and XD-439 that were now designated as JP-15 and JP-16. The entire fleet was re-painted in an all-aluminum scheme from 1964.

Plans to acquire a further 10 to 14 aircraft were cancelled after evaluation of a number of standard safety features on the T-33s, such as a pressurized canopy, and ejection seats, proved the Vampires to be obsolete. Furthermore in December 1966, JP-08 was lost over Pachuca in Hidalgo state and this was followed by a second accident only a few days later. By late 1967, the FAM had lost another Vampire in an accident. Furthermore, Vampires JP-03, JP-09, and JP-14 had been written off after they suffered irreparable damage to their undercarriages in hard landings. Vampire operations were suspended in 1967 although they remained officially on the order of battle until the early 1970s.

Manufacturer	Aircraft Type	Delivered	Number	Serial Numbers	Remarks
English Electric	Vampire F.Mk.3	1961	15	JP-01 to JP-14	ex-RCAF; one used as spares
De Haviland	DH-115 Vampire T.11	1962	2	JP-15 & JP-16	ex-RAF

Lockheed T-33 (1961–2007)

In March 1961, the Mexican government acquired a batch of 15 Lockheed T-33A-1 tactical jet trainers at a bargain price of under USD 40,000. This was possible thanks to the Military Assistance Program (MAP). The aircraft were surplus according to USAF requirements and had been stored in the AMARC facility at Davis Monthan AFB in the Arizona desert. They were restored to flying condition by Lockheed Aircraft Services.

The first three T-33s were delivered in September 1961 and formed the basis of the Escuadrón Jet de Pelea 202 (202nd Jet Fighter Squadron) based at Mexico City's International Airport. The aircraft received serial numbers JE-001 to JE-015 upon delivery. JE stands for Jet Entrenador or Training Jet, although the type had been converted to the armed AT-33 standard with 0.50-cal machine guns in the nose and external weapons stores.

The armed trainer AT-33A (JE-004) from Escuadrón Jet de Pelea 202 with 0.50 cal machine guns was based at Mexico City's International Airport.
(Mario Martinez collection)

T-33A (4026) in a special paint scheme commemorating incredible 45 years of operations from 1691 until 2006. All T-33s retired one year later. (Jonathan Parra)

Once the runways had been adapted to operate the new jets and new hangars built to house both squadrons, the 202nd Squadron joined its sister unit, the Vampire-equipped 200th Squadron at Santa Lucia Air Base, Mexico's main air base from late 1962. In 1967 the FAM lost its first AT-33A and from then on, with the virtual retirement of the Vampire fleet, the 202nd Fighter Squadron assumed all air defence responsibilities. In June 1970 the 202nd lost its second Tetra (JE-012).

In order to replace attrition loses as well as those caused by serviceability problems, the FAM bought seven former Royal Netherlands Air Force T-33s in 1972. However, only three aircraft arrived by 1981. They received serial numbers JE-016 to JE-018, the rest of the order wound up operating in the US civilian sector.

In 1986 the Mexican Government entered negotiations with the US for the acquisition of another 30 former USAF aircraft. The order soon rose to 40 aircraft as additional airframes were offered by the USAF from 1987. The refurbished aircraft were obtained for a total of USD 3.5 million with deliveries beginning in March 1989. They received serial numbers in the JE-019 to JE-058 range. Original plans called for these aircraft to be a stop-gap acquisition and to remain in service for ten years. These aircraft were pure-trainer versions, with no combat capabilities.

Anticipating the large Tetra delivery, the FAM created the 10th Air Group, responsible for the creation and operation of three new squadrons. The 210th Fighter Squadron was formed in January 1989 at BAM-8 Mérdia, on the Yucatan Peninsula. Two (original) Tetras were used for familiarization and conversion training. The 211th Fighter Squadron stood up at BAM-6 Tuxtla Gutierrez in Chiapas, while the 212th Fighter Squadron began operations in BAM-2 Ixtepec in Oaxaca on 24 November 1989.

These three bases became increasingly important as the Mexican Air Force focused on south and southeast bases as part of their anti-narcotic and counter-insurgency operations. By mid-1990 the three squadrons were fully operational on the type. The 212th was re-located to BAM-2 by late 1990.

A tragic accident cost the lives of several Tetra pilots, when JE-036, JE-049 (211th Squadron) and JE-050 (212th Squadron) collided with an F-5E over Mexico City, during the Independence Day parade on 16 September 1995.

From 1998 the 24 remaining aircraft were combined into the new 402nd Air Squadron based at BAM-2 Ixtepec. The remaining aircraft were re-numbered in the 4000 range. The 402nd was, from its conception was to be an operational squadron, constantly being employed in intercepting illegal flights. Tetras were armed with nose fixed 0.50-cal machine guns, MAG 7.62-mm gun pods and LAU-32 or MA2A rocket launchers. The number had been reduced to 14 operational aircraft by 2002 and another aircraft number 4032, was lost over Oaxaca on 16 April 2003.

The type continued in service until late October 2007, when the last of the 12 operational aircraft were retired and placed as gate guards and monuments.

Manufacturer	Aircraft Type	Delivered	Number	Serial Numbers	Remarks
Lockheed	AT-33A	1961	15	JE-001 to JE-015	ex-USAF
Lockheed	T-33A-1-LO	1972	7	JE-016 to JE-018	ex-KLu; just 3 delivered
Lockheed	T-33A	1987	40	JE-019 to JE-058	ex-USAF

Northrop F-5 Tiger II (1982–)

In 1977 the Mexican Air Force developed a requirement for a new tactical jet fighter. Several options were considered, including the F-4 Phantom II and IAI Kfir, but the Northrop F-5E/F Tiger II was eventually selected. An initial requirement for 36, comprising 30 single-seat F-5Es and 6 two-seat F-5Fs to equip three tactical fighter squadrons but, was turned down by the US Congress.

F-5E (4510) armed with unguided rocket pods & AIM-9B Sidewinder undergoes some maintenance.
(Inigo Guevara)

177

A special paint scheme on FAM F-5F (4501) commemorated in 2007 the 25 years of F-5 operation. Both of FAM's F-5Fs shown here will soldier on with the remaining F-5Es as sole Mexican jet fighter.
(Hector Wong & Oswaldo Flores)

The Mexican government begun negotiations with Israel for the acquisition of at least 24 IAI K-fir C.2/TC.2 fighters and there was some mention of interest in establishing a production line of the type for further requirements as well as export to the Latin American market. Wether these mentions were indeed a possibility or not, the US changed its position and authorized the sale of a dozen F-5E/F to Mexico.

The USD 110 million FMS contract, named Peace Aztec, included ground support equipment, training, AIM-9B Sidewinders, LAU-3 rocket launchers and Mk.82 and Mk.83 GP bombs. Mexican F-5E Tigers differed from standard Tigers with a prominent dorsal antenna spine.

These Tigers IIs arrived from August to December 1982, after a group of Mexican pilots received training at the 425th Tactical Fighter Training Squadron, at Williams AFB in Arizona. The single-seat Tigers were assigned the serial numbers 4001 to 4010, while the two F-5Fs were numbered 4501 and 4502. Curiously, number 4008 was the 1000th F-5 built by Northrop.

The Tigers formed the Escuadrón de Defensa Aérea 401 (401st Air Defense Squadron) at Santa Lucía Air Base, joining a squadron of veteran T-33s (the 202nd Jet Fighter Squadron) in the 7th Air Wing and filling a void left by the Vampires since their deactivation some 15 years earlier.

In November 1983 the 401st Squadron suffered its first accident when number 4002 crashed in the Chihuahua desert during a training sortie. Information on the F-5s service history in Mexico is scarce, although some sources point out that they have been used in anti-narcotic operations, intercepting unauthorized flights which lead to a reduction in drug traffic.

A minor update that involved fitting a GPS system was performed in 1995, but the planned upgrade of the ten surviving machines to Northrop-Grumman's proposed 'Tiger IV' program never materialized. Number 4003 crashed in 1995. The F-5E fleet was re-designated numbers in the 4503 to 4510 series after the GPS update.

In 2000 the FAM began a major re-structuring process designed to counter illegal flights as part of its contribution to the war on drugs. AEW and surveillance aircraft were acquired from Brazil and the USA (EMB-145SA/RS and C-26B Merlin) to enhance its detection capability. Soon it became obvious that the FAM lacked the armed resources to intercept illegal aircraft. Only four to five Tigers were available for nationwide deployments, since two aircraft are always kept on emergency alert to defend Mexico City and one or two Tigers are usually going through general maintenance. The F-5s rotate in 5-minute, 30-minute, and 2-hour alert patterns.

The Mexican government sought to obtain 14 F-5s from Switzerland during the early years of the 21st Century, in order to replace the tired T-33 in service with the 402nd Air Squadron and complete the 401st fleet. But several factors prevented this operation and the aircraft eventually found their way to US Navy and USMC Aggressor units. With the retirement of the T-33 fleet in 2007, the F-5E/F is the sole combat jet equipment in service with the Mexican Air Force.

Manufacturer	Aircraft Type	Delivered	Number	Serial Numbers	Remarks
Northrop	F-5E Tiger II	1982	10	4001 to 4010	Re-serialled 4503 to 4510 after 1995
Northrop	F-5F Tiger II	1982	2	4501 & 4502	

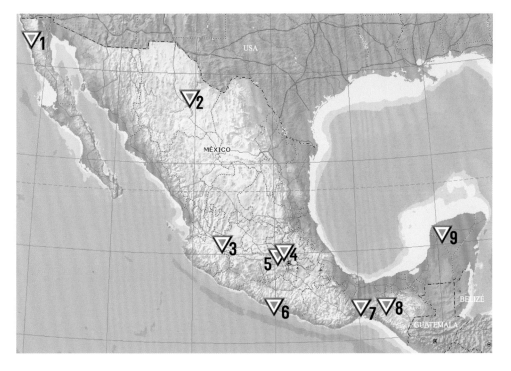

1. BAM 3 El Cipres, Baja California
2. BAM 11 Santa Gertrudis, Chihuahua desert
3. BAM 5 Zapopan, Jalisco
4. BAM 1 Santa Lucía, Estado de México
5. EAM 1 Aeropuerto Internacional de la Ciudad de México (Mexico City international Airport)
6. BAM 7 Pie de la Cuesta, Guerrero
7. BAM 2 Ixtepec, Oaxaca
8. BAM 6 Tuxtla Gutierrez, Chiapas
9. BAM 8 Merida, Yucatan

Chapter 13

NICARAGUA

Nicaragua was ruled by the Somoza family for some 43 years, until President General Anastacio 'Tacho' Somoza Debayle fled the country in 1979. The Fuerza Aérea Nicaragüense (FAN, Nicaraguan Air Force) along with the other services of the armed forces was neglected for decades. The Somoza-regime failed to introduce modern weapons in an attempt to limit the armed forces power. This proved to be his demise as Sandinista rebels took control of the country after an 18 month civil war. The air force had received a handful of armed jet trainers from the US Navy and used them against the Sandinistas. The aircraft were then taken over by the Sandinistas and formed the new Fuerza Aérea Sandinista (FAS, Sandinista Air Force).

Sandinista desires included the formation of large and powerful armed forces, numbering some 600,000 of mostly infantry, supported by at least 1,000 tanks, and 100 jet fighters. This was to become a major threat to the United States and most of Central America (mainly the Panama Canal). The Soviets and Cubans encouraged such military development and offered all their support.

In the early 1980s a group of Nicaraguan personnel, rumoured to number about 70 people, were sent to Bulgaria, to receive basic flight training. Another group was sent to Cuba. Conversion training on the MiG-21 was reportedly performed in Cuba, in anticipation for the delivery of about a dozen such fighters. The MiG-21 was to be joined apparently from 1983, by a squadron of MiG-23 fighters (probably former Cuban MiG-23BN fighter-bombers). These deliveries did not take place and by mid-1984 efforts were reportedly underway for the acquisition of second hand Mirage fighters. France had apparently been approached since 1981 to supply them these fighters.

Delivery of the MiGs would complicate the delicate balance of power in Central America in the 1980s. The Soviet Union was under intense pressure not to supply jet fighters. The Sandinistas turned restless, as they badly needed a jet fighter that could shoot down the scores of transports and utility aircraft that supported the Contra rebels.

The only recorded intent to deliver armed jet aircraft to the Sandinista regime occurred in 1983, when a flight of Libyan Arab Republic Air Force Ilyushin Il-76 heavy transports made an emergency landing in Brazil. They transported a total of 17 unassembled Aero L-39ZA Albatross armed jet trainers bound for Nicaragua. The crates were impounded and later returned to Libya. During August 1984, the Sandinista government announced that Nicaragua had the least powerful air force in Central America and the arrival of jet fighters was imminent. Punta Huete Air Base was apparently prepared for the arrival of MiG-21 jet fighters, but this did not take place.

In February 1990 Violeta Chamorro won the national elections in the country's drive into democracy. The armed forces, although still under Sandinista control, were re-

structured a shrank by about 60 per cent. The Fuerza Aérea Sandinista kept operating under such name until 1996, but deleted its plans for a jet-equipped air force.

In late 2006 Daniel Ortega returned to power through democratic elections and outlined plans to modernize the Nicaraguan armed forces, but these do not appear to include the acquisition of jet fighters.

Lockheed T-33 (1963–1982)

Somoza's Fuerza Aérea Nicaragüense (FAN), which was part of the National Guard, acquired six former US Navy Lockheed T-33B (TV-2) jet trainers in the early 1960s. The T-33 was the first jet to enter service with the Central American country after a group of Nicaraguan pilots underwent conversion training in the US.

The T-33s built in the early 1950s were refurbished before delivery, modified with two fixed 0.50-cal machine guns in the nose. The aircraft were assigned the serial numbers 304 to 309 and equipped the Escuadrón de Combate (Combat Squadron), which also doubled as an aerobatic display team. A seventh aircraft was acquired as an attrition replacement and received the serial number 310.

By the late 1970s only two aircraft were operational and they were pressed into service against the opposing Sandinista forces. They performed daily operations during 1978 and 1979. In 1979 a T-33 intercepted and downed a Sandinista aircraft that was operating from Costa Rica.

The FAN ceased operations in July and on 8 September 1979 and the Fuerza Aérea Sandinista took its place. The five surviving T-33s were re-designated as FAS-172 to FAS-176. An eyewitness reports that only two T-33s were in operational condition.

Spare parts shortage and an inadequate maintenance infrastructure limited the T-33's operational capabilities. Hopes of receiving MiGs from either the Soviet Union or Cuba pretty much prevented any desire to keep the T-birds in operation. They were withdrawn from use in the early 1980s.

A total of seven T-33B served as fighters due to installed machine guns and simultaneously for an aerobatic team.
(via Mario Martinez)

Manufacturer	Aircraft Type	Delivered	Number	Serial Numbers	Remarks
Lockheed	T-33B	1963	6	304 to 309	ex-US Navy
Lockheed	T-33B	1964	1	310	ex-US Navy

At least one picture in decent quality – FAS T-33B 310 preserved as gate guard. (Collection Martin Hornlimann/ MILPIX)

One out of two operational T-33s in service with FAS. As no MiG-21s were delivered the T-33s finally retired in 1982. (DoD)

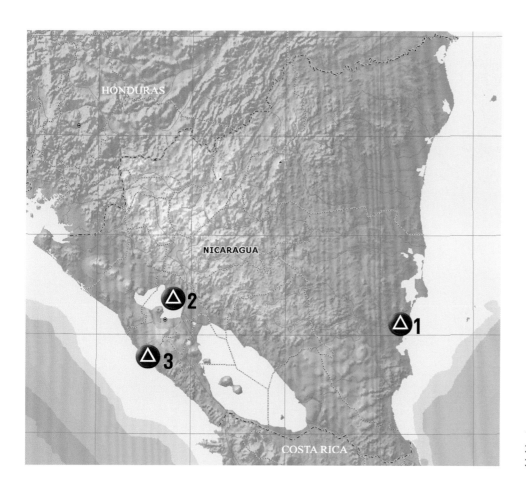

1. Bluefields
2. Punta Huete
3. Managua

Chapter 14

PARAGUAY

President Alfredo Stroessner maintained tight control of this land-locked South American country during his 35 year rule that began in 1954. A fierce anti-communist regime managed to maintain him in Washington's good side throughout the Cold War years. However, this relationship did not translate to the usual supply of MAP-funded T-33 armed jet trainers, F-80 Shooting Star fighters and A-37B Dragonflies.

Paraguay entered the jet age rather late, even by Latin American standards. A squadron of Brazilian-supplied light-attack jets formed the country's first line of defence from the late 1970s. This was the sole type of jet used throughout the 1980s. In 1990 good diplomatic relations with the Republic of China (ROC, Taiwan) led to the donation of half a dozen AT-33A armed jet trainers to complement the Xavantes in the Tactical Air Group.

The 1995 announcement for the transfer of up to 12 AIDC-built F-5E Tiger II (known as the 'Chung Cheng' in Taiwan) supersonic tactical fighters was eventually cancelled. The Fuerza Aérea Paraguaya (FAP, Paraguyan Air Force) would have to secure constant financial aid to support the fighters. Paraguay was to take delivery of the fighters from 1998-1999, forming a squadron that would replace both the Xavantes and the 1950s-era T-33. The cost of introducing this supersonic fighter proved impractical for the Paraguayan defence budget. The FAP received half a dozen former ROC Army UH-1H utility helicopters instead.

EMBRAER EMB-326 Xavante (1979–2003)

In order to replace its ageing fleet of T-6G Texan armed trainers operated by the Grupo Aerotáctico (GAT, Tactical Air Group) at Ñu-Guazú (Campo Grande) military air base, the Paraguayan Air Force selected the Brazilian-built MB-326, known as the EMB-326GB Xavante. Xavantes had replaced Brazilian T-6 Texan trainers in the FAB so they were as such, designed to take over this role.

Negotiations for the acquisition of six Xavantes started in 1977, but were interrupted when the United States offered to transfer six Cessna A-37B Dragonfly light attack fighters through the Military Assistance Program. Since the Carter administration was keen in providing these aircraft with strings attached, the proposed transfer did not go through.

In 1978 Paraguay resumed negotiations with Brazil and placed an order for nine factory-fresh Xavantes. Paraguayan pilots started training on the type at the 3° Composite Attack and Reconnaissance Squadron based in Santa Cruz and at the 1° Squadron/4°

Rather late Paraguay joined the jet community in 1979 with the delivery of nine EMB-326GB. (via AAMA)

Air Group in Fortaleza during 1978. A Brazilian military mission established a training syllabus for the Paraguayan Air Force in 1982.

Deliveries begun in late December 1978, with three aircraft joining the 1st Fighter Squadron 'Guarani' at Presidente Stroessner International Airport in Asuncion. The order was completed between January and June 1980. They were assigned the serial numbers FAP-1001 to FAP-1009. Once delivered, the 1st Fighter Squadron was organized around two operational flights, named 'Orion' and Centauro'.

Fatality struck the squadron only three months later when FAP-1008 was lost when it crashed into Lake Yparacai. A replacement for the lost Xavante was ordered in 1981 and delivered in September 1982, wearing the serial number FAP-1010. Further attrition during the 1980s included the loss of FAP-1002 during a training flight when its engine caught fire during 1985 and the loss of FAP-1003 in 1988.

Xavantes were instrumental during the 1989 cup d'état against President Stroessner led by General Andres Rodriguez. They joined tanks from the 1st Army Corps in operations against the entrenched Presidential Guard and police units loyal to Stroessner. President Stroessner surrendered and fled to Brazil in exile.

No major change for the Xavante fleet came after the 1989 revolution. Their base dropped the old Stroessner name and adopted the name Silvio Pettirossi International Airport. FAP-1001 was lost in 1990. During the 1990s their role shifted considerably (as it did in most Latin American air forces) towards counter-narcotics operations. In late 1995 the Xavantes were used to strike at covert airstrips in the heights of Parana. They operated from Ciudad del Este alongside some remaining AT-33s.

The last operational sortie flown by Paraguayan Xavantes was recorded in 2003 and the type has since been reported as stored. Due to its current economic situation, a suitable replacement will have to come in the form of second hand, and most likely, foreign aid. Negotiations for the transfer of up to four former FAB Xavantes

Combat jet operations in Paraguay were last recorded in 2003 and since the only combat capable aircraft are turboprop EMB-312 Tucanos. (Santiago Rivas)

were suspended in the early 21st Century, and a reversal policy might effectually send the remaining Paraguayan Xavantes back to Brazil, in exchange for up to six turbo-prop Tucanos.

Manufacturer	Aircraft Type	Delivered	Number	Serial Numbers	Remarks
EMBRAER	EMB-326GB Xavante	1978	3	1001 to 1003	
EMBRAER	EMB-326GB Xavante	1980	6	1004 to 1009	
EMBRAER	EMB-326GB Xavante	1982	1	1010	attrition replacement

Lockheed T-33 (1991–1998)

A ferocious anti-communist doctrine ruled in this country since Stroessner took power in the mid-1950s. This anti-communism brought about Paraguay's recognition of the Republic of China (Taiwan) as the legitimate Chinese state. So, economic and military ties soon followed diplomacy. In the late 1980s this diplomacy translated into the donation of six former Republic of China Air Force Lockheed AT-33A armed trainers by 1990. The T-33As would augment the air force's GAT Xavantes.

Taiwan had originally received some 32 Lockheed T-33s from the USAF during the 1950s. These had been built in around 1956-7. They had been converted into the AT-33A configuration, armed with two 0.50-cal machine guns and the capability to carry ground attack weapons such as rockets and GP bombs. They operated as second-line, back-up fighters, alongside F-100 Super Sabre and F-104 Starfighter fighter-bombers up until the late 1980s.

Delivery of the T-33s from Taiwan began in late 1990 and finished in 1991. The aircraft were applied the serial numbers FAP-1020 to FAP-1025 and assigned to the Indios Squadron of the Grupo Aéreo Táctico. The Squadron was divided into two flights, these being Escuadrilla Taurus and Escuadrilla Scorpio.

In 1991 FAP received six T-33s from Taiwan to augment their much newer EMB-326s. Nevertheless their operational life lasted only seven years. (Claudio Lucchesi)

The newly delivered T-33s were used for border patrol and anti-narcotic operations alongside the Xavantes. During 1995 they were used to bomb several illegal airstrips used for narcotic shipments in the Parana Heights. Some reports stated that the fleet was retired as early as 1998, but at least three aircraft were stored and kept in flying condition.

Manufacturer	Aircraft Type	Delivered	Number	Serial Numbers	Remarks
Lockheed	AT-33A-5-LO	1991	6	1020 to 1025	ex-ROCAF

After being used in anti-narcotics & border patrol role for a short time, several T-33s were stored in airworthy condition. (Antonio Sapienza)

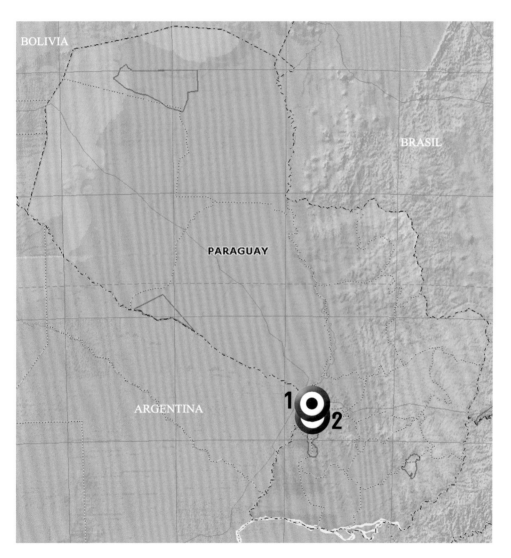

1. Silvio Pettirossi International
   Airport, (Presidente
   Stroessner International
   Airport), Asunción
2. Campo Grande, Ñu Guazú

Chapter 15

PERU

Peru was to become the third Latin American country to field jet fighters and the first to field US-built jet fighters, when it ordered four brand new Lockheed P-80C Shooting Stars in 1949. The Korean War prevented their delivery and the Fuerza Aérea del Perú (FAP, Peruvian Air Force) had to wait a few more years before receiving its first jet fighters.

As part of a major re-equipment and modernization programme initiated in the mid-1950s, the FAP sought no fewer than 64 jet fighters from the United States and the United Kingdom in order to form four squadrons. T-33s provided the first experiences of jet operations and was soon followed by the more potent F-86 Sabre and Hawker Hunter fighters. Some refurbished F-80s also joined the fleet at about the same time. With the US and UK opposed to providing supersonic fighter jets to the region during the mid-1960s, Peru turned to France and became South America's first supersonic air force. France was willing to provide Mirage fighters to the supersonic-thirsty region and Dassault soon found its production line filled with orders from Argentina, Brazil, Colombia and Venezuela.

In the early 1970s the Revolutionary Armed Forces Government started an ambitious modernization programme that would expand the current fighter fleet into a modern and potent combat force. French prices were at an all time high and the US continued to curtail its offer to simple, light attack jets. Peru set another record, becoming the first non-communist Latin American country to order defence materials from the Soviet Union. Soviet fighter-bombers began to pour into Peruvian squadrons, and were accompanied by transports, helicopters, missiles, tanks, etc.

During the 1980s Peruvian efforts to develop an indigenous aerospace industry were hampered by financial difficulties. License production of the small Italian MB-339 jet trainer was cancelled and its procurement plans centred on upgrades to its existing fleet and a squadron of new generation multi-role fighters. France was again the selected supplier and Peru again fielded the region's most advanced fighter, the Mirage 2000.

A major re-equipping programme was again implemented after a border dispute escalated into a small-scale war with neighbouring Ecuador and showed the FAP's deficiencies. A contract with the former Soviet Republic of Belarus saw the delivery of second hand MiG-29s and Su-25s amid an international corruption scandal. A small yet meaningful contract with Russia guaranteed the required service and spares for the Fulcrum fleet.

As of the early 21st century, Peru continues to field a modern air force for Latin American standards and has equipped some of its fighters with beyond-visual range

Lockheed T-33 (1955–1994)

A T-33 on exhibit at museo de la BA Las Palmas, Lima. Actually, this serial number (455) never existed. Note the nose guns. It must be one of the converted to AT-33A standard.
(Cesar Cruz)

As part of a major re-equipment and modernization programme, the FAP initiated contact with several sources for the supply of jet aircraft. The Lockheed T-33 armed trainer was the first jet aircraft to enter FAP service and would lead the way for more advanced types.

A half dozen former USAF aircraft were received in 1955 after Peruvian pilots had been through conversion training in the US. These T-33A-1-LOs formed a fighter squadron at Limatambo Air Base that began to work up on the type. With a further ten aircraft delivered they were transferred to Grupo de Caza 11 (11th Fighter Group) at Talara Air Base during 1960.

The T-33s were re-numbered 480 to 495, and after a re-organization scheme applied serial numbers in the 400 range to the trainers. The T-33 was known in FAP service as 'Tintas' and served a dual role of advanced jet training and light attack.

At least eight aircraft were upgraded to AT-33A standard, with the fitting of 0.50-cal machine guns in the nose and a pair of bomb racks. From 1971 they were transferred to the newly established Grupo Aereo 7, with their ground-attack duties taken over by Cessna A-37Bs. They remained in FAP service until 1994.

Manufacturer	Aircraft Type	Delivered	Number	Serial Numbers	Remarks
Lockheed	T-33A-1-LO	1955	16	400 to 415, later 480 to 495	ex-USAF

North American F-86 Sabre (1955–1977)

The FAP received its first six F-86F Sabre fighters in June 1955 through the US Military Assistance Program (MAP). These were former USAF F-86F-25-NH versions, built in 1951 or 1952, armed with up to 24 70-mm rockets for ground-attack duties. The fighters were delivered to Limatambo Airport after a ferry flight from their USAF base at Macon in Georgia. Six Peruvian pilots went to Nellis AFB in Nevada to receive conver-

The F-86F, here 595, has been Peru's first real jet fighter. (via AAMA)

sion training and then returned to Peru during September of 1955. In October another 12 fighters were delivered and entered service with the Escuadrón de Caza 11 (11th Fighter Squadron) at Talara Air Base. They were assigned serial numbers from 591 to 605. The first accident occurred in April 1956, when serial number 599 crashed near Arequipa in an emergency landing. This was followed by the loss of number 601 over Talara in 1957.

Following a 1960 re-organization scheme that brought about a new administrative system, fighters were issued serial numbers in the 100s range, bombers in the 200s, transports in the 300s, trainers in the 400s, miscellaneous in the 500s and helicopters in the 600s, the entire F-86 Sabre fleet was re-numbered. Known serial numbers include 130, 131, 133, 171, 176, 179, 180, and 186.

There are some rumours that up to 9 Sabres had been lost by 1964 and that the FAP received anywhere between 5 and 11 replacements taken from USAF stocks, but these deliveries have not been confirmed. The USAF apparently offered another 15 former USAF Sabres to fulfil a Peruvian requirement for a new generation fighter during 1966. The FAP eventually bought the more powerful Mirage 5. By 1971 the fleet had been

F-86 (via Cesar Cruz)

This former FAP Sabre is preserved as part of a small museum within Las Palmas Air Force Base, close to Lima. (Michael Blank)

reduced to only a few flying aircraft and the type was completely phased out by 1977. Rumours of their transfer to the Bolivian Air Force are not correct.

Manufacturer	Aircraft Type	Delivered	Number	Serial Numbers	Remarks
North American	F-86F-25-NH	1955	18	591 to 605; latter 130, 131, 133, 171, 176, 179, 180, 186	ex-USAF

Hawker Hunter (1956–1980)

As part of a programme aimed at acquiring top of the line combat aircraft, the FAP selected the Hawker Hunter F.Mk.4 fighter and the English Electric Canberra bomber in October 1955. The contract for 16 Hunters included spare engines, airframe parts, additional pairs of wing pylons (with which the aircraft were modified to use), ground equipment, and ammunition for a total of BDP2.76 million.

Deliveries of the 'export version' Hunter F.4s (re-designated as F.Mk.52) began in 1956. The aircraft being diverted from a RAF production order. They formed the Escuadrón de Caza 14 (14th Fighter Squadron) of the Grupo de Aviación 1 (1st Air Group) which began operations on 26 May 1956 from Limatambo International Airport. They were given serial numbers 630 to 645. The unit was transferred to the Grupo de Caza 12 (12th Fighter Group) during 1957, together with the Sabre and T-33 units. Four of the Hunters were used to form the aerobatic display team 'Los Cuatro Ases' (The Four Aces). This team began to perform at major air shows from late 1956 onwards.

In the early years the Hawker Hunter operated as fighter. From the early 1970s on it switched to ground attack role due to arrival of Mirage 5. Seen here technicians perform flight line maintenance on aircraft 637. (via AAMA)

The absence of a conversion trainer was addressed in 1960, when the FAP bought one Hunter T.7 directly from the RAF. This aircraft (RAF serial number WT706) was re-designated as T.Mk.62 once delivered to Peru.

The Hunter turned out to be an excellent fighter in Peruvian hands. However, their lack of supersonic speed prevented them from acquiring further Hunters to cover a 1960s requirement for a modern fighter. One Hunter crashed in September 1960 and was followed by another in early November 1963.

The Hunters were allocated to the ground-attack role from the early 1970s, once the Mirage 5Ps replaced them in the fighter role. At least ten Hunters remained in service until 1980, being used mainly as tactical trainers. They were retired from service once enough Su-22 had been delivered.

Manufacturer	Aircraft Type	Delivered	Number	Serial Numbers	Remarks
Hawker Siddley	Hunter F.Mk.52	1956	16	630 to 645	
Hawker Siddley	Hunter T.Mk.62	1960	1		ex-RAF

Lockheed F-80 Shooting Star (1958–1967)

The Peruvian government ordered four P-80C-10-LO Shooting Star fighter-bombers from Lockheed as early as 1949. These were built (c/n 49-3957 to 49-36000) but the contract was cancelled by the US government, as the USAF absorbed the jets for operations on the Korean Peninsula during 1951.

With the end of the Korean War the US government selected the F-80C as replacement for the region's P-47D Thunderbolt operators and offered over a hundred refurbished machines to several Latin America countries. They would be provided through the Mutual Defence Aid Pact (MDAP), and Peru was quick to take them into account.

The FAP sent a group of pilots to train on the type during March 1958 and took delivery of the first three F-80C Shooting Stars in June. Eventually 14 aircraft were delivered and they assigned serial numbers in the 660s range, joining two squadrons of P-47D Thunderbolts at Piura. The F-80s formed Escuadrón de Caza 13 (13 Fighter Squadron). In 1960 a re-organization of units moved the fleet to a new base. They were re-designated in the 100s range, including numbers 150 and 165. The type was retired in 1967.

Manufacturer	Aircraft Type	Delivered	Number	Serial Numbers	Remarks
Lockheed	F-80C Shooting Star	1958	14	660 to 673	ex-USAF

As usual the P-80 saw a short operational life. Peru received 14 aircraft and flew them just for nine years. Shown here are five P-80s from 13th Squadron sometime after 1960. (Beatriz López)

Dassault Mirage 5 (1968–2000)

Prompted by Argentina's acquisition of what was then regarded a modern fighter-bomber (the A-4B Skyhawk), the FAP announced its intentions of acquiring a squadron's worth of the brand new Northrop F-5A Freedom Fighter. The sale was not authorized and Peru re-evaluated its options.

Since collaboration with the RAF had been successful in the past, with the FAP acquiring the Hawker Hunter fighter as well as Canberra light bombers, the English Electric Lightning was also considered, however it was the French Mirage III/5 series that was eventually preferred and negotiations began in late 1966.

The Government of Peru signed a letter of intention to acquire a dozen Mirage 5 fighter-bombers in May 1967. This was formalized in what became known as Operation Martello, that saw an USD 28 million order for 10 single-seat Mirage 5Ps fighters and 2 two-seat Mirage 5DPs fighter-trainers in October 1967. A group of experienced Peruvian pilots were sent to France to begin their conversion training a few weeks later.

Delivery of the first pair of Mirages, an M5P and an M5DP began in July 1968. Upon delivery they were assembled by French and Peruvian technicians. The first group of aircraft were assigned the serial numbers 182 to 191 for the single-seat and the numbers 196 and 198 for the two-seat Mirages. These fighters formed the Escuadrón de Caza 611 (611th Fighter Squadron) at Chiclayo, becoming the first South American supersonic unit.

A second batch under project Martello II was delivered in 1974, and included five aircraft, composed of four single-seat M5P1s (serial numbers 192 to 195) and one two-seat Mirage 5DP1 (serial number 197) aircraft. A single-seat M5P from the original batch had crashed in early March 1971. This deal included options for s further seven Mirage 5P2 single-seat fighters (serial numbers 101 to 107) that allowed the formation of a second Mirage unit, the Escuadrón de Caza 612.

The Martello III contract was awarded in 1980 and comprised the last batch of Mirage 5 fighters produced for Peru. These comprised seven of the upgraded M5P3 versions (serial numbers 108 to 114) plus and a M5DP3 two-seat fighter trainer (serial number 199). The P3 version included new Cyrano-IV radar, Thomson-CSF HUD, Litton INS, CSR laser range finder, modern communications, additional avionics, and the ability to carry Magic II air-to-air missiles.

One of 10 Mirage 5Ps (183) before delivery in France in 1968. These Mirage formed South America's first supersonic unit.
(Dassault via Tom Cooper)

The FAP selected Dassault-Breguet to provide a comprehensive upgrade of the fleet in March 1982. An unknown number of early model aircraft were upgraded to M5P4/M5DP4 standard with new Agave radar, Exocet anti-ship and AS-30L laser-guided missile capability. The works were performed in Peru by SEMAN (Servicio de Mantenimiento, FAP's Maintenance Service).

Peru actively supported Argentina during the Falklands campaign and was the only Latin American country to provide significant military hardware. A group of ten former FAP Mirage 5Ps were transferred to the Fuerza Aérea Argentina on 14 June 1982. The known serial numbers (in numerical order) included FAP 103, 104, 105, 106, 107, (from the second batch) 183, 185, 196 (from the first batch), and possibly 195. The fighters were sold to Argentina who used them as replacement for war loses.

Re-delivery of the upgraded Mirage 5P4 models took place between 1983 and 1985 and some reports suggest that up to 14 aircraft were upgraded. Attrition of the Mirage fleet was high during the 1980s, with at least eight aircraft being written off, comprised of two in 1980, one in 1983 and, one more in 1985. A Mirage 5P4 (serial number 189) was lost on 10 March 1987, followed by another three by 1988, including a two-seat 5DP (number 196) on 18 May.

During the 1995 Condor War with Ecuador, some 14 Mirage 5s were still operational and these performed at least 12 attack missions on Ecuadorian positions. Information about their use is scarce and they were replaced by MiG-29s. The remaining fighters were concentrated in the 611th Fighter-Bomber Squadron alongside their new Russian mounts. Although at least five aircraft were grouped into a detachment and deployed to La Joya Air Base from 1998 to 2000, they were soon placed in reserve status in Las Palmas Air Base and offered for sale.

Manufacturer	Aircraft Type	Delivered	Number	Serial Numbers	Remarks
Dassault	Mirage 5P	1968	10	182 to 191	
Dassault	Mirage 5DP	1968	2	196 & 198	
Dassault	Mirage 5P1	1974	4	192 to 195	
Dassault	Mirage 5DP1	1974	1	197	
Dassault	Mirage 5P2	1976	7	101 to 107	
Dassault-Breguet	Mirage 5P3	1980	7	108 to 114	
Dassault-Breguet	Mirage 5DP3	1980	1	199	

Cessna A-37 Dragonfly (1975–)

A MAP contract for the supply of Cessna A-37B Dragonfly light attack and counter-insurgency jets were signed in 1974. Deliveries of the first of 24 aircraft started in 1975 and finished in 1976, under a project named Inca I, with the assigned serial numbers 115 to 131, as well as 133, 134, 136, 137, 139, 141, and 144. These aircraft formed two squadrons, one each with the 6th and 7th Aviation Groups.

A second contract (Inca II) made up of 12 aircraft built in 1975 started arriving a year later, with these taking serial numbers 145 to 156. The deliveries ended in March

As originally delivered, FAP A-37Bs wore a "desert" camouflage pattern - sand and dark earth. Following overhauls several years ago, the entire fleet was re-painted in two shades of green and grey. (Claudio Toselli Collection)

1977, allowing the creation of the 411th Fighter-Bomber Squadron of the 4th Aviation Group in charge of protecting the south of the country. They were replaced by Su-22s in 1980 and transferred to the 7th Aviation Group, where they formed a second squadron at Piura Air Base.

In the summer of 1986, both squadrons were used for the first time to attack a drug cartel's infrastructure. On 10 August, as part of Operation Condor III, A-37s bombed and strafed a dozen illegal airstrips used to supply cocaine paste. By 1992 the A-37B fleet had been reduced to 25 aircraft, not all of which were in flying condition so the FAP obtained a top-up batch of five A-37B Dragonflies from the USAF. These were older aircraft, built in the 1968–73 period.

In 1994 the Peruvian Air Force introduced a shoot-first, ask-questions-latter policy on illegal aircraft suspected of narcotic smuggling. The US provided radar coverage and direction through an US-operated surveillance plane that would vector-in Peruvian jets to perform the intercepts. Peruvian A-37s where selected to provide the bulk of Peruvian co-operation in anti-narcotic flights.

On 10 February 1995, a pair of A-37Bs from the 7th Fighter Group at Piura took off to attack an Ecuadorian Army outpost near Tiwinza. After dropping bombs on their target, they were intercepted by a pair of Ecuadorian Kfirs flying CAP. One of the Dragonflies was shot down by an AAM, with the pilots, Commander Valladares and Cap. Mendiola safely ejecting before the aircraft crashed into the jungle. The second aircraft, piloted by Commander Hoyos, managed to escape by flying low and stealthily over the jungle tree-tops.

In 1996 the FAP acquired via the USAF a fleet of 12 second-hand Dragonflies. These were obtained for a mere USD 1.2 million. They were easily to acquire as the remaining aircraft were being intensely used in anti-narcotic operations. When operating in this mission, the Sapito, as it is nick-named by its Peruvian crews, are armed only with their centreline machine-gun and with four long-range fuel tanks. Peruvian Sapitos are able to take fuel in flight from the FAP's Boeing 707 and from specially equipped Antonov An-32s (ASCC code Cline).

On 20 April 2001 during a joint US-Peruvian anti-narcotic operation, one A-37B shot at an unidentified light seaplane over the Amazon jungle. The Dragonfly was being directed by a US-operated Cessna 552 Citation II surveillance jet. The private aircraft turned out to be a Cessna 185 with a Baptist missionary family on board. The plane was forced down and two people on board, Veronica Bowers and her baby were killed while the pilot was injured. This turned out to be an embarrassing situation for the FAP and the US, who alleged that this was an area of heavy narcotic and guerrilla

In the first years A-37Bs served as fighter-bombers. From October 1986 onwards they were used in COIN role against drug cartels.
(Cesar Cruz)

activity and that the Cessna pilot did not comply with the radio communication or international-established instructions to land. The shoot down policy was suspended from then onwards.

In 2002, the FAP subjected 10 aircraft out of 30 survivors through a US funded USD 20 million upgrade program. The US Government offered a pair of former USAF OA-37Bs in 2002 for less than USD 250,000 but they have not seen to have been taken on charge. On 10 February 2004 one A-37B crashed during a training flight southeast of Piura Air Base, the crew escaped without harm.

During late 2007, international press reported Peruvian expressed interest in acquiring a number of A-37Bs from the Republic of Korea Air Force, which signals an intention to keep the Sapito in service for several years.

Manufacturer	Aircraft Type	Delivered	Number	Serial Numbers	Remarks
Cessna	A-37B Dragonfly	1975	24	115 to 131,133, 134, 136, 137, 139, 141, 144	Inca I
Cessna	A-37B Dragonfly	1976	12	145 to 156	Inca II
Cessna	OA-37B Dragonfly	1992	5		ex-USAF
Cessna	OA-37B Dragonfly	1996	12		ex-USAF

Sukhoi Su-22 (ASCC code Fitter) (1977–2006)

The FAP started a program to replace its remaining De Havilland Vampire and F-86F Sabre fighters in the early 1970's. The Northrop F-5E/F Tiger II was selected for this task, however, by 1974 relations between the US and Peru were at an all time low.

Peru ordered 32 Su-20MKs, which received local designation Su-22A.
(Chris Lofting)

After shopping around Europe without success the Peruvian delegation arrived in its last stop, the Soviet Union. The Soviets were keen to introduce their products to the region and offered either the MiG-21 or the Su-22. In 1975 the FAP ordered 32 Sukhoi Su-22A (ASCC code Fitter-F) variable-geometry fighter-bombers, as well as 4 two-seat Su-22U conversion trainers.

The USD 250 million contract included options on 18 additional aircraft, a full range of armament, training, and new-generation engines. Armament comprised the standard R-13 (AA-2-2 Advanced Atoll) AAMs, S-24 240-mm and S-5 57-mm rockets, FAB 250-kg and 500-kg GP bombs, BETAB anti-runway bombs, OFAB fragmentation bombs, RBK cluster bombs, ZAB incendiary bombs, and 23-mm UPK-23 gun pods. Training of Peruvian pilots started in 1977 at the Krasnodar Military Institute, in the USSR. Peru had selected the more powerful Tumansky R-29BS-300, the same engine used on the MiG-27 for its export-model Su-17. The Sukhois arrived by ship in June 1977 and sent to Capt. Victor Montes at El Pato Air Base in Talara, where Soviet technicians assembled the aircraft. They also trained the 116th Maintenance Squadron, which was put in charge of servicing these new machines. They were assigned the serial numbers 001 to 026 and 157 to 166. The Su-22As started operations as early as July that year, forming the 111th Squadron. Training was so fast, that the first joint exercise with Army and Navy units – Operation Impala – was held in 1978.

Although there are several reports that Cuba provided a dozen MiG-21Fs to be used as 'eastern bloc' familiarization training for Peruvian ground crews and pilots, this has been a myth. Peruvian pilots were reportedly flown to Cuba, and some even flew in the backseat of MiG-21Us, but no MiG-21 was ever deployed from Cuba on any kind of loan or lease agreement.

Even though the FAP complained about the Su-22's 'primitive' nature (lacking basic avionics, navigation aids, the useless Sirena-2 RWR and an IFF which was not compatible with SA-3 Goa SAMs), Peru exercised its options for these aircraft in 1978. The new order was for the more advanced Su-22M-3Ks (locally designated Su-22M-2Ds) (ASCC code Fitter-J), that had a redesigned cockpit, increased internal fuel capacity, additional pylons and more room for avionics. The two-seat version, Su-22UM-2 (ASCC code Fitter-G) has a totally different cockpit arrangement.

Delivery of 16 Su-22Ms and 3 Su-22UMs started in May 1980 to La Joya Air Base, in the southern part of the country, replacing A-37Bs in the 411th Squadron. This directly threatened Chilean air defence assets. These aircraft had a dual air and ground offensive and defensive roles. A Su-22M replaced Su-22A serial number 164 lost before 1980.

Locally designated Su-22M-2D, Su-22M-3K proved to be a much more potent asset in FAP service.
(Chris Lofting)

However, this allowed the retirement of the elder Hawker Hunters, at a time when the FAP's southern adversary, the FACH was fielding the type.

The first operational use of Peruvian Sukhois occurred on 28 January 1981, when they were used to attack an Ecuadorian Army outpost during the Paquisha conflict. The FAP mounted 107 combat sorties, including bombing runs on Ecuadorian targets. The conflict ended on January 31 and it did not produce any air battles.

A major upgrade for the 'primitive' Su-22A fleet started in 1984. This included US avionics, a laser rangefinder, and modifications to carry the French Magic air-to-air missile. A French FR probe was also installed at a later date to extend the bomber's range.

The Su-22s of the 411th were joined by Mirage 2000P fighters that formed the 412th Squadron in 1986, releasing the Su-22Ms to focus on interdiction missions and leave the air defence role to its new French stable mates.

On 24 April 1992 a USAF C-130H belonging to the 310th Airlift Squadron was conducting a photographic reconnaissance mission as part of Operation Furtive Bear, a US counter-drug operation to secretly photograph cocaine labs and airstrips in Peru's Upper Huallaga region. Two Su-22s from the 111th Squadron were sent to identify and intercept. The Sukhois opened fire after the Hercules refused to cooperate, killing 2 and wounding 4 of its 14 man crew. The repercussions were immediate, and the US froze an USD 100 million economic aid package until the FAP had paid appropriate restitution to the victim's families.

By 1993 the 411th Squadron based in La Joya was dissolved and the remaining 12 Su-22Ms were transferred to the 111th Squadron at Talara. Both air defence and strike roles were absorbed by the remaining Mirage 2000P Squadron.

The 111th Squadron was one of the first units to be pressed into action once hostilities with Ecuador turned into the 'Condor War' in January 1995. Only 7 Su-22s were still in service by late January however, the 116th Maintenance Squadron quickly put 12 Su-22M-3Ks, 4 Su-22UM-3Ks and 4 Su-22MKs in operational condition. On 10 February 1995 an attack group of 16 aircraft was directed against several Ecuadorian positions. A flight of two Su-22s and three A-37Bs was directed towards Tiwiza. They bombed their target with FAB-500 bombs, but were intercepted on their return flight by four Ecuadorian Mirage F-1 and Kfir interceptors. The Mirages went after the Sukhois and downed both aircraft (serial numbers 014 and 108).

After the Condor War, the FAP introduced a series of improvements to its combat fleet and the entire Su-22 force was subject to a 'navigation' enhancement (with new GPS), a 'self-defence' upgrade that included a new RWR (under project Cuervo), and

chaff/flare dispensers (project Luciernaga). They were also wired to fire the R-60M/MK (AA-8 Aphid) air-air missiles.

On 19 June 2001 a Su-22UM crashed some 30-km northwest of Talara, while on a training mission with three other Su-22s, killing both its crewmen. The final accident of a Su-22 occurred in mid-2006. By this time there were a dozen Su-22s in strength and they were finally de-activated during late 2006.

Manufacturer	Aircraft Type	Delivered	Number	Serial Numbers	Remarks
Sukhoi	Su-22A	1977	32	001 to 026, 157 to 166	
Sukhoi	Su-22U	1977	4		
Sukhoi	Su-22M2D	1980	16	167 to 181	
Sukhoi	Su-22UM2	1980	3	027 to 029	

Aermacchi MB-339 (1981–)

With a growing fleet of modern jet fighters, the need for an advanced jet trainer that could replace the ageing T-37 Tweet, provide advanced and lead-in fighter training as well as close air support functions (replacing the A-37B) developed into a requirement for up to 80 aircraft.

Negotiations with Aermacchi in 1980 led to a contract for the supply of 14 MB-339AP and license production of another 66 aircraft. The aircraft were to be built at a new IndAer factory to be established with Aermacchi's help. Deliveries were to spread from 1983 to 1989.

The first batch of Italian built MB-339APs were delivered from 1981 to 1983 and formed the Escuadrón 513 (513 Squadron) at the Academia del Aire (Air Academy) at the Las Palmas Air Base. The license production agreement was cancelled and these were the only MB-339s acquired by the FAP.

Two aircraft were lost over Paracas, while performing an aerobatic stunt on 7 January 1985.

By the early 21st Century, most of the fleet was in long term storage. The need to fill an air defence gap in the northern border with Chile led the FAP to relocate its MB-339AP lead-in-fighter trainers to La Joya Air Base, reactivating the 411th Fighter Squadron as a part of the 4th Air Group. In 2006 the FAP earmarked eight aircraft for

Beside its trainer role the MB-339 (480) is used in COIN role. (Hans Rolink)

One of the MB-339s in livery of the Air Academy. Nevertheless it is armed with a gun pod and unguided rocket pod. (Santiago Rivas)

an extensive overhaul which brought them back to life. They received a new glass cockpit which included three LCDs and new avionics. Up to ten aircraft were eventually brought back into service.

Manufacturer	Aircraft Type	Delivered	Number	Serial Numbers	Remarks
Aermacchi	MB-339AP	1981	14	452, 456, 467, 468, 473, 477, 479-482, 484-488, 495, 496	

Dassault-Breguet Mirage 2000 (1986–)

In the early 1980s, the Peruvian High Command started inquiries in order to launch a major modernization program that would re-equip at least three squadrons of high-performance fighters. The General Dynamics F-16 was one of the favouritesbut US policy prevented the sale of this modern fighter. The US offered Northrop F-5 tactical fighters instead. Remaining options included the Mikoyan-Gurevich MiG-23MF and the Dassault Mirage 2000. The Mirage 2000 was selected as the country's first fly-by-wire fighter. Negotiations called for a first batch of 12 fighters to be followed by another 14, with an option for a third batch of 10 additional aircraft.

Price negotiations did not go swiftly, the price of the aircraft going up to USD 38 million apiece and the order was cut back to ten single-seat Mirage 2000Es and two

Mirage 2000P with French made BAT-runway piercing bombs role and captive R.550 missile for self-defence. (Chris Lofting)

Mirage 2000DP (193) during an
exercise with USAF
(Cesar Cruz)

twin-seat Mirage 2000Bs. They were designated as 2000P and 2000DP respectively.
The Mirage 2000's capabilities were not fully exploited, as there was no AS-30L laser-
guided missiles nor Super-530 medium-range air-to-air missiles were acquired. Still,
they armed with Magic 2 AAM where more powerful than any aircraft flying in Chile
or Ecuador.

A group of four experienced pilots were sent to France for conversion training
on the type. These pilots returned in late 1986 as instructors with their new mounts
to form the 412th Fighter Squadron 'Los Halcones'. The Mirage 2000Ps were initially
tasked with air defence, ignoring their multi-role capability, and complementing the
strike-oriented Su-22Ms of its sister unit 411th Squadron.

In 1991 the FAP updated its training syllabus and started to send its Mirage 2000
fighter pilots to Mont-de-Marsan to receive advanced training on the Mirage 2000 simulator. Multi-role training on the type started soon after, in anticipation to the 411th
Squadron being disbanded.

They were kept on high alert during the 1995 Condor War. Although several sources
state they were deployed and performed CAP missions, 'chasing' away Ecuadorian
fighters from the area of operations, there is no evidence or facts to back these rumours. The Mirage 2000 was kept back as a strategic reserve. Being the country's most
expensive fighters meant that their use was limited to actual emergencies.

Since the arrival of the MiG-29 fleet in the late 1990s, the Halcones focused more
and more into strike role. The Halcones started to train against MiG-29s with both types
gaining considerable DACT experience. The Mirage 2000s were submitted to a combat
enhancement program, including ATLIS II designator pods, Lizzard LGBs, AS-30L laser-
guided missiles, FR probes and an Intertechnique 231-300 buddy-refuelling system. This
would allow them to perform interdiction missions deep into Chilean and/or Ecuadorian territory. During the 2009 Paris Air Show, Dassault and the Peruvian Ministry of
Defence announced an USD 140 million upgrade of the Peruvian Mirage 2000 fleet.

Manufacturer	Aircraft Type	Delivered	Number	Serial Numbers	Remarks
Dassault	Mirage 2000P	1986	10	050 to 054, 060 to 064	
Dassault	Mirage 2000DP	1986	2	193 & 195	

Mikoyan i Gurevich MiG-29 (ASCC code Fulcrum) (1996–)

Ecuadorian air superiority during the 1995 Condor War proved to be a real threat for the FAP. The subsequent 'Emergency Re-armament Plan 1995–2000' called for the acquisition of at least a fighter squadron that could out manoeuvre and outshoot anything in Ecuadorian or Chilean skies. Clearly F-16s were out of the question for political reasons, and buying new Mirage 2000-5s proved to be prohibiting expensive.

Pleased with the performance of Eastern Bloc aircraft, Peru began negotiations with Belarus, who had inherited over 80 MiG-29 fighters from the former Soviet Empire. The Peruvian requirement was that the second hand aircraft have at least 70 per cent of their service life left and not require major overhaul at least until 2000.

The FAP ordered 16 single-seat MiG-29 and 2 two-seat MiG-29UB fighters through a USD 252 million contract signed in April 1996. The single-seat fighters were Soviet Air Force-standard 9.13 versions. Belarus only had one operational MiG-29UB, so it acquired a stored MiG from Russia to complete the order. In June 1996 a Japanese freighter delivered crates with the engines and related equipment, while the fuselages were delivered by a Belarus An-124 transport. Close to 80 technicians from former East-bloc countries were hired to put the MiG-29s into service. The contract also included R-60 (AA-8 Aphid), R-27R-1 (AA-10 Alamo), and R-73E (AA-11 Archer) missiles, the S-8 and S-24 unguided rockets and a wide variety of bombs. Although assembled at La Joya Air Base, the MiG-29s formed the 612th Fighter Squadron at Chiclayo, replacing the old Mirage 5Ps from the 611th Squadron in the air defence role. The 606th Maintenance Squadron was trained in Belarus to service the MiG-29s, but the contract did not include a post-sale support package and spare parts began to be a problem.

The 612th Squadron was declared operational in November 1997 and suffered its first accident on 2 December, when one aircraft crashed over the Naylamp Valley, some 70 km from its base. In order to replace the lost MiG and to obtain a direct-support package, the FAP signed a USD 117 million contract with RSK MiG in July 1998.

MiG-29S (045) with captive R-27 & R-73 missiles (Cesar Cruz)

205

MiG-29SE (041) with OFAB-250
and RBK-250 at Chiclayo AB. In
early 2007 a rare view.
(Edurado Cardenas)

The contract provided three brand new MiG-29SE aircraft, spares for the entire fleet, and the R-77 (AA-12 Adder) medium range air to air missile. Three of the original MiGs were also wired to fire the R-77. The delivery of the missiles was delayed for political reasons, although at least a dozen were delivered as early as January 1999.

On 13 March 2001 another MiG-29S crashed into a rice-field, while it was being tested for obsolescence. An inquiry report indicated that the 1988-built MiG-29S fleet had been acquired with very low flying hours remaining. They had served with the Group of Soviet Forces Germany and the Southern Group of Forces in Hungary. This generated a USD 48 million international scandal that involved Belarus government officials, former President Fujimori and his Intelligence Chief, Vladimiro Montesinos.

In September 2001 David Waissman, Peru's Defence Minister, announced that it had taken delivery of R-77 medium range air-to-air missiles, although he did not disclosed how many had been acquired. At least 12 missiles were bought with up to 30 probably delivered eventually. When Chile selected the F-16C Fighting Falcon, the FAP announced that it would need six more MiG-29s, armed with R-77 medium range missiles; whether this meant modifying the original Byelorussian fighters or buying new MiGs was not specified.

During 2005 the Russian government offered a USD 200 million modernization package that included a mid-life update and R-77 capability all around. The upgrade would include 'the works' (new N010 radars, avionics, RWR, TVC engines, FR probes, etc.). According to a source close to the FAP, there were only four MiG-29s in operational condition by early 2006.

Manufacturer	Aircraft Type	Delivered	Number	Serial Numbers	Remarks
MiG	MiG-29S	1996	16	030 to 045	ex-Belarus AF
MiG	MiG-29UB	1996	2	046 & 047	ex-Belarus AF
MiG	MiG-29SE	1999	3	048, 049, 055	

Sukhoi Su-25 (ASCC code Frogfoot) (1998–)

In the aftermath of the Condor War, the FAP 'Emergency Re-armament Plan 1995-2000', elected the Su-24 (ASSC code Fencer) to replace the older English Electric Canberra bombers of Grupo Aereo 9 flying from Pisco. Such an acquisition was considered alarmingly de-stabilising for the region, and would have plunged it into an expensive and unnecessary arms race.

A re-evaluation of its attack needs brought the Su-25 into the picture. Peruvian fighter and attack aircraft suffered heavily from Ecuadorian air defence systems, and the FAP needed an aircraft that could take a large amount of punishment and still be able to provide close air support to ground forces. The link with Belarus was already in place and the FAP ordered 18 second-hand Su-25s during 1997. The deal was linked a few years aft with a huge fraud scandal that involved the MiG-29s, former President Fujimori, his Chief Intelligence Officer, the Belarus Government and millions of dollars.

Delivery of the ten single-seat Su-25K (serial numbers 070 to 079) and eight two-seat Su-25UBK (numbers 080 to 087) subsonic attack-fighters started in 1998 to the 112th Squadron, at Talara. They joined the 111th Squadron's Su-22s at the same base, releasing them for pure interdiction duties. For political reasons, the Su-25s were introduced as 'anti-narcotic' aircraft! There was an immediate response from Ecuador, who strengthened its air defences.

The 'K' designation (Kommyerzyeskij, Commercial) is a mere marketing designation, as Belarus had inherited some 85 Soviet-standard Su-25s from the USSR. About half of them were in service with the 206th Air Assault Regiment and the rest were up for sale. They were delivered with a large cache of weapons that included R-60MK air-air missiles, SPU-22 30-mm gun pods, a wide variety of un-guided rockets and guided ASMs.

The Tigers began to work up on the Su-25s in January 1999, with IOC obtained by early 2000 and the 112th Squadron was declared operational in June. On 1 June, one Su-25 shot down a light aircraft north of Lima during an anti-narcotic operation. All

All 18 Su-25s were officially assigned to anti-narcotics role, although delivered weapons would allow a pure interdiction role.
(Cesar Cruz)

the Sukhoi fighter-bombers were assigned the anti-narcotic role as they are perfectly suited to intercept and chase single and twin-engine light aircraft.

Manufacturer	Aircraft Type	Delivered	Number	Serial Numbers	Remarks
Sukhoi	Su-25K	1998	10	070 to 079	ex-Belarus AF
Sukhoi	Su-25UBK	1998	8	080 to 087	ex-Belarus AF

In 2008 the fleet of Su-25 received a new two-tone grey colour scheme. (Eduardo Cardenas)

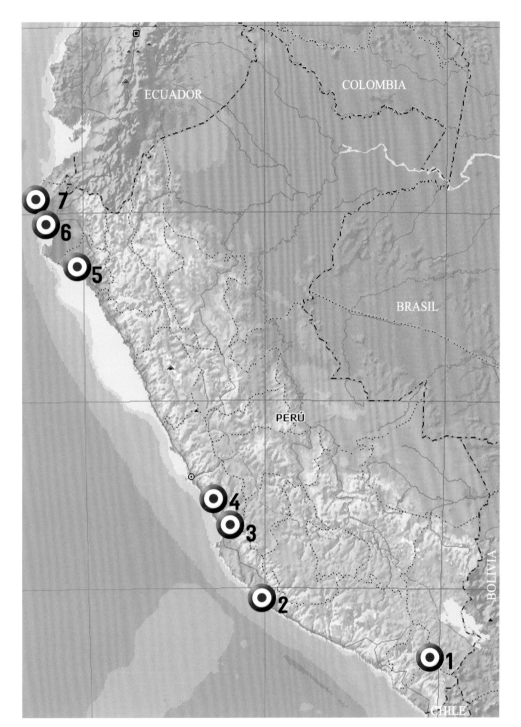

1. Coronel FAP Víctor Maldonado Begazo Air Base, La Joya
2. Capitan FAP Renán Elias Oliveira, Pisco
3. Las Palmas Air Base, Santiago de Surco
4. Jorge Chavez IAP, Lima-Callao (Limatambo Air Base)
5. Capitán FAP José Abelardo Quiñonez Gonzalez Air Base, Chiclayo
6. Capitán FAP Guillermo Concha Ibérico Air Base, Piura
7. El Pato Air Base, Talara

Chapter 16

URUGUAY

Sandwiched between two regional powers, Argentina and Brazil, the Uruguayan military have been small but effective defensive service.

The United States has been a major influence in the country's airpower since it established a U.S. Air Force mission in December 1951. The first jets arrived in the mid-1950s, as Korean War surplus equipment, they formed the main component of a fighter group. The T-33/F-80 combo formed the mainstay of Uruguayan airpower up until the mid-1970s. Several top-up batches were received from the US via Military Aid Programmes during this time.

Efforts to acquire a squadron of US-built Argentine fighters suffered under US pressure, even though a group of Uruguayan pilots received training on the type. The US eventually offered a number of new built COIN examples and these remain the sole jet equipment in service with the FAU to date.

Lockheed T-33 (1956–1997)

The recently created Fuerza Aérea Uruguaya (FAU, Uruguayan Air Force) entered the jet age on 23 October 1956, when four Lockheed T-33A-1-LO armed trainers arrived at Carrasco Air Base. The factory-fresh jet trainers, displaying Uruguayan serial numbers 201 to 204, complemented North American P-51D Mustangs that had been in service with the Grupo de Aviación No.2 Caza (2nd Fighter Air Group) from 1951. Their previous USAF (transfer) identities were serial numbers 55-4441 to 55-4444.

Lockheed's P-80 and T-33 have been a typical ramp line up of Latin American air forces from the 1950s onwards. FAU was no exception to the rule: one P-80 (218) and three T-33s (203, 202 & 201) at Carrasco AP in 1986. (Eduardo Luzardo)

FAU T-33 (204) in the standard silver overall paint scheme off the Uruguayan coast. In the very early years it was even used in air defence role!
(Eduardo Luzaro)

T-33s formed the Escuadrilla de Transición y Entrenamiento (Transition and Training Flight), in charge of converting the first group of former Mustang pilots into jet fighter pilots. Once enough pilots were in place, the T-33s took over the air defence role and the Mustangs were transferred to the Grupo de Aviación No.1 Ataque (1st Attack Air Group).

In order to augment its fleet, a pair of former USAF T-33A-1-LOs (serial numbers) 53-5860 and 52-9521) arrived in early 1964, and assigned serial numbers 205 and 206 respectively.

In 1969 another pair of T-33s joined the FAU. These comprised two of the T-33-1-LOs that had been upgraded to AT-33A-20-LO standard (numbers 53-4919 and 53-4928). They had served with the Dominican Republic from 1967, but had been re-assigned by the US Mutual Defence Assistance Program (MDAP) to Uruguay after strained diplomatic relations ended their Dominican career. The 'exiled' T-33s received serial numbers 207 and 208. MDAP delivered another pair (numbers 53-5344 and 53-5422) of T-33A-20-LO which arrived in 1970. These two aircraft had assigned serial numbers 209 and 210, but they never flew, instead were used as a source of spares parts.

AT-33 207 has been one of the few survivors when FAU retired its T-33s after 41 years.
(AAMA via Eduardo Luzardo)

In 1971 an aerobatic display team, named 'Cocodrilos' (Crocodiles), was organized with aircraft serialled 201, 204, 207, and 208. On 17 December 1971, 204 was lost when it crashed near Carrasco Air Base, and was followed by 206 which crashed during 1972. The last air display of the Cocodrilos was during 1976, over Durazno Air Base.

The T-33 fleet remained in operation throughout the 1980s. In 1989 the FAU acquired a batch of five former USAF aircraft comprising two T-33A-1-LOs and three T-33A-5-LOs for USD 900,000. Three aircraft (serial numbers 57-707, 52-9667, and 53-5959) were put in operational conditions, comprising two of the –5-LOs and one –1-LOs. They were designated the serial numbers 209 to 211, while the remaining two aircraft were designated numbers 212 and 213. These last two aircraft were used as a spare parts source. This delivery would allow the retirement of number 205 during 1990. The last six T-33s (serial numbers 203, 207, 208, 209, 210, and 211) stopped flying in 1994 and were officially retired in 1997.

Manufacturer	Aircraft Type	Delivered	Number	Serial Numbers	Remarks
Lockheed	T-33A-1-LO	1956	4	201 to 204	
Lockheed	T-33A-5-LO	1964	1	205	ex-USAF
Lockheed	T-33A-20-LO	1964	1	206	ex-USAF
Lockheed	AT-33A	1969	2	207 & 208	
Lockheed	AT-33A	1970	2	209 & 210	ex-USAF
Lockheed	T-33A-5-LO	1989	2	213	one used as spares
Lockheed	T-33A-20-LO	1989	3	211 & 212	one used as spares

Lockheed F-80 Shooting Star (1958–1971)

Uruguay was one of the many Latin American countries that took up an offer from United States for F-80 Shooting Star fighter bombers in the late 1950s. The first former USAF F-80C-10-LOs arrived in August 1958, equipping the Grupo de Aviación No.2 (Caza) [Aviation Group 2 (Fighter)] Uruguayan Mustang pilots received F-80 conversion training by USAF personnel in Carrasco. The 14 aircraft were Korean War veterans and received serial numbers 210 to 223. The first write-off occurred that same year, when number 215 crashed.

As in most Latin American air forces, the Korean War veteran P-80 replaced the P-51 Mustangs.
(Eduardo Luzardo)

FAU's first jet fighter: a Lockheed P-80. (Eduardo Luzardo)

The Grupo's first base was the military side of Carrasco Airport, the only airfield in the country capable of handling jet aircraft. Once they obtained their initial operational capability (IOC) in 1960, they replaced the surviving P-51D Mustang piston-engine fighters, which had been relegated to attack functions since 1956. Once the runway at Base Aerotáctica 1 'Capitán Boiso Lanza' at Paso de Mendoza had been lengthened, the unit began deploying aircraft there.

On 28 February 1963, a pair of F-80s (numbers 214 and 222) suffered a mid-air collision and both aircraft were lost. The remaining 11 aircraft soldiered on until 1969, when they began to be withdrawn from active service. They were some of the last surviving F-80C Shooting Stars in operational service.

The FAU had selected the North American F-86F Sabre jet fighter to replace its Shooting Stars, and started negotiations with Argentina to buy a dozen second hand examples. However, the U.S. vetoed the sale in 1976 and offered new A-37B Dragonflies. Most of the aircraft were retired by 1971, although some reports indicate that at least two aircraft were kept in service until replaced by A-37B Dragonflies in 1976.

Manufacturer	Aircraft Type	Delivered	Number	Serial Numbers	Remarks
Lockheed	F-80C Shooting Star	1958	14	210 to 223	ex-USAF

Cessna A-37B Dragonfly (1976–?)

Although the FAU's original plans called for a squadron of former Argentine Air Force F-86F-30 Sabre jet fighters to replace its elder F-80s, the United States' policy at the time prevented the deal. This policy was directing Latin American air forces towards a COIN role, in an effort to drive them away from any type of inter-American confrontation. At the time, the main COIN aircraft being supplied to Latin American air forces was the A-37B Dragonfly, and Uruguay soon joined the Dragonfly club.

The first batch of eight aircraft was delivered to Carrasco International Air Port (IAP), near Montevideo, on 31 October 1976, and they joined the old T-33As in the Grupo de Aviación No.2 (caza) (No.2 Aviation Group –Fighter-). The Dragonflies received serial numbers 270 to 277 (USAF serial numbers had been 75-410 to 417) and were christened as 'Alfas' in local FAU jargon.

A good view from above on a OA-37B. FAU modified them to carry up to six 375 litres auxiliary fuel tanks.
(Cees-Jan van der Ende/alfakilo.nl)

In 1980 the Alfa unit was transferred from Carrasco IAP to its new base, Teniente Segundo Mario W. Parallada Military Airfield at Santa Bernardina, Durazno. The first accident claimed two aircraft, serial numbers 271 and 272, which crashed into a mountain range during a night training flight on 6 October 1983. During the next four years, the FAU was restricted to six Alfas.

On 7 September 1987, the FAU lost another pair of Alfas, when serial numbers 270 and 276 crashed. This limited the fleet to four aircraft, with only two operational at any time. A 1987 order for two attrition replacements brought two former USAF OA-37Bs to the Alfa squadron. They were delivered on 17 January 1988 and were allocated serial numbers 278 and 279.

One of FAU's OA-37B (273) with 2 underwing fuel tanks and 1 unguided rocket pod on each side.
(Cees-Jan van der Ende/alfakilo.nl)

A programme to replace the attack jets with the more powerful Northrop F-5E Tiger II was scrapped on financial reasons and in 1989 additional OA-37Bs were made available by the USAF. The FAU obtained half a dozen second hand Alfas. They were assigned the serial numbers 280 to 285.

Uruguayan Alfas have been modified by FAU technicians to carry six 375 litres auxiliary fuel tanks. They were used for a variety of mission, including air superiority, counter-air (offensive and defensive), surface attack, close air support, and maritime patrol. These last two missions are constantly exercised with army and navy units respectively. Reconnaissance is another role, and one aircraft is equipped with an indigenous reconnaissance pod. This pod consists of a modified T-33 travel pack with photo and video cameras.

On 31 January 2003 Alfa number 283 piloted by Colonel Heber Tome and Captain Gustavo Varela crashed after an electrical failure.

By 2009 there were ten Alfas operational with the Escuadrón Aereo No.2 (caza). This was the only jet powered combat aircraft in the FAU's inventory, alongside turboprop powered IA-58 Pucarás of the Escuadrón Aéreo No.1 and AT-92s (PC-7Us) of the Escuadrón de Vuelo Avanzado, all three units at Durazno. Although the Alfas went through a slight modification that included the installation of GPS, they are in dire need for an avionics upgrade.

Manufacturer	Aircraft Type	Delivered	Number	Serial Numbers	Remarks
Cessna	A-37B Dragonfly	1976	6	270 to 276	
Cessna	OA-37B Dragonfly	1988	2	278 & 279	ex-USAF
Cessna	OA-37B Dragonfly	1989	6	280 to 285	ex-USAF

One of FAU's OA-37s (280) participated in October 2008 at multinational exercise CRUCEX IV.
(Johnson Barros)

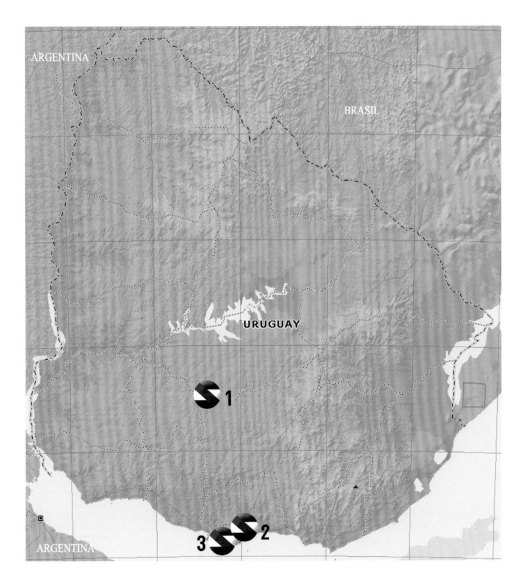

1. Base Aérea Teniente. 2do. Mario W. Parrallada, Santa Bernardina, Durazno
2. Aerodomo General Artigas, Pando
3. General Cesareo L. Berisso International Airport, Carrasco

Chapter 17

VENEZUELA

With a growing oil-based economy, the Venezuelan armed forces started a process of expansion and modernization in the early 1950s. As several Latin American nations of that time did, the United Kingdom became its main source for modern military aircraft. The Fuerza Aérea Venezolana (FAV, Venezuelan Air Force) bought an entire generation of aircraft to create fighter, fighter-bomber, trainer, and bomber squadrons. These units were in service by the mid-1950s and were soon followed by US-built jets.

British-built bombers remained at the forefront of Venezuelan striking capabilities through the 1960s, while the defensive arm of the FAV obtained enough funds to replace most of its older aircraft with second-hand, US-built interceptors obtained from West Germany. Venezuela was also the second country in Latin America (after Argentina) to include jets in its training syllabus.

As in most of the region, the need for supersonic fighters was fulfilled by France with the popular Mirage series. The Canadian-built CF-5 Freedom Fighter proved to be a good addition to the air force, with US companies strongly objecting the sale, arguing that the Venezuelan market was their turf. However, US policy at the time denied the sale of modern jet fighters to Latin America and limited it to COIN-oriented aircraft. The extremely popular A-37 attack jet, strangely, did not find its way into FAV squadrons.

With a growing communist presence in Central America and the Caribbean during the early 1980s, the Reagan administration finally agreed to sell two squadrons of modern F-16 fighters to equip the FAV. Venezuela wanted at least four and as much as six squadrons. Further requirements for modern ground attack fighters to replace the ageing Canberra light bombers as well as modern jet trainers failed to materialize.

In the early 1980s, the Venezuelan Navy set a requirement for a squadron of jet fighters to be used primarily in the anti-ship attack role. Attempts to acquire a small fleet of 8 to 12 Spanish designed light fighters from the Chilean assembly line, armed with anti-ship missiles, failed due to internal politics, with the air force pledging to provide a solution. The requirement was vaguely met by the upgrade of the Mirage fleet with an Exocet anti-ship missile capability. The upgraded Mirage squadron was assigned to provide the naval fleet with anti-air and anti-ship support, thus ending the Navy's quest to join the jet fighter club.

Venezuelan fighter jet acquisitions resumed in the early 1990s, with the air force taking additional Mirages and Freedom Fighters from France and the Netherlands respectively, however, these served mainly as attrition replacements.

In the early 21st Century several requirements remained outstanding, for new tactical trainers to multi-role fighters. Venezuela announced several selections to meet its

From mid to late 1950s onwards FAV operated two De Havilland Vampires T.Mk.55 out of El Liberator Air Base. See here T.Mk.55 (IE35) with several Vampires FB.Mk.52 in the background.
(via AMAA)

Their usual armament fix comprised up to eight unguided rockets and two 227 kg bombs. The 35th Fighter Squadron and its Vamps moved to the new Palo Negro Air Base in 1953. Some of the new Vampires formed the first jet aerobatic demonstration team: 'Panteras del 35' (Panthers of the 35th). In September 1957 the FAV ordered a further six Vampires, together with a fresh order for the enhanced Venoms. These were two-seat D.H. 150 T.Mk.11 trainer versions, designated T.Mk.55 for export. They were delivered in 1959 and assigned the serial numbers 1E35 to 6E35. 'E' identified them for 'Entrenamiento' (Training). There are reports of at least two two-seat Vampires operating in Venezuela as early as 1955.

In 1961 a major re-organization of the entire FAV brought all the jet fighter squadrons under No.12 Group, headquartered in Barquisimento, but the 35th Fighter Squadron moved to Generalisimo Francisco de Miranda Air Base at La Carlota. They applied a new serial number, the T.Mk.55s was designated 0023.

The Vampire fighter-bombers started to be retired from front-line service as soon as the former West German F-86Ks began to take their place in 1967-68. The last Vampire FB.52 was retired in 1973, while the last T.55 was kept in service as a transition trainer until 1981.

Manufacturer	Aircraft Type	Delivered	Number	Serial Numbers	Remarks
De Havilland	Vampire FB.Mk.52	1949	24	1A35 to 8A35, 1B35 to 8B35, 1C35 to 8C35	
De Havilland	Vampire T.Mk.55	1959	6	1E35 to 6E35	ex-RAF

The same T.Mk.55 (IE35), but now retired and exhibited at Museo Aeronautico de la Fuerza Aerea Venezolana.
(Steve Homewood)

De Havilland Venom (1955–1973)

As part of a major oil-funded re-equipment programme, the FAV acquired a total of 44 new jet fighters in 1955. This order included 22 Venom F.Mk.54 fighter-bombers from the De Havilland production line. The aircraft was an improved export version of the Venom FB.Mk.1, itself a development from the earlier Vampire series, featuring ejection seats (which the earlier Venezuelan Vampires lacked) and a new tail unit.

Venoms were acquired via CIRCA (Corporación Internacional de Representaciones C.A.), a private company that represented De Havilland in Caracas. The contract was worth BPD1.6 million and included eight spare engines, airframe spares, and ground equipment. The Venoms formed flights A, B and C of the new 34th Fighter Squadron 'Indios', and designated serial numbers accordingly to the flights: 1A34 to 7A34, 1B34 to 7B34, and 1C34 to 8C34. The squadron was established at El Libertador Air Base near Palo Negro.

On 1 January 1958, the Venoms of 34th Squadron were activated as part of an FAV-inspired uprising against then (Dictator) President General Marcos Pérez Jimenez. Air force officers had been quite alienated by the President's clear preference towards the Army. Two Venoms made several passes over Caracas that morning, while a second flight of three aircraft did the same in the early afternoon. Loyal (to Perez) AAA managed to damage at least one of the rebel Venoms. The FAV actions soon gave way to several other military units in joining the anti-Perez rebellion. Perez fled the country on 23 January.

In 1961 a major re-organization of the entire FAV brought all the jet fighter squadrons under No.12 Group, headquartered in Barquisimento. It also brought a new serial number system that included random numbers used to this day. Known Venom serial numbers included 0099, 0325, 5232, 7090, 7125, 8331, and 9418. The Venoms were replaced by supersonic Mirages in 1973.

FAV's first jet fighter, a D.H. Venom FB.Mk.54, was possible due oil revenues, much to contrary to other Latin American countries. (via Mario Martinez)

Manufacturer	Aircraft Type	Delivered	Number	Serial Numbers	Remarks
De Havilland	Venom FB.Mk.54	1955	22	1A34 to 7A34, 1B34 to 7B34, 1C34 to 8C34	

North American F-86 Sabre (1956–1976)

The FAV ordered 22 F-86F-30 Sabre fighters during 1955 in an effort to augment its combat capability. They were part of a modernization and expansion programme that envisioned the acquisition of more jet fighters from a variety of sources. First deliveries started in 1956, replacing the old P-47D Thunderbolts in the Escuadrón de Caza 36 (36th Fighter Squadron) Los Diablos, which was then re-named Jaguares.

The 36th Squadron was also divided into three flights: A, B, and C. The aircraft were assigned a serial number depending of the flight it belonged to; examples being 1A36, which identified it as the #1 aircraft, 'A' flight, 36th Squadron and 3B36, being the #3 aircraft of 'B' flight, 36th Squadron. The 3B36 was written off in June 1957, just months after delivery.

The aircraft were armed with 227 kg and 450 kg bombs as well as HVAR rockets. Problems immediately emerged with the service and maintenance of the AN/APG-30 radar. Four of the Sabres were used alongside Venoms by rebel forces in a coup attempt against General Marcos Pérez Jimenez on 1 January 1958. They attacked the Presidential Palace with machine gun fire.

In 1961 a major re-organization of the entire FAV brought all the jet fighter squadrons under No.12 Group, headquartered in Barquisimento, with the 36th Fighter squadron based at El Libertador in Palo Negro. The squadron operated at El Libertador until 1969, when it was transferred to the new Teniente Vicente Landeta Gil Air Base near Barquisimento. During 1974, the serial numbers 0900 and 3335 were destroyed in accidents.

The growing presence of Cuban MiGs in the mid-1960s over Caribbean waters led the Venezuelan government to strengthen its air defences. Project Ventura included positioning new early warning radars in the Paraguaná Peninsula and expand the jet fighter force. The FAV selected the radar-equipped F-86K fighter, several aircraft became available as they were surplus by the West German Luftwaffe starting in 1965. The USD 11 million order included 78 second hand Fiat-built Sabres. Deliveries were not problem-free, as four aircraft were impounded in Curaçao. Only 51 F-86K Sabres were eventually placed in operation. Some reports indicate only 30 aircraft were available at any one time.

The F-86K Sabres replaced the old British Vampires and supplemented Venoms in the 34th and 35th Fighter Squadrons and the Venom F models in the 36th Fighter Squadron.

One of the 22 North American F-86F Sabres (0674) ordered in 1955. The random assigned serial number system was established in 1966 and is still active today.
(via AAMA)

Radar-equipped F-86Ks were a welcome addition to Venezuela's air defence capability, especially with an increasing number of MiG's in the region. Today this Italian built F-86K (0931) is exhibited in perfect conditions at EAM Venezuela, Maracay. (Andre DuPont)

In 1966 random serial numbers were applied to the 15 surviving F-86F-30s including 0310, 0493, 0521, 0674, 0900, 0921, 1382, 1465, 1508, 2162, 3335, 4549, 6271, 9478, and 9518, replacing the older 'coded' numbers which identified the aircraft with each flight.

In July 1969 a large part of the fleet was grounded, including ten of the F-86F models and at least seventeen F-86Ks. The remaining aircraft were concentrated at El Libertador in Palo Negro. From 1971 the Sabres began to be withdrawn from service, as the more potent Mirage interceptors began to be delivered by late 1972. Disposal of a number of aircraft started in the early 1970s, with nine F-86Fs going to the Bolivian Air Force and six 'crated' F-86Ks to Honduras.

Manufacturer	Aircraft Type	Delivered	Number	Serial Numbers	Remarks
North American	F-86F-30 Sabre	1955	22	0310, 0493, 0521, 0674, 0900, 0921, 1382, 1465, 1508, 2162, 3335, 4549, 6271, 9478, 9518	
Fiat	F-86K Sabre	1966	74		78 ordered; ex-West German AF

BAC 145 Jet Provost (1962–1975)

With a growing fleet of jet fighters, some 70 per cent of which came from the United Kingdom, the FAV selected the BAC Jet Provost as its led-in jet trainer. Jet Provosts would transition young pilots from the T-6 Texan and its replacement, the T-34 Mentor to the twin-seat Vampire, before going on to the Vampire, Venom or, F-86F Sabre.

Up to 15 BAC 145 Jet Provost T.Mk.52 advanced trainers were acquired in 1961, with deliveries commencing in 1962. They were assigned serial numbers E040 to E054.

The BAC 145 Jet Provost T.Mk.52 became FAV's first led-in trainer. During his rather short career of 12 years none was lost. (Arturo Celestino Soto / FAV-CLUB)

The BAC 145 Jet Provost T.Mk.52 could also be used for tactical support. Seen here exhibited at Museo Aeronautico de la Fuerza Aerea Venezolana serial number 040 being equipped with unguided rockets. (Delso Lopez / FAV-CLUB)

The export version of the Jet Provost could also be used for tactical support when armed with rockets, twin 12.7 mm guns and 91 kg bombs.

The aircraft were re-numbered after 1966 in random numbers. Known serial numbers included 4332 and 6780. Their service began to wind down once the more modern T-2D Buckeyes took their place in 1972, and they were relegated to the basic jet trainer scheme. They were withdrawn from use in 1975 and replaced by a new batch of T-2Ds from 1977. Not a single Jet Provost was lost in accidents.

Manufacturer	Aircraft Type	Delivered	Number	Serial Numbers	Remarks
BAC	Jet Provost T.Mk.52	1962	15	E040 to E054	

Dassault Mirage III (1972–1990)

In the late 1960s the FAV developed a requirement for a new multi-role fighter that could outmatch the growing numbers of MiG-21 fighters deployed by Cuba. Several types were considered, including the French Mirage IIIE, American F-4E Phantom II, Swedish J-35 Draken, British Hunter F.Mk.6 and Lightning. The FAV selected the

FAV's Mirage IIIEV (2843) proved to be an excellent interceptor, but had also a secondary ground attack role.
(via Santiago Rivas)

Mirage IIIEV fighters began to be delivered in 1972 and formed the 33rd interceptor squadron. (Adolfo Alonzo, via Arturo Soto)

French deltawing fighter. Israeli victory over Arab MiGs in the 1967 Six-Day War and a clear US refusal to provide modern combat aircraft (the F-4) to Latin American countries were deciding factors.

The Venezuelan government signed a contract with Dassault for the supply of nine single-seat Mirage IIIEV fighters in 1971. Deliveries were scheduled to start in 1972 to the 33rd Halcones Fighter Squadron. Serial numbers were random, comprising 0624, 2473, 2843, 3039, 4058, 6732, 7381, 8940, and 9325.

Some sources state that Venezuela acquired 3 two-seat versions referred to as Mirage IIIDV, however, they have been confused with two-seat Mirage 5DV fighter-trainers at the same time. These two-seat fighters and another four single-seat Mirage 5V fighter-bombers completed the Mirage order. The total Mirage contract (including armament) was worth some USD 60 million.

In 1973 the 34th and 35th Fighter Squadrons were grouped with the 33rd Fighter Squadron, to form the 11th Fighter Group. This unit became responsible for providing national air defence coverage and eventually disbanded the 35th Squadron, re-organizing its assets as the 33rd (interceptor), 34th (fighter-bomber) squadrons, supported by the 117th Maintenance Squadron, and at the time, with the sole Mirage simulator in the Americas.

Modern weapons were a priority as the FAV followed the USAF philosophy of 'quality over quantity', as a deterrent to the larger number of MiGs operating over the Caribbean. The Mirage IIIEVs were equipped with the Cyrano IIB radar and armed with a pair of dog-fighting AIM-9B Sidewinders and the medium range Matra R.530 missiles. Interception was their primary mission, although ground-attack was their secondary role when armed with Mk-82 GP bombs and Matra JL-100 68-mm rocket launchers.

In 1977 the FAV ordered a second batch of Mirage 5s and included an IIIEV as an attrition replacement for serial number 2473, which was lost in an accident. The Mirage IIIEV proved to be a good interceptor, protecting Venezuelan airspace until the mid-1980s, when they were supplemented and eventually replaced by F-16s. The type suffered from some attrition, and by 1988 the Mirage III fleet had been reduced to five flying aircraft.

These survivors were earmarked for a considerable upgrade negotiated with Dassault under a USD 300 million contract that brought all up to Mirage 50 standard. The last Mirage III, serial number 0624, crashed in 1990.

Manufacturer	Aircraft Type	Delivered	Number	Serial Numbers	Remarks
Dassault	Mirage IIIEV	1972	9	0624, 2473, 2843, 3039, 4058, 6732, 7381, 8940, 9325	
Dassault	Mirage IIIEV	1977	1	2473	Attrition replacement

Dassault Mirage 5 (1972–1990)

In order to maximize the number of aircraft available to the FAV, the 1971 contract with Dassault included six 'simplified' Mirages. These lacked the Cyrano radar comprised of four single-seat Mirage 5Vs and two twin-seat Mirage 5DVs.

The single-seat fighters received serial numbers 1297, 7162, 7712, and 9510, while the two-seat fighter-trainers received the numbers 5471 and 7512. These fighters formed the nucleus of the 34th Fighter Squadron, replacing the old Venoms from December 1972.

Records are not that clear, but apparently the FAV ordered an additional two single-seat Mirage 5V and one two-seat 5DV in 1977 (probably serial numbers 0155, 0240, and 1225).

Mirage 5V (5706) in a pure exhibition shot can be seen with a variety of weapons: an Exocet AM.39 under centreline, which cannot be supported by M5. In front a Matra JL-100 combined rocket pod & fuel tank, joined by Mk.82 bombs and a R.550 Mk.1 missile under the wing. Oddly, this particular serial number 5706 never showed up any M III or V list. Later there has been a 5706 – as Mirage 50DV! (Jesus Antonio Aveledo / via AAMA)

Mirage 5V 2473 still in France during a test flight prior to delivery in 1973.
(Adolfo Alonzo, via Arturo Soto)

The first loss to the Mirage 5 fleet occurred on 30 July 1982, when number 9510 suffered an accident. The fleet's worse accident year was in 1986, when number 7712 was lost in August, followed by number 0240 on 2 December.

The FAV decided to upgrade its four surviving Mirages (three 5Vs and one 5DV) to the Mirage 50 version in the late 1980s.

Manufacturer	Aircraft Type	Delivered	Number	Serial Numbers	Remarks
Dassault	Mirage 5V	1972	4	1297, 7162, 7712, 9510	
Dassault	Mirage 5DV	1972	2	5471 & 7512	
Dassault	Mirage 5V	1977	2	0240 & 1225	
Dassault	Mirage 5DV	1977	1	0155	

North American Rockwell T-2 Buckeye (1972–1999)

In order to replace its ageing fleet of Jet Provost trainers, the FAV selected the T-2C Buckeye. It was to be a stepping stone between the Beech T-34 Mentor basic trainer and Venezuela's brand-new fleet of CF-5 and Mirage supersonic fighters. They should also be capable of tactical support missions therefore the basic T-2C Buckeye advanced trainer produced by North American Rockwell for the US Navy had to undergo minor surgery. The result was the T-2D export-version, capable of carrying over 1,500-kg of bombs and rockets on six under wing hard points. It had a different avionics fit and lacked the carrier-capable landing gear.

A first batch of 12 aircraft was acquired in 1971, with deliveries commencing in late 1972 to the Grupo de Entrenamiento 14 (Training Group) of the Escuela de Aviación Militar (Military Flight School, EAM) at Mariscal Sucre Air Base. These aircraft had USN Bureau numbers 159330 to 159341 (construction numbers 358-1 to 12). They were applied Venezuelan serial numbers 0048, 0219, 1316, 2155, 3499, 4821, 5612, 7532, 7744, 8763, 8991, and 9187.

From 1972 onwards FAV received the much needed trainer T-2 Buckeye to bridge the gap between T-34 and F-5/ Mirage III/ Mirage V. In total 24 were ordered.
(via Santiago Rivas)

A second batch was ordered from Rockwell International and these arrived in 1977. They formed a second training squadron within the 14th Training Group, which replaced the old Jet Provost trainers. New serial numbers included 0070, 0250, 2240, 3500, 3580, 3605, 3750, 3861, 4150, 4290, 4380, and 5625. Number 4290 was lost on 14 July 1978.

In the early 1980s a modernization and expansion plan called for a new trainer to supersede and latter replace the T-2Ds. The FAV studied several aircraft including the Franco-German Alpha Jet, the Northrop T-38 Talon, and the BAe Hawk. The Hawk advanced trainer was selected to become the new lead-in fighter trainer for a new generation of F-16 pilots. At least 24 were required for tactical training duties, while a further 24 would perform training duties for a light attack group. The Hawk deal was cancelled for several reasons, from the short number of F-16s acquired to post-Falkland's war politics, and Venezuelan advanced jet training remained at the hands of the trusty T-2D Buckeye for almost two more decades.

In late 1986 the remaining 20 T-2Ds were transferred to the 35th Squadron at Teniente Vicente Landeta Gil Air Base, forming the 12th Air Group together with the resident CF-5 unit. Once the T-2Ds were replaced by turboprop EMB-312 Tucanos in the training syllabus, they were assigned to the newly created Escuela de Combate (Fighter School). This organization was designed to enhance the Venezuelan pilot's combat capabilities.

In 1996 the remaining Buckeyes were transferred to the 13th Air Group, forming two squadrons. This group had been Venezuela's main offensive unit, when equipped with English Electric Canberra bombers, and now it assumed the role of a combat conversion unit.

By the late 1990s there were only six Buckeyes in service, and the air force selected the Italian MB-339FD to replace them. A July 1998 order for eight aircraft was to be followed by two similar orders, to be placed in 1999 and 2000 for a total requirement of 24 new LIFTs. Negotiations stalled and were later cancelled, in favour of what turned out to be another failed negotiation. This time it was for the Brazilian-built AMX-T attack trainers. The last Buckeyes were placed in storage during 1999.

Manufacturer	Aircraft Type	Delivered	Number	Serial Numbers	Remarks
North American Rockwell	T-2D Buckeye	1972	12	0048, 0219, 1316, 2155, 3499, 4821, 5612, 7532, 7744, 8763, 8991, 9187	
Rockwell International	T-2D Buckeye	1977	12	0070, 0250, 2240, 3500, 3580, 3605, 3750, 3861, 4150, 4290, 4380, 5625	

Canadair CF-5 Freedom Fighter (1972–)

In 1969 the FAV started a program to replace its large F-86K Sabre fleet with a new multi-role light fighter. The Canadian government offered a package of 20 surplus CF-5 Freedom Fighters, since some 64 of these lightweight fighters had been put in storage by the Canadian Air Force due to financial constraints and operational requirements.

The 16 CF-5As (serial numbers in Venezuelan service are quite odd, they range from 2950 to 9538) together with two CF-5Ds (numbers 1269 and 2327) were delivered in 1972. These came straight from CAF stocks, replacing Sabres of the 12th Fighter Group (35th and 36th Squadrons at Barquisimento and Barcelona). They were followed by an order for 100 AIM-9B Sidewinder missiles. In 1974 the last two CF-5Ds (numbers 2985 and 5681) were delivered from the Canadair production line, as Canadian stocks could not fulfil the requirement. It costed Canadair Ltd. a USD 9 million lawsuit from Northrop, since the Canadian company did not have any export rights to South America as part of its F-5 license agreement.

The CF-5 was nicknamed Zancudo (mosquito) in Venezuelan service. It was upgraded with a new VOR communications system in the late 1970s. This led to a change in its designation to VF-5A, the 'V' standing for 'Venezuelan'. The VF-5As performed well in Venezuelan skies, and the FAV set a requirement for another 19 aircraft to form

Canadair CF-5A, called VF-5A within FAV, can carry a detachable four-camera nose. (Ivan Pena Nesbit)

VF–5D 5681 is ready for a life-firing mission with unguided rockets.
(Ivan Nesbit)

a new fighter group. However, preference for a modern fighter such as the F-16 led this requirement to be cancelled. Two of the VF-5As (serial numbers 9124 and 9456) were converted to day reconnaissance configuration, with four KS-92 cameras in a detachable nose, and as so were re-designated RVF-5As in 1983.

By the late 1980s only seven single-seat F-5s where operational, and the FAV started to look for additional aircraft on the second hand market to fill the gap left by attrition and low serviceability. The Royal Netherlands Air Force (KLu) had bought some 105 Freedom Fighters from the same Canadian production line in 1969, and was in the process of replacing them with new F-16 Fighting Falcons. Six NF-5B and one NF-5A Freedom Fighters were bought in 1991 and received an extensive overhaul before delivery in late 1992. The NF-5s where the most advanced Freedom Fighters ever built and during the course of service with the KLu had been constantly upgraded.

During a coup attempted by forces loyal to Lt. Col. Hugo Chavez (later to become President) in late November 1992, three of the VF-5As (6719, 8707, and 9215) were destroyed while parked in their base by rebel Mirages and OV-10E Broncos.

In 1993 the FAV selected Singaporean company ST Aerospace to perform a major upgrade to its remaining VF-5 fleet. The USD 30 million Project Griffo included a new mission computer, IFF, TACAN, VR, new HUD and chaff/flare dispenser. This comprised 1 two-seater and 13 surviving single-seat fighters. Further improvements included fitting a FR probe and a major engine overhaul performed by General Electric. The upgraded VF-5s were armed with AIM-9P-3 Sidewinder missiles, 70-mm rocket launchers, Durandal anti-runway bombs, Mk-82, Mk-84, and M-117 GP bombs.

Elbit was contracted in the early 21st century to upgrade the three remaining NF-5Bs, as the other NF-5Bs and the NF-5A had come to the end of their structural service life. This upgrade included the installation of new colour MFDs in a NVG compatible cockpit, GPS and a new INS will be provided for the entire fleet. A further structural re-fit to the entire fleet would had provided an additional 8,000 hour lifespan. However, the program was plagued by problems and delays.

Student fighter-pilots are usually attached to the 12th Fighter Group for a LIFT course involving air-to-air and air-to-ground training before moving on to the VF-16. The VF-5s also serve as tugs for aerial targets and gunnery training for the VF-16 and Mirage 50V fighter pilots.

As late as 2004, the Canadian government and Bristol Aerospace Limited offered 36 refurbished CF-5s, comprising 11 single-seat CF-5As and 25 two-seat CF-5Ds for USD105 million. The aircraft were said to be in prime condition and have a 6,000 hour life-span remaining. This option was discarded by the Venezuelan government, as any new acquisitions would be of a new generation of aircraft, not 1960s vintage fighters.

Manufacturer	Aircraft Type	Delivered	Number	Serial Numbers	Remarks
Canadair	CF-5A Freedom Fighter	1972	16	2950, 3264, 3318, 5276, 6018, 6323, 6539, 6719, 7200, 8708, 8792, 9124, 9215, 9348, 9456, 9538	ex-RCAF
Canadair	CF-5D Freedom Fighter	1972	2	1269 & 2327	ex-RCAF
Canadair	CF-5D Freedom Fighter	1974	2	2985 & 5681	
Canadair	NF-5B Freedom Fighter	1991	6	1711, 2111, 4002, 6292, 6340, 6372	ex-KLu
Canadair	NF-5A Freedom Fighter	1991	1	6324	ex-KLu

General Dynamics F-16 Fighting Falcon (1983–)

In order to cope with a prolific communist presence in the Caribbean, armed mainly with supersonic MiG-21 and MiG-23 fighter-bombers, the Venezuelan Air Force organized a commission to review available modern Western fighters in the late 1970s.

The plan was to form three fighter groups equipped with two squadrons each of multi-role fighters, strategically placing each of them in the east, centre and west of the country. Among the reviewed candidates were the Israeli Kfir C.7, the Swedish JA-37 Viggen, the American F-16 Fighting Falcon, the French Mirage 50, and the Mirage 2000. Total value of the contract was to be worth some USD1.5 billion and comprised 72 aircraft. This ambitious program was later cut back to 48 aircraft due to financial difficulties.

The United States tried to market the downgraded F-16/79 version to its non-NATO allies, including Venezuela, Singapore and Thailand, but the version was not accepted by the FAV (nor any other country). In May 1982 the Venezuelan government signed an order for 18 single-seat F-16A Block 15 OCU and 6 two-seat F-16B Block 15 OCU Fighting Falcons under a Foreign Military Sales (FMS) contract named Peace Delta.

A F-16B (1715) in interesting missile configuration: left one AIM-9L Sidewinder and right one Python Mk.4.
(Cees-Jan van der Ende/alfakilo.nl)

Deliveries of the F-100-engined F-16s commenced in September 1983 to the 16th Fighter Group 'Dragones' based at El Libertador Air Base, near Palo Negro. They formed two squadrons, the 161st Caribes and 162nd Gavilanes. The new fighters came to strengthen the Air Defence Command, which had just fielded five new radar sites that were linked to Roland SAM sites and AAA batteries.

Their main air-to-air armament was the AIM-9P Sidewinder missile, while air-to-ground armament included the standard Mk-82/Mk-84 GP bombs, and rocket launchers. The single-seat fighters received the serial numbers 1041, 0051, 6611, 8900, 0678, 3260, 7268, 9068, 8924, 0094, 6023, 4226, 5422, 6426, 4827, 9864, 3648, and 0220, while the B versions were allocated serial numbers 1715, 2179, 9581, 2337, 7635, and 9583. All aircraft were delivered by 1985.

In the early 1990s the FAV replaced its F-16's AIM-9Ps with the newer AIM-9L Sidewinder missiles. More important by this time however, was the Dragones baptism of fire. On 27 November 1992, a group of Venezuelan Air Force and Army officers, participated in a coup d'état against President Carlos Andres Perez. Rebel forces took several military and strategic installations, but two F-16As managed to escape from El Libertador Air Base, which had fallen to a rebel assault. They landed at Barquisimento Air Base, where they refuelled and took off again to attack their overrun home base. The fighters raced back to Barquisimento, which was being bombed by rebel aircraft. They then proceeded to fly CAP over Caracas, where they engaged a recently delivered Mirage 50 and forced it to retreat. The Dragones shot down two rebel OV-10 Broncos that attempted to bomb Barquisimento and another Bronco over El Libertador, all of them with their 20-mm cannons.

The first F-16 casualty occurred in April 1994, when an F-16B (serial number 9581) on its landing approach suffered a bird strike ingestion and lost control. In November 1995, F-16B serial number 2179 crashed while performing an aerobatic display at an air show. In October 1997 the US Congress agreed to sell two former USAF F-16B Fighting Falcons as attrition replacements as well as to provide a Mid-Life Update (MLU) to the

After many years of embargo still in action: VF-16 (4226) armed with a Python Mk.4 missile during CRUCEX IV in Brazil.
(Chris Lofting)

fleet. However, the political tension between the new Venezuelan government, in the hands of former Parachute Colonel Hugo Chávez, and the Clinton Administration and the subsequent Bush Administrations put a hold on both deals.

In September 2001, F-16A serial number 6611 crashed after ingesting a vulture on its landing approach to Barcelona Air Base.

As the desired MLU was not approved by the US Government, the Venezuelan Dragones obtained a considerable weapons and systems enhancement from Israel. This included a DASH helmet, Python 4 air-to-air missiles, Rafael Litening targeting pods, Elisra RWR, and a new MFD. An engine upgrade to the F100-PW-220E standard was done by Samsung in South Korea. However, a larger upgrade, known as the Falcon ACE and set to include the Elta EL/M-2032 multi-mode radar and Derby medium-range missiles was cancelled by Israel due mainly to U.S pressure. Allocated funds were diverted for the acquisition of a new Airbus Presidential plane.

Rumours surrounding the replacement of the F-16 fleet, as well as the Mirage 50, and CF-5s with up to 50 new MiG-29M2 multi-role fighters in 2004 proved to be false. The F-16 will continue in service with the FAV until 2020, or as far as US-provided spares allow.

Manufacturer	Aircraft Type	Delivered	Number	Serial Numbers	Remarks
General Dynamics	F-16A Block 15 Fighting Falcon	1983–1985	18	1041, 0051, 6611, 8900, 0678, 3260, 7268, 9068, 8924, 0094, 6023, 4226, 5422, 6426, 4827, 9864, 3648, 0220	
General Dynamics	F-16B Block 15 Fighting Falcon	1983–1985	6	1715, 2179, 9581, 2337, 7635, 9583	

Dassault Mirage 50 (1991–2009)

As Venezuela's Mirage III/5 fleet became obsolete by the late 1980s, the FAV decided to acquire a new multi-role fighter that could supplement its F-16s and pose a direct counter balance to Cuban MiG-23s over the Caribbean. Additional F-16s were desired, but these proved to be politically unreliable, depending on the mood of US (and latter Venezuelan) administrations.

The requirement was for an aircraft in the same class as the current Mirage fleet, but with longer range, enhanced attack systems, survivability, and engine performance. FAV selected Dassault's proposal for the Mirage 50 fighter-bomber. This was the latest and last development of the Mirage III series.

In 1989 the Venezuelan government signed a contract worth USD 300 million that included seven new-built Mirage 50s (including one two-seat trainer) and the conversion of nine former Venezuelan Air Force Mirages. This included all the survivors from the original fleet, five Mirage IIIEV, three Mirage 5Vs and, one Mirage 5DV. A further 3 former Armée de l' Air Mirages (including 2 twin-seaters) were also converted to Mirage 50 standard, to reach the total requirement for 19, comprised of 15 single-seat fighters, and 4 dual-seat fighter-trainers.

The Mirage 50EV was the standard version, with Thomson-CSF Cyrano IV-M3 multi-mode radar capable of guiding an anti-ship AM-39 Exocet missile, as well as the new R.555 Magic II air-to-air missile. An integrated ECM suite was also added. Upgraded single-seat Mirages were designated Mirage 50M. The twin-seat Mirage 50DVs were pure fighter-trainers, lacking radar or, Exocet missile capability. The Mirage 50EV was the most capable newly-built Mirage in the III/5/50 series.

Flight refuelling capability was included through a fixed probe, allowing them to take fuel from the Boeing 707 converted tanker in service with the FAV since 1991. Among the new commodities were also canards, a navigation and attack control system, new HUD, HOTAS, Thomson-CSF Sherlock RWR, chaff/flare dispensers and most importantly, a new and powerful engine. The FAV's main source of complaints with the earlier Mirage III/5 series was the Atar 9C. Therefore the new Atar 9K-50, with increased thrust and better take-off and climb rate was an appreciable improvement. Mirage 50EVs performed so well, that witness reports state it out performed Mirage F-1Cs during DACT tests in France. Deliveries began in 1991 and included the last seven Mirage fighters built at the Mirage III/5/50 production line. They were received by the

Mirage 50EV (3373) during pre-flight check before another CRUCEX mission.
(Cees-Jan van der Ende/alfakilo.nl)

Mirage 50DV (7512)
(Chris Lofting)

11th Fighter Group, with the 34th Fighter Squadron becoming the main combat unit and the 33rd Squadron becoming an operational conversion unit.

By November 1992 the FAV had only received three new built fighters, with the rest of the earlier Mirage III/5 fleet being shipped to France for conversion. Two Mirages were used by FAV Brigadier General Visconti in a coup attempt led by Hugo Chavez against President Carlos Andres Perez on 27 November. The new Mirages were used to lead an attack on Barquisimeto Air Base. The coup attempt was frustrated by loyal forces and the rebel Mirages were reportedly 'chased-away' from Caracas by a pair of F-16As loyal to government forces. Both Mirages fled to Aruba, where the pilots asked for political asylum. The aircraft were returned to Venezuela soon afterwards.

By the early 21st Century the 11th Combat Group had some 11 single-seat Mirage 50EVs and 3 two-seat Mirage 50DVs. Their main mission was anti-ship attack, armed with the Exocet missile. They would constantly train with and against Venezuelan Navy Lupo frigates in this role. Serial number 6732 crashed near Maracay on 18 September 2004, its pilot ejected and landed safely. This was followed in June 2007 by the crash of number 5145 reducing the fleet to nine single-seat fighters. Grupo 11 ceased Mirage operations in March 2008 and switched to operating six Su-30MKVs, flying from Capitan Manuel Rios Air Base at El Sombrero. The Mirage was officially phased out of Venezuelan service during 2009. New Su-30MKV or Su-35 will eventually replace the Mirages.

Manufacturer	Aircraft Type	Delivered	Number	Serial Numbers	Remarks
Dassault	Mirage 50EV	1991	6	0160, 2056, 2353, 3373, 3414, 5145	
Dassault	Mirage 50DV	1991	1	4212	
Dassault	Mirage 50EV(M)	1993	9	0155, 0624, 1297, 2191, 2212, 2473, 3033, 4058, 6732	ex-FAV & ex-ADLA; upgraded
Dassault	Mirage 50DV(M)	1993	3	5706, 6732, 7512	

Sukhoi Su-30MKV (ASCC code Flanker) (2006–)

After several years of speculation about the acquisition of a new front line fighter and the cancellation of an USD 100 million upgrade programme scheduled for Venezuela's ageing F-16 fleet, the Aviación Militar Venezolana (AMV) selected the Sukhoi Su-30MK2 Flanker multi-role air superiority fighter in 2006. In early July 2006, a pair of Russian Air Force (VVS) Su-30MKK fighters accompanied by a single Ilyushin Il-76TP (ASCC code Candid) deployed to Base Aérea El Libertador for trails.

A successful evaluation led to the signature of an USD 1.3 billion contract with Russian state export company Rosoboronexport during 2006 for 24 Su-30MKVs.

The first two Su-30MKVs, produced at the Komsomolsk-na-Amur (KnAAPO) plant were delivered by an An-124 Ruslan air freighter and arrived on 30 November 2006 to Base Aérea Teniente Luis del Valle García in Barcelona. They were designated serial numbers 1259 and 0460. Another two aircraft arrived on 20 December 2006, designated numbers 1075 and 1265. Delivery of another 12 aircraft during 2007 was followed by the last 8 in 2008.

They formed the Grupo de Caza 13 Simon Bolivar based at Base Aérea Teniente Luis del Valle García, Barcelona comprising two squadrons, the 131st Ases and the 132nd 'Pumas' fighter squadrons. Venezuela also acquired a comprehensive arms package that includes the RVV-AE BVR-AAMs, R-73Es (though it's uncertain whether these are "vanilla" R-73Es or R-73ELs), KAB-500Kr EO-homing bombs, Kh-59ME EO-homing missiles with OVOD-ME systems (including APK-9E and TEKON-E guidance systems for Kh-59MEs), Kh-29TE EO-homing missiles, Kh-31P ARMs and L-005S Sorbtsiya-S ECM-pods. Venezuela has announced its intention to acquire the Sukhoi Su-35 Super Flanker once this is made available for export.

Manufacturer	Aircraft Type	Delivered	Number	Serial Numbers	Remarks
Sukhoi	Su-30MKV	2006	24	0167, 0457, 0460, 0462, 0564, 0962, 1075, 1161, 1175, 1259, 1265, 1457, 1783, 2564, 3564, 5790, 5812, 8953, 8963, 9463, 9958, 9959, ????	

Su-30MKV (1161) takes-off in full afterburner, armed with one KAB-500T (left) and one Kh-29T (AS-14 Kedge) (right). (Ivan Pena Nesbit)

Su-30MKV 1783 wears a fin-flash design with the logo of the Group (Simón Bolivar's portrait) and a serial number is honouring the year of birth of Simón Bolivar.
(Ivan Pena Nesbit)

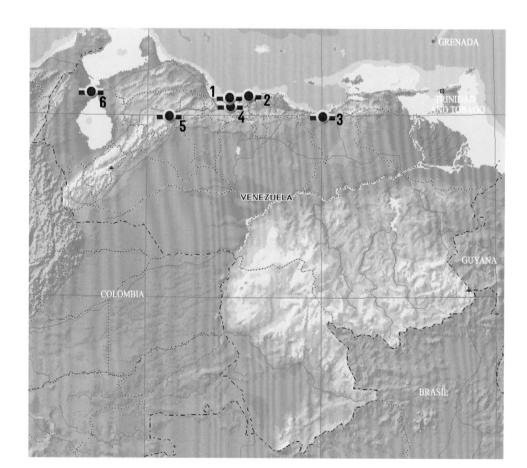

1. Base Aerea Mariscal Sucre, Boca del Rio
2. Base Aerea Generalisimo Francisco de Miranda, La Carlota, Caracas
3. Base Aerea Teniente Luis del Valle Garcia, Barcelona
4. Base Aerea El Libertador, Maracay, Palo Negro
5. Base Aerea Teniente Vicente Landaeta Gil, Barquisimento
6. Base Aerea Rafael Urdaneta, Maracaibo

APPENDIX I

Bibliography

Books

ANDRADE, J. M., *Latin American Military Aviation* (UK: Midland Counties Publications (Aerophile) 1982)

BENDALA, M. & SEOANE, P., *La Campaña De Las Malvinas* (Madrid: San Martin, 1985)

BONDS, R. (Editor) *The Illustrated Directory of Modern Weapons* (UK: Salamander Books, 1985)

CORNEJO, D., *La Aviación Nacional – Historia De La Fuerza Aérea Salvadoreña* (San Salvador: Concultura, 2002)

DONALD, D., *The Complete Encyclopedia of World Aircraft* (New York: Barnes & Noble Books, 1997)

ENGLISH, A. J., *Armed Forces of Latin America* (UK: Jane's Publishing Inc., 1984)

PEACOCK, L., *The World's Air Forces* (UK: Salamander Books Ltd., 1991)

TAYLOR, M. J. H., *Encyclopedia of the World's Air Forces* (USA: Multimedia Books Limited, 1988)

TOPERCZER, I., *MiG-17 and MiG-19 units of the Vietnam War* (Osprey Publishing, 2001)

Magazine Articles

CRUZ, C. & GUEVARA, I., Ecuador Airpower Survey *Air Forces Monthly*, 218 (May 2006): 80–81

Operation Fenix: Colombian Air Raid at Dawn, *AIR International*, (May 2008): 52–55

Mex to the Max, *Air Forces Monthly*, (May 2008): 60–68

Visiting Cuscatlán, *Air Forces Monthly*, 237 (December 2007): 40–41

Mexican Air Force seeks replacement for long serving T-33 jet trainer aircraft, *Jane's Defence Weekly* (1 October 2007)

Socialism: alive and well in the new Venezuela, *Jane's Defence Weekly*, (27 September 2007)

The Latin Dragons, *Air Forces Monthly*, 233 (August 2007): 48–53

Force Report: Mexican Naval Aviation; Mexico's Nautical Needs, *Air Forces Monthly*, (November 2006): 63–66

Mexico Airpower Survey *Air Forces Monthly*, 219 (June 2006): 78–80

Honduras Airpower Survey *Air Forces Monthly*, 219 (June 2006): 77

Dominican Republic Airpower Survey *Air Forces Monthly*, 218 (May 2006): 79

México: panorama militar, Fuerzas Militares del Mundo, *Ikonos Press SL*, Madrid, Spain, (June 2003): 23–31

Internet Articles

ALFONZO, A., Dassault Aviation Mirage, *FAV-CLUB*, (15 December 2002)
http://www.fav-club.com/articulos/PDF/Modelmiragerev2.pdf

ALVAREZ, C. J., Recuerdos de un piloto de Sabre, *FAV-CLUB*, (November 2004)
http://www.fav-club.com/articulos/sabrecazador/sabrecazador.htm

ANGERMAN, H., The Honduran Air Force Today, *LAAHS*, (10 May 2003)
http://www.laahs.com/artman/publish/article_29.shtml

AGUILAR, P., The History of the "Escuadrilla Cocodrilos", *LAAHS*, (16 December 2003)
http://www.laahs.com/artman/publish/article_66.shtml

CHAVEZ, G., Ecuadorian Meteors, *LAAHS*, (2 October 2004)
http://www.laahs.com/artman/publish/article_57.shtml

COOPER, T., Peru vs. Ecuador, Alto Cenepa War 1995, *ACIG*, (August 2007)
http://s188567700.online.de/CMS/index.php?option=com_content&task=view&id=97&Itemid=47

COOPER, T. & J. SOSA, Venezuelan Coup Attempt 1992, *ACIG*, (August 2007)
http://s188567700.online.de/CMS/index.php?option=com_content&task=view&id=95&Itemid=47

COOPER, T., Guatemala since 1954, *ACIG*, (August 2007)
http://s188567700.online.de/CMS/index.php?option=com_content&task=view&id-91&Itemid-47

COOPER, T., Argentina 1955-1965, *ACIG*, (August 2007)
http://s188567700.online.de/CMS/index.php?option=com_content&task=view&id=80&Itemid=47

FAV-CLUB STAFF, El Proyecto Grifo, *FAV-CLUB*, (2005)
http://www.fav-club.com/articulos/grifo/grifo.htm

FOURT, O. & A. CUENCA, Caribbean MiGs, *ACIG*, (August 2007)
http://s188567700.online.de/CMS/index.php?option=com_content&task=view&id=82&Itemid=47

FUGUETT, E., Caribes y Gavilanes, *FAV-CLUB*,
http://www.fav-club.com/articulos/cyggac16/cyg.htm

FUGUETT, E., Los 25 años del Mirage en Venezuela, *FAV-CLUB*
http://www.fav-club.com/articulos/mirageaniver/mirage25.htm

FUGUETT, E., Northrop F-5 con la Fuerza Aérea Venezolana, *FAV-CLUB*
http://www.fav-club.com/articulos/f5vzla/f5vzla.htm

GASIA, M., Un Aguila caída, *FAV-CLUB*, (January 2005)
http://www.fav-club.com/articulos/aguilacaida/aguilacaida.htm

GUAJARDO, M., Airplanes of the Mexican Air Force's Museum, *LAAHS*, (10 May 2003)
http://www.laahs.com/artman/publish/article_8.shtml

GUEVARA, I., Fuerza Aerea Colombiana, *ACIG*, (August 2007)
http://s188567700.online.de/CMS/index.php?option=com_content&task=view&id=93&Itemid=47

GUEVARA, I., Forca Aerea Brasileira, *ACIG*, (August 2007)
http://s188567700.online.de/CMS/index.php?option=com_content&task=view&id=84&Itemid=47

HOLSEN, P. J., Honduras F-86/T28 Venture, *LAAHS*, (10 May 2003)
http://www.laahs.com/artman/publish/article_41.shtml

LAYA, J., AMX, *FAV-CLUB*
http://www.fav-club.com/articulos/amx/amx.htm

LEIVA, L. & M. OVERALL, El Salvador Air Force: Return of the Mystic, *LAAHS*, (10 May 2003)
http://www.laahs.com/artman/publish/article_52.shtml

LONGONI, H., Cruz del Sur: High Aerobatics Squadron, *LAAHS*, (10 May 2003)
http://www.laahs.com/artman/publish/article_89.shtml

LÓPEZ, D., Misiels aire-aire en la FAV, Pasado, presente y futuro, *FAV-CLUB*
http://www.fav-club.com/articulos/misilesfav/misiles.htm

LÓPEZ, D., Los F-16 y la guerra fría, *FAV-CLUB*, (2001)
http://www.fav-club.com/articulos/f16coldwar/f16coldwar.htm

LUGO, J. J., Grupo Aéreo de Caza No-16 Fuerza Aérea Venezolana, *FAV-CLUB*, (May 2003)
http://www.fav-club.com/articulos/gac16/gac16.htm

LUGO, J. J., La FAV en busca de un entrenador avanzado de combate, *FAV-CLUB*, (September 2004)
http://www.fav-club.com/articulos/trainerfav/trainerfav.htm

MEJÍA, L., Farewell to the Peruvian Fitters, *LAAHS*, (11 February 2007)
http://www.laahs.com/artman/publish/article_198.shtml

MEJÍA, L., Peruvian Sabres, *LAAHS*, (10 May 2003)
http://www.laahs.com/artman/publish/article_100.shtml

OLGUÍN, J., Bolivia's Grupo Aéreo de Caza 31, *LAAHS*, (29 April 2006)
http://www.laahs.com/artman/publish/article_179.shtml

OVERALL, M., The 100 Hour War, *LAAHS*, (11 March 2004)
http://www.laahs.com/artman/publish/article_19.shtml

OVERALL, M., Guatemala's Combat Dragons, *LAAHS*, (10 May 2003)
http://www.laahs.com/artman/publish/article_30.shtml

PICO, A., ¿Un sustituto para el Mirage 50?, FAV-CLUB
http://www.fav-club.com/articulos/sustitutom50/sustitutom50.htm

QUEVEDO, J. A., Mexico Northrop F-5E/F, *LAAHS*, (10 May 2003)
http://www.laahs.com/artman/publish/article_10.shtml

SIMINIC, I., A Walk in the Clouds: the Chilean Dragonflies, *LAAHS*, (10 May 2003)
http://www.laahs.com/artman/publish/article_91.shtml

SIMINIC, I., The Hawker Hunter ex-Fach 736, *LAAHS*, (10 May 2003)
http://www.laahs.com/artman/publish/article_88.shtml

SOTO, T. R., The Guatemalan Air Force Today, *LAAHS*, (10 May 2003)
http://www.laahs.com/artman/publish/article_43.shtml

URRIBARES, R., & M. LITTLE, The Cuban MiGs, *LAAHS*, (7 August 2003)
http://www.laahs.com/artman/publish/article_46.shtml

VAN DER ENDE, C.-J., Cicalesi, Juan Carlos & Rivas, Santiago,
The New Hawks of the Argentine Air Force, *LAAHS*, (10 May 2003)
http://www.laahs.com/artman/publish/article_93.shtml

VIANA, L., **Venom sobre Caracas: 1ero. de Enero de 1958**, *FAV-CLUB*
http://www.fav-club.com/articulos/venonoverccs/venonccs.htm

WISER, M. & COOPER, T., Cuban Crisis, ORBATs and OPLANs 1962, *ACIG*, (August 2007)
http://s188567700.online.de/CMS/index.php?option=com_content&task=view&id=85&Itemid=47

APPENDIX II

Kit & Decal Lists

Compiled with kind help of Mario Martínez, the following list includes most of the currently available plastic kits, as used for replicating Latin American jet fighters.

Table 1: Aircraft Kits

Model	1/72 Scale Brand	1/48 Scale Brand	1/32 Scale Brand
Aermacchi MB.326/ EMBRAER XAVANTE	Supermodel	Esci, Italeri	n/a
Aermacchi MB.339	Supermodel	Supermodel	n/a
Aero L-39	Eduard, KP	Special Hobby	n/a
AMD Mirage F.1	Airfix, Esci, Hasegawa, Heller	Esci, Italeri	n/a
AMD Super Etendard	Academy, Airfix, Heller	Monogram	n/a
BAC 167 Strikemaster	Airfix, MPC	n/a	n/a
Cessna A-37B Dragonfly	Academy, Hasegawa	Monogram	n/a
Dassault Ouragan	Heller	FM Models	n/a
Dassault Super Mystere B2	Heller	Fonderie Miniatures	n/a
Dassault Mirage IIICJ	Airfix, AML, High Planes, PJ Productions	Eduard, Hobbyboss	n/a
Dassault Mirage IIIE / EA / F-103(EDR)	Heller, High Planes, PJ Productions, Revell	Esci, Italeri	Revell
Dassault Mirage IIIDEA	High Planes, PJ Productions	n/a	n/a
Dassault Mirage 5 / ELKAN / PANTERA	Heller, High Planes, PJ Productions	Esci	n/a
Dassault Mirage 2000P/2000-5	Airfix, Heller, Italeri	Eduard, Heller, Italeri, Monogram	n/a
Dassault Mirage 2000D	Heller, Italeri	Eduard, Heller	n/a
De Havilland Vampire Mk.III	Heller	Classic Airframes, Hobbycraft	n/a
Douglas A-4Q(B) / P	Airfix, Fujimi	Hasegawa, Hobbycraft	n/a
Douglas A-4C	Fujimi	Hasegawa, Hobbycraft	n/a
McDonnell Douglas A-4M / OA-4M	Fujimi, Hasegawa	Hasegawa, Hobbycraft	Hasegawa
Fouga Magister	Heller	Fonderie	n/a
Gloster Meteor F.Mk.4	Airfix	Tamiya	n/a
Gloster Meteor F.Mk.8	Airfix, Extrakit	n/a	n/a
Grumman F-9 F2 Panther / Cougar	Hasegawa	AMT, Monogram, Trumpeter	n/a
Hawker Hunter FGA.9	Airfix, Revell Germany	Academy	Revell
IAI Nesher / Dagger	High Planes, PJ Productions	n/a	n/a
IAI KFIR	Hasegawa, Italeri	Esci	n/a

Model	1/72 Scale Brand	1/48 Scale Brand	1/32 Scale Brand
General Dynamics F-16A BLOCK 15	Fujimi, Hasegawa, Hobbyboss, Revell	Hasegawa, Kinetic	Hasegawa
Lockheed-Martin F-16C BLOCK 50/52	Academy, Hasegawa, Revell Germany	Hasegawa, Kinetic, Tamiya	Tamiya
General Dynamics F-16B BLOCK 15	Fujimi, Hasegawa, Hobbyboss, Revell Germany.	Hasegawa	n/a
Lockheed-Martin F-16D BLOCK 50/52	CMK /Model Alliance (Hasegawa & Revell) - spine dorsal added conversion	Hasegawa, Kinetic	n/a
Lockheed P-80	Airfix, RVHP	Monogram	Classic Airframes
Lockheed T-33 and AT-33	Hasegawa, Heller	Academy	n/a
MiG-15	Airfix, Dragon, KP	Tamiya, Trumpeter	AA Models, Trumpeter
MiG-17	AML, Dragon, KP	Heller, Hobbyboss, SMER	AA Models, Trumpeter
MiG-19	Bilek, KP, Trumpeter	Trumpeter	AA Models, Trumpeter
MiG-21F-13	Academy, Bilek, Hasegawa, Revell	n/a	Trumpeter
MiG-21PF	Bilek, Fujimi, Zvesda	Academy, Revell	Revell
MiG-21MF	Fujimi.KP,Kondor	Academy, Kopro, OEZ	Revell, Trumpeter
MiG-21bis	Fujimi, Kondor, Zvesda	Kopro	n/a
MiG-23MF	Academy, Airfix, Hasegawa, Zvesda	Esci, Italeri	Trumpeter
MiG-23BN	Zvesda	n/a	n/a
MiG-23 Flogger G	Zvesda	n/a	Trumpeter
MiG-29 Fulcrum A9-12	Airfix, ICM, Italeri	Academy, Monogram	Revell
MiG-29 Fulcrum A9-13	ICM, Pantera	n/a	n/a
MiG-29UB	Heller, Italeri	Academy	n/a
Morane-Saulnier MS570	Heller	Fonderie	n/a
North American F-86 E/F	Academy, Fujimi, Hasegawa, Heller	Academy, Hasegawa, Monogram	Hasegawa, Kinetic
North American F-86 K	Special Hobby	Hasegawa	n/a
Northrop F-5A	Esci, Hasegawa, PM Models	Classic Airframes	n/a
Northrop F-5B	Esci	Classic Airframes, Fujimi	n/a
Northrop F-5E	Airfix, Italeri	Italeri, Monogram	Hasegawa, Revell
Northrop F-5F	Italeri	Monogram	n/a
Rockwell T-2 Buckeye	Matchbox	En Resina Desconcido	n/a
SEPECAT Jaguar ES/EB	Hasegawa, Italeri	Airfix, Heller	n/a
Sukhoi Su-20 Fitter-F	Pantera	n/a	n/a
Sukhoi Su-22M-3/UM	Bilek, Pantera, SMER	Kopro	n/a
Sukhoi Su-25A/UB	Italeri, Pantera, Zvesda	Kopro, OEZ	n/a
Sukhoi Su-30MKI/-27UB	Heller, Italeri, Nacotne, Trumpeter	Academy, Trumpeter	Trumpeter

Table 2: Decals

Manufacturer	Reference	Content & Comentary
Scale 1:72		
Albatros Decals	72-001 (out of print)	The Southern Flying Tigers - Peruvian MiG-29, Mirage 2000, Su-22
Albatros Decals	72-002 (out of print)	The Caribean Falcons - Cuban MiG-15/ -17/ -21/ -23/ -29 & Peruvian M2000
Albatros Decals	72-007 (out of print)	A-37B Dragonfly - A-37s from Chile, Colombia, Dom Rep, Ecuador, El Salvador, Guatemala, Honduras, Uruguay, Peru.
Atzec Models	D72/031	Mexican AF T-33 45 Years
Atzec Models	D72-001 (out of stock)	Latin American T-33s Set I & II -
Atzec Models	D72-003	Ecuadorian Air Force II - A-37B, Strikemaster Mk.89, Mirage F.1
Atzec Models	D72-004 (out of stock)	Ecuadorian Air Force I - Jaguar, Kfir C2
Atzec Models	D27-005	Peruvian Air Force I - MiG-29, Mirage 2000
Atzec Models	D72-006 (out of stock)	Peruvian Air Force II - A-37, F-86F, Mirage 5, Su-22M-3
Atzec Models	D72-007 (out of stock)	Latin Eagles I - Argentinian A-4, Chile Hunters, Colombian Kfir & Mirage
Atzec Models	D72-008 (out of stock)	Latin Eagles II - Brazilian F-5E, Cuban MiG-21, Venezuelan F-16
Atzec Models	D72-011 (out of stock)	Latin Eagles III - Dominican A-37, Mexican F-5E
Atzec Models	D72-015	Freedom Tigers - Venezuelan VF-5
Atzec Models	D72-017 (out of stock)	COIN Warriors 1 (Guatemalan Air Force)
Atzec Models	D72-018 (out of stock)	Stunning Sabres 1 - Argentina, Bolivia, Colombia, Venezuela
Atzec Models	D72-020	Mexican Air Force - F-5 20 Years
Atzec Models	D72-021	Amazonia Mirages - Brazil & Colombia
Atzec Models	D72-023	Venimous Vipers 1 - Venezuelan F-16s, anniversary schemes
Zotz	72-016	Vivacious Vipers #2 - Chile F-16A & B
Zotz	ZTZSP-3	Roundels of the World Part 3 - Central America
Zotz	ZTZSP-4 (sold out)	Roundels of the World Part 4 - South America
Scale 1:48		
Albatros Decals	48-001 (out of print)	The Southern Flying Tigers - Peruvian MiG-29, Mirage 2000, Su-22
Albatros Decals	48-002 (out of print)	The Caribean Falcons - Cuban MiG-15/ -17/ -21/ -23/ -29 & Peruvian M2000
Albatros Decals	48-007 (out of print)	A-37B Dragonfly - A-37s from Chile, Colombia, Dom Rep, Ecuador, El Salvador, Guatemala, Honduras, Uruguay, Peru.
Atzec Models	D48-001 (out of stock)	Latin American T-33s Set I -
Atzec Models	D48-002 (out of stock)	Latin American T-33s Set II - Brazil, Mexico
Atzec Models	D48-003	Ecuadorian Air Force II - A-37B, Strikemaster Mk.89, Mirage F.1
Atzec Models	D48-004 (out of stock)	Ecuadorian Air Force I - Jaguar, Kfir C2
Atzec Models	D48-005	Peruvian Air Force I - MiG-29, Mirage 2000
Atzec Models	D48-006 (out of stock)	Peruvian Air Force II - A-37, F-86F, Mirage 5, Su-22M-3
Atzec Models	D48-007 (out of stock)	Latin Eagles I - Argentinian A-4, Chile Hunters, Colombian Kfir & Mirage
Atzec Models	D48-008 (out of stock)	Latin Eagles II - Brazilian F-5E, Cuban MiG-21, Venezuelan F-16
Atzec Models	D48-011 (out of stock)	Latin Eagles III - Dominican A-37, Mexican F-5E
Atzec Models	D48-015	Freedom Tigers - Venezuelan VF-5
Atzec Models	D48-020	Mexican Air Force - F-5 20 Years
Atzec Models	D48-021	Amazonia Mirages - Brazil & Colombia
Atzec Models	D48-022	Venezuelan Air Force
Atzec Models	D48-023	Venimous Vipers 1 - Venezuelan F-16s, anniversary schemes

Atzec Models	D48-025	Argentine Gloster Meteors F.Mk.4
Atzec Models	D48/031	Mexican Air Force T-33 45 Years
Atzec Models	D48/017	Mexican Air Force & Navy. New Release
Zotz	48-016	Vivacious Vipers #2 - Chile F-16A & B
Zotz	ZTZSP-3	Roundels of the World Part 3 - Central America
Zotz	ZTZSP-4 (sold out)	Roundels of the World Part 4 - South America

Scale 1:32

Atzec Models	D32-001	Mexican Air Force - F-5 20 Years
Zotz	32-008	Vivacious Vipers #2 - Chile F-16A & B
Zotz	ZTZSP-3	Roundels of the World Part 3 - Central America
Zotz	ZTZSP-4 (sold out)	Roundels of the World Part 4 - South America

INDEX

Carlos Filipe Operti

www.carlosoperti.fot.br

Silver Wings – Serving & Protecting Croatia

by Katsuhiko Tokunaga & Heinz Berger

160 pages, 30x22 cm, hardcover w jacket

48,00 Euro ISBN 978-0-9825539-1-6

The world-famous Japanese aviation photographer Katsuhiko Tokunaga covers the activities of today's Croatian Air Force in his well known and destinctive, nearly artistic style.

Following a brief introduction into the history of Croatian Air Force from 1991 until 2009, this exclusive, top quality photo monography provides dozens of high-quality photographs of the aircraft currently in service, and rich detail about the life, work and action of the men and women serving and protecting Croatia.

Appendices list the technical data of all aircraft in service and the current order of battle, together with all the unit insignia.

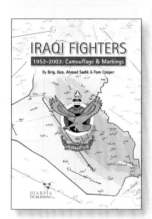

Iraqi Fighters 1953–2003 Camouflage & Markings

by Brig. Gen. Ahmad Sadik & Tom Cooper

156 pages, 28x21cm, softcover

29,95 Euro ISBN 978-0-615-21414-6

Richly illustrated with photographs and artworks, this book provides an exclusive insight into service history of 13 fighter jet types – from Vampires and Hunters to MiG-29s and Su-24s – that served with Royal Iraqi Air Force (RIrAF) and Iraqi Air Force (IrAF) between 1953 and 2003.

The result is a detailed history of RIrAF and IrAF markings, serial numbers and camouflage patterns, the in-depth history of each Iraqi fighter squadron, their equipment over the time as well as unit and various special insignias.

An appendix lists the exisiting plastic scale model kits in 1/72, 1/48 and 1/32 scale as well as decals sheets in regards to Iraqi Air Force.

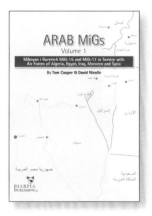

Arab MiGs Volume 1, MiG-15s and MiG-17s, 1955–1967

by Tom Cooper & David Nicole

272 pages, 28x21 cm, softcover

35,95 Euro ISBN 978-0-9825539-2-3

This study – the first in a series of similar publications – provides a unique and previously unavailable insight into the service of both types with five Arab air forces, including Algeria, Egypt, Iraq, Morocco and Syria. It tells the story of people that flew MIG-15s and MiG-17s, several of whom became dominant political figures in most recent history of these countries, and completes this with a review of combat operations in Yemen, as well as in three wars between the Arabs and the Israelis. Over 200 photos, colour artworks, maps and tables illustrate the story of the aircraft and their crews, as well as unit insignia in unprecedented detail. Extensive lists of serial- and construction numbers are provided as well.

THE AVIATION BOOKS OF A DIFFERENT KIND

UNIQUE TOPICS I IN-DEPTH RESEARCH I RARE PICTURES I HIGH PRINTING QUALITY